Lecture Notes in Computer Science   1007

Edited by G. Goos, J. Hartmanis and J. van Leeuwen

Advisory Board: W. Brauer   D. Gries   J. Stoer

Springer
Berlin
Heidelberg
New York
Barcelona
Budapest
Hong Kong
London
Milan
Paris
Santa Clara
Singapore
Tokyo

Antoon Bosselaers   Bart Preneel (Eds.)

Integrity Primitives
for Secure
Information Systems

Final Report of
RACE Integrity Primitives Evaluation
RIPE-RACE 1040

 Springer

Series Editors

Gerhard Goos
Universität Karlsruhe
Vincenz-Priessnitz-Straße 3, D-76128 Karlsruhe, Germany

Juris Hartmanis
Department of Computer Science, Cornell University
4130 Upson Hall, Ithaca, NY 14853, USA

Jan van Leeuwen
Department of Computer Science,Utrecht University
Padualaan 14, 3584 CH Utrecht,The Netherlands

Volume Editors

Antoon Bosselaers
Bart Preneel
Department Elektrotechniek - ESAT, Katholieke Universiteit Leuven
Kardinaal Mercierlaan 94, B-3001 Heverlee, Belgium

Cataloging-in-Publication data applied for

Die Deutsche Bibliothek - CIP-Einheitsaufnahme

Integrity primitives for secure information systems : final RIPE
report of RACE integrity primitives evaluation (R1040) /
Antoon Bosselaers ; Bart Preneel (ed.). - Berlin ; Heidelberg ;
New York ; Barcelona ; Budapest ; Hong Kong ; London ;
Milan ; Paris ; Tokyo : Springer, 1995
  (Lecture notes in computer science ; Vol. 1007)
  ISBN 3-540-60640-8
NE: Bosselaers, Antoon [Hrsg.]; GT

CR Subject Classification (1991): D.4.6, E.3, K.6.5

ISBN 3-540-60640-8 Springer-Verlag Berlin Heidelberg New York

© Springer-Verlag Berlin Heidelberg 1995
Printed in Germany

Typesetting: Camera-ready by author
SPIN 10487165   06/3142 – 5 4 3 2 1 0   Printed on acid-free paper

RIPE Integrity Primitives

Final report of RACE Integrity Primitives Evaluation (R1040)

A. Berendschot, *PTT Research, Leidschendam (NL)*

B. den Boer, *Philips Crypto B.V., Eindhoven (NL)*

J.P. Boly, *PTT Research, Leidschendam (NL)*

A. Bosselaers, *ESAT Lab, K.U. Leuven (B)*

J. Brandt, *Aarhus Universitet, Århus (DK)*

D. Chaum (chairman), *CWI/Digicash, Amsterdam (NL)*

I. Damgård, *Aarhus Universitet, Århus (DK)*

M. Dichtl, *Siemens AG, München (D)*

W. Fumy, *Siemens AG, München (D)*

M. van der Ham, *CWI, Amsterdam (NL)*

C.J.A. Jansen, *Philips Crypto B.V., Eindhoven (NL)*

P. Landrock, *Aarhus Universitet, Århus (DK)*

B. Preneel, *ESAT Lab, K.U. Leuven (B)*

G. Roelofsen, *PTT Research, Leidschendam (NL)*

P. de Rooij, *PTT Research, Leidschendam (NL)*

J. Vandewalle, *ESAT Lab, K.U. Leuven (B)*

Abstract

This is a manual intended for those seeking to secure information systems by applying modern cryptography. It represents the successful attainment of goals by RIPE (RACE Integrity Primitives evaluation), a 350 man-month project funded in part by the Commission of the European Communities. The recommended portfolio of integrity primitives, which is the main product of the project, forms the heart of this volume.

By integrity, we mean the kinds of security that can be achieved through cryptography, apart from concealment. Thus included are ways to ensure that stored or communicated data is not illicitly modified, that parties exchanging messages are actually present, and that "signed" electronic messages can be recognised as authentic by anyone.

Of particular concern to the project were the high-speed requirements of broadband communication. But the project also aimed for completeness in its recommendations. As a result, the portfolio contains primitives, i.e., building blocks, that can meet most of today's perceived needs for integrity.

AMS Subject Classification (1991): 94A60

CR Subject Classification (1991): D.4.6

Keywords & Phrases: Integrity Primitives, Security Services, Integrity Mechanisms, Data Origin Authentication, Entity Authentication, Access Control, Data Integrity, Non-repudiation, Signature, Key Exchange.

Note: The work described in this report is the result of a research project carried out during the period 1 November 1988 to 30 June 1992. While the project received support under the EC RACE programme, the results should not be interpreted as a given view on the Community policy in this area.

Table of Contents

Part I

Introduction and Background

Table of Contents

1 Introduction

This is a manual intended for those seeking to secure information systems by applying modern cryptography. It represents the successful attainment of goals by RIPE (RACE Integrity Primitives Evaluation), a 350 man-month project funded in part by the Commission of the European Communities. The recommended portfolio of integrity primitives, which is the main product of the project, forms the heart of this volume.

By integrity, we mean the kinds of security that can be achieved through cryptography, apart from concealment. Thus, included are ways to ensure that stored or communicated data is not illicitly modified, that parties exchanging messages are actually present, and that "signed" electronic messages can be recognized as authentic by anyone.

Of particular concern to the project were the high-speed requirements of broad-band communication. But the project also aimed for completeness in its recommendations. As a result, the portfolio contains primitives, i.e., building blocks, that can meet most of today's perceived needs for integrity.

1.1 Perspective on the Project Results

Six leading European research groups in the field made up the RIPE consortium; however, much of the input was drawn from experts around the world who responded to two widely circulated calls for submissions. These responses were then extensively evaluated according to a work plan that involved multiple stages of review for each submission and independent verification of decisions. We were fortunate that those submissions remaining, after some adjustments, gave essentially the same breadth of coverage as the original set.

Most of the project's effort is regrettably not directly reflected in this report. The majority of submissions had to be, after substantial efforts in many cases, rejected because of weaknesses uncovered during the project.

In the cryptographic world today there are few absolute guarantees, however. Primitives with provable security such as the so called one-time pad are rare and of limited applicability. A few others have security that can be reduced to certain established assumptions, as with many minimum disclosure protocols. But security of the overwhelming majority of primitives is based simply on the lack of any known successful attack. In this respect our portfolio contains a representative sampling, which means that ongoing monitoring will continue to be necessary for most of the primitives we recommend.

The project was of course confronted with the question of what kinds of primitives are really needed. Unable to find an acceptable answer elsewhere, we developed a taxonomy of primitives which we believe is well suited to currently perceived needs for integrity. But as integrity techniques continues to be more widely applied, the need for more sophisticated capabilities can be expected to grow.

1.2   Relationship to Standardization

Standardization of integrity primitives has proven to be rather difficult in practice. Though substantial efforts have been made over the last decade, the specificity of the results is far less than what we propose here. And specificity is key to cryptographic standards, since compatibility and interoperability of systems are major requirements and are often the main motivation for standardization in the first place.

Part of the reason our efforts have gone further is that we could apply substantial research effort which usually is not available to support standardization activities. Also, we have had the benefit of relevant standardization proposals at various stages.

We expect that parts of our portfolio will be serious candidates for international standardization in ISO. As a European project, however, we are particularly focused on standardization activities such as ETSI and CEN, as well as de facto standardization that may result from adoption within CEC DG XIII funded programs such as RACE II.

1.3   Organization of this Report

The remainder of Part I describes the background, structure, and actual experience of the RIPE project itself.

Part II is intended as a survey of the kinds of problems generally encountered in information security and the particular kinds of solutions offered by integrity primitives. The approach is structured by our taxonomy of primitives. For the newcomer to the field, references to introductory literature are provided.

The actual recommended integrity primitives are contained in Part III. They are briefly introduced in Chapter 1. Each of Chapters 2 through 8 covers a different recommended integrity primitive. Although the description of individual primitives is self-contained, they all follow a common format. They each have a section on definitions, in the style of standardization documents; a description of the primitive itself; recommended ways to use it; indications of the claimed properties as well as the extent to which they have been verified; performance estimates and software implementation guidelines. In addition four of them have an appendix containing a sample software implementation and test values. Finally, Chapters 9 and 10 contain guidelines to, respectively, RSA key generation and arithmetic computations with large integers.

2   The RIPE Project

2.1   Integrated Broad-band Communication for Europe

The European Community plans to set up a unified European market of about 300 million customers. In view of this market Integrated Broad-band Communication (IBC) has been planned for commercial use in 1996. This communication network will provide high-speed channels and will support a broad spectrum of services. In order to pave the way towards commercial use of IBC, the Commission of the European Communities has launched the RACE program (Research and Development in Advanced Communications Technologies in Europe) [RAC88]. Under this program pre-competitive and pre-normative work is going on. It is clear that the majority of the services offered as well as the management of the network are crucially dependent on the use of cryptographic techniques for security.

Within RACE, the RIPE project (RACE Integrity Primitives Evaluation) had the goal of putting forward a portfolio of techniques to meet the anticipated security requirements of IBC. (See [FLCJ92] for RIPE seen from an IBC perspective.)

The members of the RIPE project are: CWI, the Centre for Mathematics and Computer Science, Amsterdam (prime contractor); Siemens AG; Philips Crypto BV; Royal PTT Nederland NV, PTT Research; Katholieke Universiteit Leuven; and Aarhus Universitet.

2.2 An Open Call for Integrity Primitives

The project's motivation was the unique opportunity to attain consensus on openly available integrity primitives. In order to achieve wide acceptance for a collection of algorithms, the RIPE consortium decided to disseminate an open call.

The scope of the project and the evaluation procedure were fixed after having reached consensus with the main parties involved. The scope includes any digital integrity primitive, except for those offering data confidentiality. (It should be noted, however, that in some documents, e.g., [ISO83], integrity is used in a very much narrower sense than we use it.)

In response to the first call—which was circulated in a mailing of around 1250 brochures, announced by presentations at Eurocrypt'89 and Crypto'89 [VCFJ89], published in the IACR Newsletter [RIP89a] and the Journal of Cryptology [RIP89b]—fifteen submissions were received. Most common types of primitives were represented, but three additional primitives were invited for more comprehensive coverage. In the end, many well known primitives were submitted as well as proprietary ones from major suppliers.

From the eighteen submissions, ten came from academic submitters and the other eight from industry. The division over different countries was as follows: West Germany 5; U.S.A. 4; Denmark 3; Canada and Japan 2; Belgium and Australia 1. In October 1989, many of the submitters attended special meetings aimed at clarifying their submissions.

2.3 Evaluation Results

The evaluation was carried out following a carefully designed procedure. The submissions were evaluated with respect to three aspects: functionality, modes of use, and performance. The evaluation comprised computer simulation, statistical verification and analysis of mathematical structures, particularly to verify the integrity properties. Because of the limited resources and time period, it was decided that if any flaw was identified, the submitter would not be allowed to patch the flaw, thus preventing moving targets.

Five submissions already had to be rejected in a preliminary screening. After the main phase of the evaluation, and after taking into account deficiencies implied by work done in the cryptographic community, ten primitives (six submissions) remained.

These submissions showed significant potential, but each required modification and/or further specification by the submitters. Four of the six had minor functional problems. In most cases, it was clear how the problems could be avoided. Further evaluation was postponed, in accordance with the policy of not allowing modifications by submitters during evaluation. Permission was obtained from six submitters to publish the problems we had uncovered.

2.4   A Second Call for Integrity Primitives

At the inception of the project, it was already foreseen that some submissions to the first call would require adjustment and re-submission to the second call, although it was not anticipated that no result of the first call would be recommended and that all results would come from the second call. It was circulated in essentially the same ways as the first call [PCFJ91], and resulted in fifteen submissions all told. About seven of these could be considered improved versions of submissions from the first call.

Of the fifteen submissions, ten came from academic submitters and the other five from industry. The division over different countries was as follows: Germany 6; U.S.A. 3; Belgium and the Netherlands 2; Canada and Denmark 1. In June 1991 meetings with submitters were again held.

Essentially the same evaluation techniques were used as for the first call. Five submissions could be rejected in a preliminary screening. After the main phase of the evaluation six primitives (four submissions) remained. Three more primitives were adapted from the literature for more comprehensive coverage. The final nine primitives resulting comprise Part III of this report.

3   Conclusion

The RIPE project carried out its planned acquisition and evaluation of integrity primitives. It has been able to put forward a comprehensive yet carefully evaluated and specified portfolio of integrity primitives.

References

[FLCJ92] W. Fumy, P. Landrock, D. Chaum, C.J.A. Jansen, G. Roelofsen and J. Vandewalle, "Integrity Primitives for IBC," *Proceedings of IWACA'92– International Workshop on Advanced Communications and Applications for High Speed Networks*, Munich, Germany, 1992, pp. 133–138.

[ISO83] ISO International Standard 7498, *Information processing - Open systems interconnection - Basic reference model*, 1983.

[PCFJ91] B. Preneel, D. Chaum, W. Fumy, C.J.A. Jansen, P. Landrock and G. Roelofsen, "Race Integrity Primitives Evaluation (RIPE): A Status Report," *Advances in Cryptology, Proc. Eurocrypt'91, LNCS 547*, D.W. Davies, Ed., Springer-Verlag, 1991, pp. 547–551.

[VCFJ89] J. Vandewalle, D. Chaum, W. Fumy, C.J.A. Jansen, P. Landrock and G. Roelofsen, "A European call for cryptographic algorithms: RIPE (RACE Integrity Primitives Evaluation)," *Advances in Cryptology, Proc. Eurocrypt'89, LNCS 434*, J.-J. Quisquater and J. Vandewalle, Eds., Springer-Verlag, 1990, pp. 267–271.

[RAC88] Commission of the European Communities, *RACE Workplan '89*, Rue de la Loi/Wetstraat 200, B-1049, Brussels, Belgium, 1988.

[RIP89a] RIPE, "Call for Integrity Primitives", *IACR Newsletter*, Vol. 6, No. 2, 1989.

[RIP89b] RIPE, "Call for Integrity Primitives", *Journal of Cryptology*, Vol. 1, No. 3, 1989.

Part II

Integrity Concepts

Table of Contents

1   Introduction

Information integrity is essential for many envisaged applications of broadband communication. In former days, the protection of information was mainly an issue of physical security and trust. The protection of authenticity relied on the difficulty of forging certain documents and/or signatures. In the electronic age, letters, contracts and other documents are replaced by sequences of bits, but the demand for authenticity and integrity existing in the 'old' world has in no way been diminished. On the contrary, with open and untrusted networks, it is relatively easy to commit all kinds of frauds unless precautions are taken [DaPr89].

There are several types of security measures. Security measures based on cryptographic techniques can provide efficient and flexible logical protection of information, which yields crucial advantages for most applications. To achieve a high level of communications security in a network, cryptographic mechanisms are to be employed. Encipherment e.g., supports data confidentiality, whereas cryptographic integrity check values can be used to protect data integrity. The use of cryptographic methods can prevent wiretapping, masquerading, and modification attacks, and does additionally allow for some access control policy to be implemented [PoKl89], [VoKe85].

The security measures employed for a specific system of course have to meet the user requirements. The set of those requirements is growing with the number of electronic communications facilities. However, a substantial part can be met by a fixed set of security services as identified in [ISO88].

The aim of this chapter is to establish a relationship between security services, security mechanisms and integrity primitives. Speaking in general terms, at the user end security services are offered. These security services are provided by security protocols or mechanisms, which are built up from basic building blocks called security primitives.

The RIPE project has selected a set of integrity primitives, the ingredients needed to solve a wide range of integrity problems. These techniques are concerned with protecting against non-trusted or potentially malicious disruption of the integrity in information systems. Some illustrative example uses of integrity primitives are as follows:

- *Accessible password files*: a publicly accessible 'password' list can allow anyone to check whether a particular password is allowed by the list, but nobody to discover what any of the passwords actually are.
- *Fingerprinted data*: a small fingerprint can be produced of an arbitrarily large amount of data when it is stored, so that when the data is later retrieved, the fingerprint can be checked and no modification of the data will escape detection.
- *Authenticated messages*: a message can be communicated through a hostile environment, in such a way that the intended receiver can be sure that it has not been modified and was sent by the intended sender.

- *Identification protocols*: one party can verify that a certain other party is really at the other end of the line during a conversation.
- *Public key digital signatures*: a message can be digitally signed so that anyone can verify its signature and even convince a judge that it really was signed by a particular party.

The following section details the concept of security services and describes how security mechanisms can be used to provide those services. A taxonomy of security primitives is given in Section 3. This allows security mechanisms to be built up from primitives as described in Section 4. General references for further reading are [Bra88, DaPr89, FuRi94, MeMa82].

2   Security Services

Security measures for information systems can be realized in various ways. In particular, there are many options for the integration of security services into a communications architecture. A system *Security Architecture* constitutes an overall security blueprint for a system. It describes security services and their interrelationships, and it shows how the security services map onto the system architecture.

In order to extend the field of application of the Basic Reference Model for Open System Interconnection [ISO83], ISO (the *International Organization for Standardization*) has identified a set of security services and possibilities of integrating them into the seven layers of the OSI architecture. The *OSI Security Architecture* [ISO88] recognizes five primary security services: authentication, access control, confidentiality, integrity, and non-repudiation. These services form the basic building blocks for other security architectures as well.

- *Data Origin Authentication* provides corroboration that the claimed origin of the data received is indeed the real origin of the data, while *Entity Authentication* is the verification that the communicating entities are the ones claimed.
- *Access Control* provides protection against unauthorized use of resources (e.g., network services).
- *Confidentiality* provides protection of information from unauthorized disclosure.
- *Integrity* ensures that data is accurately transmitted from source to destination. The system must be able to counter equipment failure as well as actions by persons or processes that are not authorized to alter the data.
- *Non-Repudiation* protects against denial by one of the entities involved in a communication of having participated in all or part of the communication. Non-repudiation with proof of origin e.g., protects against any attempt by the sender to repudiate having sent a message, while non-repudiation with proof of delivery protects against any attempt by the recipient to falsely deny having received a message.

Security services describe natural user requirements. The relevance of a particular service depends on a number of factors. In ISO 7498-2 [ISO88] there is a detailed discussion on which services are relevant for which layers. But even if this is clarified other factors may be of importance. An example is whether users are communicating in connection oriented or connectionless mode. In connectionless mode data is transmitted without a connection being established explicitly. As each packet is sent on its own, connectionless data integrity is strongly related to data origin authentication. Therefore mechanisms are required which are able to provide data origin authentication and integrity. However, there is no protection against replay or deletion. Connection oriented mode applies to the situation in which a connection between two entities is established before user data is transmitted via the connection. In addition to the connectionless case one can think of mechanisms that prevent against insertion, replay, and deletion.

According to ISO 7498-2, types of *Security Mechanisms* that can be used to provide the security services identified include encipherment, digital signature, access control, data integrity, authentication exchange, traffic padding, routing control, and notarization. The specification of suitable mechanisms is not within the scope of a security architecture. This is for instance dealt with in the ISO subcommittee ISO/IEC/JTC1/SC27 ("Security Techniques"). In the following we briefly discuss which type of cryptographic mechanism suits which security service.

- *Data Origin Authentication* implies that the originator of the information performs a transformation of the data out of which the receiver can unambiguously verify its origin. This requires the message to be linked to the identity of the sender. It has to be assured that neither changing the originator's identity nor changing the message will result in a successful data origin authentication. The latter condition implies that data origin authentication is based on a data integrity mechanism.
- *Entity Authentication* requires that the entity in question proves to know or to have something which makes the interrogator believe that he deals with the specific entity. Entity authentication can be considered as the sum of data origin authentication and a guarantee that it is not a replay of a previous transfer. The latter can be prevented by taking care that never the integrity of the same message has to be assured (e.g., by incorporating a date/time stamp into the data block) or that the mechanisms to provide entity authentication are never applied in exactly the same way (e.g., by changing the keys).
- *Access Control* can be realized in many different ways. One example is a process where a subject interrogates an Access Control List (ACL) stating the access rights of each entity to each object. For this, it is necessary that the object managing the ACL can verify the authenticity of the inquirer. Thus, the access control mechanism utilizes an authentication mechanism.
- *Data Confidentiality* can e.g., be realized by a data routing mechanism that takes care that confidential data is not passing malicious entities, or by an encipherment mechanism where the corresponding decipherment operation

can only be performed by authorized entities. Data confidentiality is excluded from the scope of RIPE.

- *Data Integrity* shall enable the receiving entity to detect any modification, insertion, deletion or replay of data (see Data Origin Authentication).
- *Non-Repudiation* can take at least four forms: non-repudiation with proof of origin, receipt, delivery and submission. *Non-repudiation with proof of origin* enables the receiver of data to prove that the claimed sender of the data really sent the data. This service is a specific combination of data integrity and entity or data origin authentication. Such a service is not only useful for the receiver but also important for the sender who is protected from being accused of sending data he did not send. Because a third party has to be able to make a distinction between sender and receiver, non-repudiation services suggest the use of asymmetric mechanisms. In an asymmetric cryptographic mechanism it is computationally infeasible to deduce the enciphering key from the deciphering key and/or vice-versa. In a symmetric cryptographic algorithm those keys are equal, or can easily be deduced from one another. Computationally infeasible refers to a computation that is theoretically achievable, but not feasible in terms of the time taken to perform it with the current or predicted power of technology. The most common mechanisms are digital signatures. However, it should be noted that non-repudiation services can also be based on symmetric authentication mechanisms, by involving a trusted third party. *Non-repudiation with proof of receipt* enables the sender of data to prove that its receiver really received the data. *Non-repudiation with proof of submission* enables the sender to prove that he submitted specific data. *Non-repudiation with proof of delivery* finally enables to prove that specific data was delivered (e.g., to a mailbox). Until recently, delivery and receipt were one service since a need to have both functions had not been identified.

3   Integrity Primitives

Security primitives are the basic building blocks of security services and mechanisms. Security primitives can be widely applied to protect information systems. This section introduces different types of primitives together with various kinds of uses that can be made of them. Figure 1 gives a taxonomy of security primitives. In this figure the primitives offering data confidentiality are shown in italics, and the integrity primitives are shown in boldface (note that in some documents, e.g., [ISO88] the term integrity has a much more restricted meaning). The given list of integrity primitives is not considered to be complete. Integrity primitives for which little immediate practical significance is foreseen (e.g., claw-free permutations or randomized mappings) are omitted from the taxonomy.

Integrity primitives are of course ultimately intended to be useful to people. But computerized equipment will often be performing the actual computations, perhaps even automatically. It will thus be convenient to abstract from the

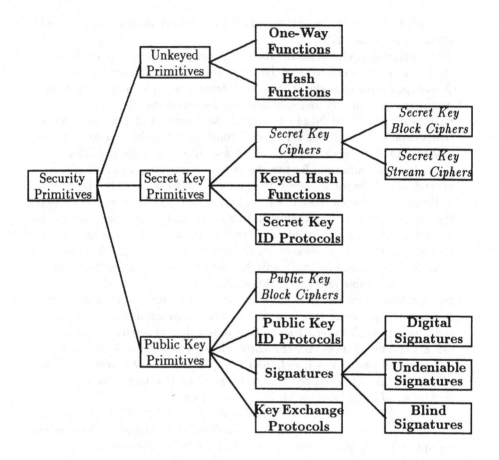

Fig. 1. Taxonomy of security primitives

distinction between a person, a person directly controlling a computerized piece of equipment, or a computer autonomously playing a similar role. Accordingly, the active agents using the integrity primitives will simply be referred to as 'parties'.

The subsections—unkeyed, secret key, and public key integrity primitives— correspond to the second level of the taxonomy in the figure. The essential idea is that keys of secret key primitives are known to more than one party, but not to an adversary, whereas public keys of public key primitives are known to all parties including any adversary.

3.1 Unkeyed Integrity Primitives

There are two types of integrity primitives that are not parameterized by a cryptographic key. Both are essential for a broad spectrum of security services:

- A *One-Way Function* is a mapping for which it is in general infeasible given an image to find a function argument that results in that image, or given a function argument and its corresponding image to find a second argument having the same image. A *One-Way Permutation* is a bijective one-way function. One-way functions can be used to protect password files. Instead of storing passwords themselves in a file, they are transformed by a one-way function before being stored. The applied transformation can be public, so that anyone can verify that a particular password is in the file. But due to the properties of the one-way function nobody can discover what any of the other passwords actually are. For a one-way permutation the result of applying the function naturally has to be as large as its input. In many practical applications, however, potential inputs are large, and producing a relatively small output is desirable.
- A *Hash Function* derives from an input of arbitrary length (the 'message') an output of fixed length (the 'hashcode') in such a way that it is practically infeasible given a hashcode to find a message that results in that hashcode, or given a message and its corresponding hashcode to find a second message having the same hashcode. If in addition it is practically infeasible to find two different messages that hash to the same result the hash function is called *collision resistant*. Since a hash function is a function that maps a string of arbitrary bit length to a result of fixed bit length, in general many inputs will be mapped to the same output. A hash function can be used in a way similar to the way one-way functions were used for passwords above. This would have the advantage that instead of passwords of a limited size, arbitrarily long 'passphrases' could be used. In fact, just by looking at the password file, no clue would be given as to the length of the corresponding password or passphrase. Another important field of application for hash functions are signature mechanisms that ask for a cryptographic 'footprint' of the data to be signed rather than applying the costly signature primitive to large amounts of data (such a signature mechanism often is called *Digital Signature with Appendix*). For a hash function based on a secret key block cipher a standard is submitted for publication [ISO94b].

3.2   Secret Key Integrity Primitives.

If not only the integrity of information is to be protected, but the information is also to be linked to an originator, a key has to be involved in the security mechanism, assuming that some coupling between a person and his or her key is established. There are two classes of security primitives that are parameterized by a cryptographic key: secret key primitives and public key primitives. Secret key primitives are based on the fact that the parties involved share a (secret) key. This key would be established by the parties in advance, for instance by one party creating the key at random and supplying it to the other party without letting anyone else learn it. By secret key techniques, parties can protect themselves against outsider attacks. If protection from insider fraud is required, a third party has to be able to distinguish between entities and the capabilities of the entities have to be different. This effect can be achieved with public key primitives. For both classes the basic security primitives parameterized by a key are block ciphers.

- A *Block Cipher* is an invertible function parameterized by a key that maps message blocks of a fixed block length into ciphertext blocks of the same length. Block ciphers are keyed one-way permutations. There are secret key block ciphers (e.g., the Data Encryption Standard, DES [ANS81], [NBS77]) and public key block ciphers (e.g., the Rivest-Shamir-Adleman algorithm, RSA [RSA78]). The evaluation of block ciphers used to provide confidentiality is excluded from the scope of RIPE. But, given a block cipher there are several ways to construct other integrity primitives, such as one-way functions, keyed hash functions, or identification protocols. Such a construction is denoted as a 'mode-of-use' of the keyed one-way permutation. Mode of use usually refers to the manner in which a block cipher may be operated (e.g., electronic code book, cipher block chaining, etc.). Note that a block cipher must be a one-way function with respect to its key input, but it need not be with respect to its data input.

- A *Stream Cipher* produces a long sequence that is unpredictable to those without its secret key, and can be used to obtain data confidentiality. Typically, the sender of a message adds the unpredictable sequence to the message before transmitting it; the recipient, having the same secret key and recreating the same sequence, subtracts the sequence from the data received to recover the original message. Synchronization must of course be maintained and care must be taken to prevent sequences from being re-used, since confidentiality of the data is ensured by the unpredictability of the sequence [Rue86].

Keyed hash functions play an important role for the authentication of messages, while identification protocols are to authenticate entities (e.g., persons, or devices).

- A *Keyed Hash Function* is a hash function parameterized by a (secret) key. Such a hash function can be used to add controlled redundancy to information and to thus protect the integrity of the information. Before a message is sent, the secret key is used to compute a keyed hashcode from it. This value is sent along with the message and can be checked by the legitimate recipient using the common secret key. Since the hash function is parameterized by a secret key it ties the originator to the information and therefore provides both data integrity and data origin authentication. For that reason, keyed hash functions often are called *Message Authentication Codes* (MAC's). Of course these same techniques may be applied to messages that are stored before they are ultimately received. A specific way to use a block cipher for the calculation of a MAC has been standardized [ISO93a] (see also [ANS86], [ISO87]). Another important application for keyed hash functions are identification schemes.

– *Secret Key Identification Protocols* are based on the assumption that the parties involved share a common key prior to the application of the protocol. In a 2-way authentication scheme the basic ingredients of the protocol are a challenge from one entity which is answered by a token, that is a set of data items formed for an authentication exchange, from the other entity (e.g., a dynamic password scheme). In a 1-way authentication protocol a token from one entity to another is simply transmitted. A *token* is a set of data items formed for an authentication exchange and transmitted from one entity to another. In this case the challenge answered is implicitly given by a time-stamp or a sequence number. For secret key identification protocols based on a secret key block cipher a standard is under development [ISO93b].

3.3   Public Key Integrity Primitives

As indicated above, the use of secret key primitives cannot solve disputes between sender and receiver, because they share the same secret information. The idea of public key primitives is that an entity is associated with a pair of related keys. One of the keys is called the 'private key' and is kept secret by its owner; the other key of the pair, called the 'public key', is made known in a way that ensures that it is genuine. Public keys might, in principle, be published in a newspaper. An essential part of the concept is that it must be infeasible to compute or simulate possession of the private key using only the public key, which is reminiscent of the one-way property described above.

Public key techniques are in some sense more powerful than the unkeyed and secret key techniques already described, but they also are more costly. That is, in general their computational complexity is considerably higher. With public key techniques, the pre-arrangement of each participant publishing a public key allows any pair of participants to ensure the integrity of their communication. This flexibility would require one pair of keys for each possible pair of participants using only secret key techniques, which rapidly becomes impractical as the number of participants grows. An even more fundamental advantage is that every party can verify that a message must have been sent by the party owning a particular secret key. This allows the recipient of such a 'signed' message to provide the signature for verification by any other participant, even a judge.

– *Public Key Identification Protocols* are based on the fact that each entity owns a private-public key pair. A party that has published its public key can identify itself to any other party. Suppose a challenging party has obtained the public key of the identifying party. Then the challenging party can form a random challenge, encode it with the public key of the identifying party, and send the result to the identifying party. The identifying party can then use its private key to compute the inverse operation to recover the original challenge value, which can be returned to the challenging party. Thus the challenging party is convinced that the identifying party is the only one that could have made the computation. Public keys are typically certified by a *Certification Authority*, i.e., they are rendered unforgeable by a third party. A common procedure is to sign the public key of an entity together with some additional information used to authenticate that entity using the private key of the certification authority. The set of data items assigned to an entity and used to authenticate that entity is called its *credentials*. A set of credentials together with the certification authority's signature of those credentials is called a *certificate*. For public key identification protocols also a standard is under development [ISO93c]. As for secret key identification protocols, the timeliness of the tokens can be established via timestamps or sequence numbers, or by answering explicit challenges as described above. In any case, public key identification protocols are based on public key block ciphers.

- A *Digital Signature* is to serve as the electronic equivalent of a written signature. It allows to 'sign' a message so that anyone can verify the signature, i.e., prove that a message has been created by a specific entity. Since the receiver must not be able to construct the signed message, the process of signing requires secret information. The validation of the signature, however, only requires access to public information. For digital signatures that provide message recovery the additional specification of a special transformation introducing redundancy is necessary, while digital signatures with appendix require a collision-resistant hash function. One specific way to calculate a digital signature with message recovery has been standardized [ISO91].

- An *Undeniable Signature* allows its signer to control who can verify it. Like a plain digital signature, it is a number that can only be formed using the private key of the signer. But an undeniable signature is only verifiable by a party if the signer cooperates with that party in a protocol. This differs from ordinary digital signatures, which are verifiable without limitation by anyone who obtains a copy of the signature. In case of dispute, the signer of an undeniable signature can prove to any party, such as a judge, whether or not a purported signature is valid or false. Extensions allow the signer to convince a recipient that an agreed party whose public key is known can confirm or deny (but would be unable to create) signatures [Cha90].

- *Blind Signatures* can be used to protect personal privacy. They prevent the signer from being able to see the message signed. One example use is for electronic bank notes, whose digital signatures allow them to be accepted by retailers. To withdraw such a note, the payer chooses a note number at random, blinds it, and sends it to the bank for signing. The bank withdraws a corresponding amount from the payer's account, signs the note, and returns it. The payer can then unblind the signed note and later spend it. When the note is returned to the bank by the retailer, it must be honored because of its signature, but the bank cannot trace it to the payer's account. Other uses are for untraceable credentials, allowing transfer of information between unlinkable pseudonyms [Cha92].

- *Key Exchange Protocols* are to establish a secret key between the communicating parties. In many cases identification protocols can easily be modified to provide additionally for key exchange. An example for a key establishment protocol is given in [DiHe79]. Standards for key exchange protocols are currently under development [ISO93d, ISO93e].

4   Security Mechanisms

In this section we will establish a relationship between security mechanisms and security primitives.

- *Data Origin Authentication* and *Data Integrity* mechanisms make use of unkeyed hash functions (Manipulation Detection Code, MDC), or of keyed hash functions (Message Authentication Code, MAC). In the case of an MDC the integrity of the hashcode has to be protected, e.g., by encipherment or by an integrity channel (e.g., a phone when people know each other's voice). With a MAC protection of authenticity is independent of confidentiality but requires its own key. With an MDC authentication is separated from encipherment but compromised when the cipher is broken.
- *Entity Authentication* mechanisms are based on secret key or public key encipherment schemes, or on keyed hash functions. In the symmetric case the parties have to share the same secret information. If this cannot be assumed they each have to share some secret information with an on-line trusted center. In the asymmetric case the identities of the entities can be certified by an off-line trusted center that issues credentials. With zero knowledge (minimum knowledge) authentication, the asymmetric protocol between prover and verifier is designed such that the verifier learns nothing but the validity of the assertion (gets only minimum additional knowledge).
  Authentication in general is based on proving/verifying specific knowledge or possession of something (e.g., a secret key). Such a proof typically requires a protocol with a number of interactions (passes). Two-pass authentication for instance involves a challenge (e.g., a random number) from one entity and a response from the other entity which convinces the challenging entity (e.g., that the challenged entity has a specific secret key). One-pass authentication makes use of the same principle but employs an implicit challenge (e.g., a time stamp or a sequence number).
- *Signature* mechanisms are based on asymmetric block ciphers. Signature mechanisms with message recovery need the additional specification of a special transformation introducing the required redundancy. Signature mechanisms with imprint/appendix as well as signature mechanisms based on zero knowledge proofs require a collision-resistant hash function. Undeniable signatures are based on commutative one-way functions, while blind signatures are based on commutative one-way permutations.
- *Encipherment* mechanisms are based on block ciphers in various modes of use.
- *Key Exchange* mechanisms are based on commutative one-way functions or on zero-knowledge techniques and will typically be integrated into entity authentication mechanisms.

References

[ANS81] ANSI X3.92-1981, *Data Encryption Algorithm*, 1981.

[ANS86] ANSI X9.9-1986, *Financial Institution Message Authentication*, 1986.

[Bra88] G. Brassard, *Modern Cryptography*, Lecture Notes in Computer Science 325, Springer-Verlag, Berlin-Heidelberg-New York, 1988.

[Cha90] D. Chaum, "Zero-knowledge Undeniable Signatures," *Advances in Cryptology, Proc. Eurocrypt'90, LNCS 473*, I.B. Damgård, Ed., Springer-Verlag, 1991, pp. 458–464.

[Cha92] D. Chaum, "Achieving Electronic Privacy," *Scientific American*, Vol. 267, No. 2, 1992, pp. 96–101.

[DaPr89] D.W. Davies and W.L. Price, *Security for Computer Networks, 2nd ed.*, Wiley & Sons, New York, 1989.

[DiHe79] W. Diffie and M.E. Hellman, "New Directions in Cryptography," *IEEE Trans. on Information Theory*, Vol. IT–22, 1976, pp. 644–654.

[FuRi94] W. Fumy and H.P. Riess, *Kryptographie, 2. Auflage*, Oldenbourg, Munich, 1994.

[ISO83] ISO International Standard 7498, *Information processing - Open systems interconnection - Basic reference model*, 1983.

[ISO87] ISO International Standard 8731-1, *Banking - Approved algorithms for message authentication, Part 1: DEA*, 1987.

[ISO88] ISO International Standard 7498-2, *Information processing - Open systems interconnection - Basic reference model - Part 2: Security Architecture*, 1988.

[ISO91] ISO/IEC International Standard 9796, *Information technology - Security techniques - Digital signature scheme giving message recovery*, 1991.

[ISO93a] ISO/IEC International Standard 9797, *Information technology - Data cryptographic techniques - Data integrity mechanism using a cryptographic check function employing a block cipher algorithm*, 1993.

[ISO93b] ISO/IEC Draft International Standard 9798-2, *Information technology - Security techniques - Entity authentication mechanisms, Part 2: Entity authentication using symmetric techniques*, 1993.

[ISO93c] ISO/IEC International Standard 9798-3, *Information technology - Security techniques - Entity authentication mechanisms, Part 3: Entity authentication using a public key algorithm*, 1993.

[ISO93d] ISO/IEC Committee Draft 11770-2, *Information technology - Security techniques - Key management, Part 2: Key management mechanisms using symmetric techniques*, 1993.

[ISO93e] ISO/IEC Committee Draft 11770-3, *Information technology - Security techniques - Key management, Part 3: Key management mechanisms using asymmetric techniques*, 1993.

[ISO94a] ISO/IEC International Standard 10118-1, *Information technology - Security techniques - Hash-functions, Part 1: General*, 1994.

[ISO94b] ISO/IEC International Standard 10118-2, *Information technology - Security techniques - Hash-functions, Part 2: Hash functions using an n-bit block cipher algorithm*, 1994.

[MeMa82] C.H. Meyer and S.M. Matyas, *Cryptography: A New Dimension in Computer Data Security*, Wiley & Sons, New York, 1982.

[NBS77] National Bureau of Standards, *Data Encryption Standard*, Federal Information Processing Standard, Publication 46, US Department of Commerce, January 1977.

[PoKl89] G.J. Popek and C.S. Kline, "Encryption and secure computer networks," *ACM Computing Surveys*, Vol. 11, 1979, pp. 331–356.

[Rue86]   R.A. Rueppel. *Analysis and Design of Stream Ciphers*, Springer-Verlag, Berlin-Heidelberg, 1986.

[RSA78]   R.L. Rivest, A. Shamir and L. Adleman, "A method for obtaining digital signature and public key cryptosystems," *Communications of the ACM*, Vol. 21, 1978, pp. 120–126.

[VoKe85] V.L. Voydock and S.T. Kent, "Security in high level network protocols," *IEEE Communications Magazine*, July 1985, pp. 12–24.

Part III

Recommended Integrity Primitives

Chapter 1

Introduction to Part III

Table of Contents

1   Introduction

This part of the RIPE final report contains full descriptions, detailed analysis as well as guidelines for the implementation and use of the RIPE primitives. Each of the next seven chapters is devoted to one of the recommended primitives. The last two chapters contain guidelines on RSA key generation and on arithmetic computations with large integers.

All chapters on primitives have the same outline. Each starts with a short introduction (Section 1). In order to avoid ambiguities in the descriptions, notation and relevant definitions are then given (Section 2). After this, the primitive is described (Section 3), followed by the recommended modes of use (Section 4). Next, the security aspects including claimed properties and a presentation of the main results of the evaluation are discussed (Section 5). Finally, hardware and software implementation are considered (Section 6) and some guidelines for software implementation are given (Section 7). Four chapters have appendices containing sample software implementations in the programming language C and test values for the primitives to allow verification.

The chapters on primitives are organized according to the taxonomy introduced in Section 3 of Part II. Chapters 2 and 3 contain unkeyed integrity primitives, Chapters 4 through 6 secret key integrity primitives and Chapters 7 and 8 two public key integrity primitives. First, we briefly indicate how each of the recommended primitives made it into the portfolio. Figure 1 illustrates how the RIPE primitives fit in the taxonomy tree introduced in Part II of this report. This chapter does not contain any references, as they, and many more, can be found in the chapters describing the recommended primitives.

2   Unkeyed Integrity Primitives

First, we present two hash functions, MDC-4 and RIPEMD. The former is especially suited for hardware implementation, the latter for software implementation.

MDC-4 (MDC stands for Manipulation Detection Code), designed by D. Coppersmith, S. Pilpel, C.H. Meyer, S.M. Matyas, M.M. Hyden, J. Oseas, B. Brachtl, and M. Schilling, is a hash function based on a symmetric block cipher and is recommended for use with a DES-engine.

RIPEMD (MD in this case stands for Message Digest) is based on the publicly known hash function MD4, which was submitted to RIPE by RSA Inc. However, due to partial attacks on the first two out of three rounds (found by R. Merkle) and also on the last two rounds (discovered by the RIPE-team), it was decided to apply to MD4 a design principle of MDC-4, viz., the use of two parallel rounds. This makes RIPEMD a sufficiently secure unkeyed hash function, which at the same time is very fast in software. The use of MD4 was preferred over its follow-up MD5, which has been discovered to have weak collisions (found by B. den Boer and A. Bosselaers).

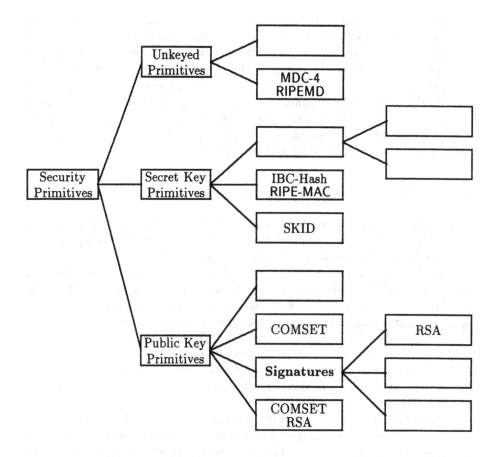

Fig. 1. Mapping of the RIPE primitives on the taxonomy tree.

3   Secret Key Integrity Primitives

Next, we present three secret key primitives, two of which are keyed hash functions (RIPE-MAC and IBC-Hash), whereas the third (SKID) is a secret key identification protocol.

The design of **RIPE-MAC** (MAC stands for Message Authentication Code) is inspired by the standardized "CBC-MAC" function (see, e.g., ISO/IEC 9797). Like CBC-MAC, RIPE-MAC is based on the block chaining mode of a block cipher. It has the additional feature that it cannot be directly used for concealment. Two variants of **RIPE-MAC** are given, which are based on single and triple encryption—corresponding to increasing levels of security.

The second keyed hash function, IBC-hash, has been designed by members of the RIPE-team, David Chaum, Maarten van der Ham and Bert den Boer. IBC-Hash has the distinguished feature of being both provably secure and rather fast in both hardware and software.

The primitive named SKID actually contains two secret key identification protocols that can be used to provide entity authentication. The two variants are for unidirectional and bidirectional authentication. Both are based on a keyed one-way function rather than on a block cipher. Their design emphasizes the integrity oriented approach of the project. These protocols have been used as a contribution to ISO-standardization and are to be incorporated in future versions of the proposed set of entity authentication standards specified in ISO/IEC 9798. The SKID primitives are not the result of a submission but have been selected and enhanced by Markus Dichtl and Walter Fumy.

4   Public Key Integrity Primitives

Finally, the RIPE portfolio contains two public key primitives. One of them is the well-known RSA algorithm, while the other one (COMSET) is a public key identification protocol based on the Rabin variant of RSA.

The chapter on RSA is based on the RSA public key scheme, which has been submitted to RIPE by RSA Inc. It includes an evaluation of the ISO/IEC 9796 standard for a digital signature with message recovery. This standard was developed by an ISO editorial group and has now been independently evaluated for the first time. The digital signature based on ISO/IEC 9796 is one recommended mode of use for RSA, where the input typically would be the result of one of the RIPE unkeyed integrity primitives applied to a message. Another recommended mode of use provides key forwarding, which would find its application typically in batch settings, such as EDIFACT.

COMSET is a public key identification protocol, which has been designed and submitted by a research group at Aarhus University, Jørgen Brandt, Ivan Damgård, Peter Landrock and Torben Pedersen. It was originally developed for DANSECT, a secure system developed by the Danish Telecommunication Companies. COMSET is a zero-knowledge mutual identification scheme, which in addition allows for secret key exchange. One of the foreseen applications of COMSET is interactive EDI.

5   Guidelines

The RIPE report concludes with two useful chapters, respectively on RSA key generation and on arithmetic computations with large integers.

After formulating the top level algorithm and the security constraints for RSA key sets, the guide to RSA key generation basically follows a bottom-up approach. It starts with algorithms for generating probable and provable primes, and incorporates these in algorithms for generating primes that satisfy the necessary security constraints for RSA key sets. Therefore it can be used for generating the primes and key sets of the primitives IBC-Hash, RSA and COMSET.

In the last chapter guidelines for arithmetic computations with large integers are given. These computations form the basis of an implementation for both the primitives IBC-Hash, RSA and COMSET, as for the generation of the necessary primes and key sets used in these primitives.

Chapter 2

MDC-4

Table of Contents

1   Introduction

This chapter describes the integrity primitive MDC-4 [MeSc88, Mey89, Mat91]; we observe that it has been patented, see [CPMM90].

MDC-4 is a so-called *modification detection code* (MDC) or *hash function* that compresses messages of arbitrary length to a 128-bit output block, the *hashcode* of the message. It is claimed that it is computationally infeasible to produce two messages having the same hashcode, or to produce any messages having a given prespecified target hashcode. Hash functions with these properties are used in message authentication applications such as the protection of the integrity and the origin of data stored or transmitted using secret-key or public-key techniques (see Part II of this report).

MDC-4 processes the data in blocks of 64 bits. The name MDC-4 is derived from the four DES [NBS77] encryptions that are required to process a single message block. The algorithm itself specifies no padding rule. The padding algorithm used is that of RIPEMD (see Chapter 3), which is the same as that of MD4 [Riv90].

Since the MDC-4 algorithm uses four DES encryptions per message block, its design is oriented towards implementations using hardware realizations of the DES. The performance of a pure software implementation will suffer noticeably from the low software performance of the DES, especially since each DES application involves a change of the key.

The structure of this chapter is as follows. In order to avoid any ambiguities in the description of the primitive, the notation and definitions in this chapter are fixed in Section 2. Section 3 contains a description of the primitive and in Section 4 the possible modes of use of the primitive are considered. The security aspects of the primitive are discussed in Section 5. These include the claimed properties and the results of algebraic evaluations of the primitive. Finally, in Section 6 the performance aspects of MDC-4 are considered, and Section 7 gives some guidelines for software implementation.

This chapter has two appendices. Appendix A contains a straightforward software implementation of MDC-4 in the programming language C and in Appendix B test values for the primitive are given.

2   Definitions and Notation

2.1   Introduction

In order to obtain a clear description of the primitive, the notation and definitions used in this chapter are fully described in this section. These include the
representation of the numbers in the description, and the operations, functions
and constants used by the primitive.

2.2   General

The symbol ":=" is used for the assignment of a value or a meaning to a variable
or symbol. That is, $a := b$ either means that the variable a gets the value of the
variable b, or it means that a is defined as "b". It will be obvious from the context
which meaning is intended.

   The equality-sign "=" is used for equality only. That is, it indicates that the
two entities on either side are equal.

   Note that in C-source code, "=" denotes assignment, while comparison is
denoted by "==".

   An ellipsis ("...") denotes an implicit enumeration. For example, "$i = 0, 1,$
$\ldots, n$" is meant to represent the sentence "for $i = 0$, $i = 1$, and so on, up to
$i = n$".

2.3   Representation of the Numbers

In this chapter a *byte* is defined as an 8-bit quantity and a *word* as a 64-bit
quantity. A byte is considered to be a nonnegative integer. That is, it can
take on the values 0 through $2^8 - 1 = 255$. Likewise, a word is considered
to be a nonnegative integer, hence it takes on the values 0 through $2^{64} -$
$1 = 18\,446\,744\,073\,709\,551\,615$. The value of a word can be given in decimal
as well as in hexadecimal form. In the latter case the number is written as '0x'
followed immediately by at most 16 hexadecimal digits, the most significant
one first. For example, the hexadecimal representation of the 64-bit number
$5\,931\,894\,172\,722\,287\,186$ is 0x5252525252525252.

   A sequence of $8n$ bits $b_0, b_1, \ldots, b_{8n-1}$ is interpreted as a sequence of n bytes
in the following way. Each group of 8 consecutive bits is considered as a byte B_i,
the first bit of such a group being the most significant bit of that byte. Hence,

$$B_i := b_{8i}2^7 + b_{8i+1}2^6 + \cdots + b_{8i+7}, \quad i = 0, 1, \ldots, n - 1. \tag{1}$$

A sequence of $8l$ bytes $B_0, B_1, \ldots, B_{8l-1}$ is interpreted as a sequence of words
$W_0, W_1, \ldots, W_{l-1}$ in the following way. Each group of 8 consecutive bytes is
considered as a word W_i, the first byte of such a word being the most significant
byte of that word. Hence,

$$W_i := B_{8i}(256)^7 + B_{8i+1}(256)^6 + \cdots + B_{8i+6}(256) + B_{8i+7}, \quad i = 0, 1, \ldots, l - 1. \tag{2}$$

In accordance with the notations above, the bits of a word W are denoted as

$$W = (w_0, w_1, \ldots, w_{63}),\tag{3}$$

where

$$W = \sum_{i=0}^{63} w_i 2^{63-i}.\tag{4}$$

In this chapter words are always denoted by uppercase letters and the bits of this word by the corresponding lowercase letter with indices as in Equation (3). Likewise, bytes are indicated by uppercase letters and the bits that constitute this byte by lowercase letters with indices as in Equation (1). The ordering of bytes in a word is given by Equation (2).

2.4   Definitions and Basic Operations

- A *string* is a sequence of bits. If X is a string consisting of n bits, then those bits are denoted from left to right by x_0, x_1, $\ldots$, x_{n-2}, x_{n-1}.
- The *length* of a string X is the number of bits in the string X. A string of length n is called an n-bit string.
- For two strings X and Y of length n, the $2n$-bit string $W = X \parallel Y$ is defined as the *concatenation* of the strings X and Y. That is, according to the definition of a string above,

$$\begin{aligned} w_i &:= x_i \\ w_{i+n} &:= y_i \end{aligned} \qquad i = 0, 1, \ldots, n-1.$$

- Strings of length 64 will also be considered as words according to the representation defined by (4), and vice versa. Hence, if X is a string of length 64, then the corresponding word is equal to

$$X = \sum_{i=0}^{63} x_i 2^{63-i}.$$

Note that the same symbol is used for both the string and the corresponding word. It will be clear from the context which representation is intended.
- For an integer N, the *length* of N is defined as the length of the shortest binary representation of N. This is the representation with most significant bit equal to 1. (All "leading zeros" are removed.)
- For a nonnegative integer A and a positive integer B, the numbers A div B and A mod B are defined as the nonnegative integers Q, respectively R, such that

$$A = QB + R \quad \text{and} \quad 0 \le R < B.$$

That is, A mod B is the *remainder*, and A div B is the *quotient* of an integer division of A by B.
- For two words X and Y, the words $U = X \oplus Y$ is defined as the bitwise *XOR* of X and Y. Hence, according to Equation (3):

$$u_i := (x_i + y_i) \bmod 2, \qquad i = 0, 1, \ldots, 63.$$

2.5   Functions used by MDC-4

MDC-4 uses two basic functions $E_1^{\oplus}(\cdot)$ and $E_2^{\oplus}(\cdot)$ that each map two words onto a single word. They are both one-way functions based on the Data Encryption Standard (DES) [NBS77] in which certain key bits are kept constant. A DES encryption operation $E(\cdot)$ will be graphically represented as shown in Figure 1 and mathematically written as

$$Y = E(K, X),$$

where K is the key and X is the 64-bit plaintext block to be encrypted. The key K is represented as a word $(k_0, k_1, \ldots, k_{63})$, but in the DES encryption operation the key bits $k_7, k_{15}, k_{23}, k_{31}, k_{39}, k_{47}, k_{55}$ and k_{63} are ignored.

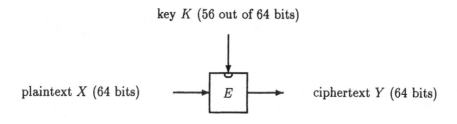

Fig. 1. The basic DES encryption operation.

A DES based one-way function $E^{\oplus}(\cdot)$ is obtained by combining the plaintext and the DES ciphertext with an XOR-operation:

$$Y = E^{\oplus}(K, X) := E(K, X) \oplus X.$$

This function is depicted in Figure 2, together with a shorthand.

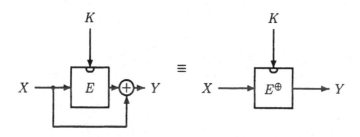

Fig. 2. The DES based one-way function $E^{\oplus}$, together with a shorthand.

The one-way functions $E_1^{\oplus}(\cdot)$ and $E_2^{\oplus}(\cdot)$ used in MDC-4 are defined in terms of this DES based one-way function $E^{\oplus}(\cdot)$ as follows. Let K' be equal to K

except that bits k_1' and k_2' are set equal to respectively 1 and 0. Similarly let K'' be equal to K except that bits k_1'' and k_2'' are set equal to respectively 0 and 1.

$$E_1^\oplus(K, X) := E^\oplus(K', X)$$
$$E_2^\oplus(K, X) := E^\oplus(K'', X)$$

They will be graphically represented like the DES based one-way function $E^\oplus(\cdot)$, with $E^\oplus$ replaced by $E_1^\oplus$ or $E_2^\oplus$.

In the description of the MDC-4 scheme, the one-way functions $E_1^\oplus(\cdot)$ and $E_2^\oplus(\cdot)$ can be substituted by two other one-way functions. However, the security of such a scheme would have to be re-evaluated, as it heavily depends on the properties of these new one-way functions. This chapter only considers the DES-based one-way function.

3   Description of the Primitive

3.1   Outline of MDC-4

MDC-4 is a hash function that maps a message M of arbitrary length onto a 128-bit block MDC-4(M). The basis of MDC-4 is the compression function compress. This function compresses a three word input to a two word output. This function is used in the following way.

First, the message M is expanded to an appropriate length and represented as a sequence of words X. Then, starting with a two-word *initial vector*, the sequence X is compressed by repeatedly appending a message word and compressing the resulting three words to two words by applying compress until the message is exhausted. Thus, a two-word result is obtained. Below this is explained in detail.

Let $M = (m_0, m_1, \ldots, m_{n-1})$ be a message of n bits long. The hashcode MDC-4(M) of M is computed in two steps.

expansion: M is expanded to a sequence X consisting of N words X_0, X_1, ..., X_{N-1}, where $N = (n \text{ div } 64) + 2$. That is, the message is expanded such that it becomes a multiple of 64 bits. This expansion is done even if the original message length is a multiple of 64 bits.

compression: Define the words $H1_0$ and $H2_0$ as

$$H1_0 := 0x5252525252525252$$
$$H2_0 := 0x2525252525252525 .$$

For $i = 0, 1, \ldots, N-1$, the words $H1_{i+1}$ and $H2_{i+1}$ are computed from the words $H1_i$ and $H2_i$ and the message word X_i as follows:

$$(H1_{i+1}, H2_{i+1}) := \text{compress}((H1_i, H2_i), X_i) .$$

hashcode: The hashcode MDC-4(M) is equal to the 128-bit string $H1_N \parallel H2_N$, where the interpretation of the words $H1_N$ and $H2_N$ in terms of bit strings is given by Equation 3.

3.2   Expanding the Message

Let $N = (n \text{ div } 64) + 2$. The n-bit message $M = (m_0, m_1, \ldots, m_{n-1})$ is expanded to the N-word message $X = (X_0, X_1, \ldots, X_{N-1})$ in the following three steps.

1. Append a single "1" and $k = 63 - (n \bmod 64)$ zero bits to the message M:

$$m_n := 1 ,$$
$$m_{n+1} := m_{n+2} := \cdots := m_{n+k} := 0 .$$

This step expands the message M to a message that is a multiple of 64 bits. Note that padding is done even if the length of M is already a multiple of 64 bits.

2. Transform this $(n + k + 1)$-bit extended message into the $\frac{n+k+1}{64} = N - 1$ words $X_0, X_1, \ldots, X_{N-2}$ according to the conventions defined in Section 2.3. Hence

$$X_i := \sum_{j=0}^{63} m_{64i+j} 2^{63-j}, \qquad i = 0, 1, \ldots, N - 2.$$

3. Complete the expansion by appending the length n of the original message:

$$X_{N-1} := n \bmod 2^{64}.$$

3.3   The Compression Function compress

For the 2-word number $(H1_i, H2_i)$ and the message word X_i the 2-word function value

$$(H1_{i+1}, H2_{i+1}) := \mathsf{compress}((H1_i, H2_i), X_i)$$

is computed as follows (see also Figure 3).

$$T1_i = LT1_i \parallel RT1_i := E_1^\oplus(H1_i, X_i)$$
$$T2_i = LT2_i \parallel RT2_i := E_2^\oplus(H2_i, X_i)$$
$$U1_i := LT1_i \parallel RT2_i$$
$$U2_i := LT2_i \parallel RT1_i$$
$$V1_i = LV1_i \parallel RV1_i := E_1^\oplus(U1_i, H2_i)$$
$$V2_i = LV2_i \parallel RV2_i := E_2^\oplus(U2_i, H1_i)$$
$$H1_{i+1} := LV1_i \parallel RV2_i$$
$$H2_{i+1} := LV2_i \parallel RV1_i$$

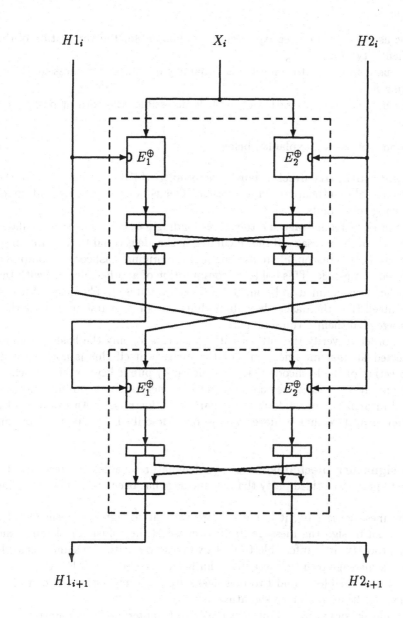

Fig. 3. Outline of the compression function **compress**.

4   Use of the Primitive

The primitive MDC-4 (and any other hash function) has the following intended applications:

- to be used in a data integrity mechanism, namely for the verification of the authenticity of a message.
- to be used in a signature mechanism, namely to compress a message before signing it.
- to be used for the generation of publicly accessible password or passphrase files.

These modes of use are explained below.

Use in data integrity mechanisms The primitive MDC-4 can be used for the verification of the authenticity of a message. This is done as follows, and under the following constraints.

After receipt of a message and the corresponding hashcode, one (re)calculates the hashcode of the message. If the calculated hashcode is equal to the value originally received, it is reasonable to assume that the original hashcode is computed from the same message. This holds, as computation of another message with the same hashcode is claimed to be infeasible (see Section 5.1). Therefore, if it can be guaranteed that the hashcode is unmodified, it is reasonable to assume that the message is authentic (unmodified).

So, in order to verify the authenticity of a message, only the hashcode must be protected against modification. For the message itself this is not required. The protection of the hashcode may be achieved by public key methods, such as digital signatures, by secret key methods, such as encryption, or through physical or logical means. For more details, see Part II of this report. An example of a public key primitive that achieves this is RSA described in Chapter 7 of this report.

Use in signature mechanisms A digital signature enables the receiver of a message to prove to a third party that the message has been created by a specific entity.

If the message is long, it is much more efficient to sign the hashcode of a message than to sign the message itself. Because of the collision resistance and one-way property, it is infeasible to find two messages with the same hashcode or to find a message resulting in a given hashcode (see Section 5.1). As a consequence, it is infeasible to find two messages with the same signature, or to find a message resulting in a given signature as well.

For a digital signature primitive we refer to Chapter 7 of this report.

Use for readable password files Because of the collision-resistance and the one-way property, MDC-4 can be used for the generation of publicly accessible (readable) password or passphrase files. This is done by storing MDC-4(*password*) in this file, instead of the password itself. Because of the one-way property, it is infeasible to derive a valid password from an entry in the file. Because of the collision resistance, this holds even if valid passwords are known.

5 Security Evaluation

5.1 Claimed Properties

MDC-4 is conjectured to be a one-way collision resistant hash function. That is, it is conjectured to satisfy the following two conditions:

1. It is computationally infeasible to compute two distinct messages M_1 and M_2 that have the same hashcode (message digest), i.e., MDC-4(M_1) = MDC-4(M_2). A hash function that satisfies this property is called *collision resistant*.

2. It is computationally infeasible, given a message and the corresponding hashcode, to compute a different message with the same hashcode. That is, given a message M, it is infeasible to compute a message $M' \neq M$ such that MDC-4(M') = MDC-4(M). A hash function that satisfies this property is called *one-way*.

By "computationally infeasible" we mean to express the practical impossibility of computing something with the technology that is currently available or can be foreseen to become available in the near future.

It is hard to give a bound beyond which a computation is infeasible, but currently, a computation requiring 2^{60} (or 10^{18}) operations is computationally infeasible. On the other hand, a computation taking 2^{40} (about 10^{12}) operations is hard, but not impossible.

In view of the past development of computing power and the relatively new possibility of using huge amounts of computing power of for example idle workstations in a network, one should cater for a substantial increase in the bound for computational infeasibility on the longer term.

Open literature provides ample proof that DES or the mode in which it is used here establish no statistical deficiencies. Therefore, no statistical evaluation was performed. Since a proof for the conjectured strength of MDC-4 cannot be given, the rest of this section is dedicated to the algebraic evaluation of the algorithm.

5.2 Algebraic Evaluation

5.2.1 One-wayness and Collision Resistance of compress

The properties of compress heavily depend on the properties of the DES, or, more precisely, on those of the $E^{\oplus}$-operation. Since its introduction in 1977, DES has been studied extensively, but to date no significant weaknesses have been found. The most effective known attack on DES is the so-called *differential cryptanalysis* attack of Biham and Shamir [BiSh91a, BiSh91b].

In this section we first consider some general attacks on compress. After that the resistance of compress against differential cryptanalysis is investigated and finally, the best known (second) preimage and collision attacks on compress are discussed.

An obvious attack on compress is to make use of so-called 'weak keys' of DES [MoSi87] or to try to force $H1_i$ and $H2_i$ to the same value. Such attacks do not work because of the following reasons.

- As $H1_i$ and $H2_i$ are used as keys in DES, the value of the DES-keys cannot easily be forced.
- Because bits 1 and 2 of the keys are forced to different values, it is impossible to have identical DES-keys in $E_1^{\oplus}$ and $E_2^{\oplus}$ or to have weak keys in one of the applications of DES.

Furthermore, because of the extra XOR in the $E^{\oplus}$-operations, it is hard to 'work backwards' through MDC-4. If this was possible, brute force attacks could be made considerably faster than mentioned below. Finally, it is worth mentioning that the switching of the half blocks increases the dependency between the halves.

Due to the internal structure of compress, a collision for the upper part, i.e., two message blocks X_i and X_i' that yield the same value for $T1_i$ and $T2_i$ for a given value of $H1_i$ and $H2_i$, is also a collision for compress. Below we investigate whether this property and differential cryptanalysis of DES can be used to find collisions in compress.

Differential cryptanalysis is a probabilistic attack on DES-like algorithms based on the relation between the XOR of two different inputs and the XOR's of the respective intermediate results and outputs. Note that two inputs such that their XOR is preserved by DES yield the same output of the first $E^{\oplus}$-operation, as the XOR's cancel out. Hence, differential cryptanalysis in principle is applicable to compress, and might yield two blocks compressing to the same result. Furthermore, the key is fixed and known (or even chosen by the cryptanalyst). Since only one pair of input blocks is needed, this might be chosen to optimize the probability of success.

However, since the keys used in the first $E_1^{\oplus}$ respectively $E_2^{\oplus}$-operation are different by definition, an XOR of a pair of inputs has to be preserved by DES for both keys simultaneously. Essentially, the probability of success is the product of the probabilities for both keys $H1$ and $H2$ separately. This roughly squares the number of steps of an attack. Furthermore, there are some unsolved technical problems, the main one being the fact that known attacks work for an odd number of rounds of DES only. This implies that without a major breakthrough, a differential attack will be far slower than a brute force attack. The current estimate for the complexity of finding a collision for compress with a differential attack is about 2^{90} DES encryptions.

The best known way to find an input or a second input to compress that yields a prespecified output requires 2^{90} DES encryptions and a storage of 2^{28} 54-bit quantities. It is based on the observation that $V1_i$ depends only on $H1_i$ through 26 bits of $LT1_i$, and that 10 bits of $H1_i$ (namely the 8 parity bits and the 2 bits that are fixed in the key port) only influence the output in the second half of the algorithm.

1. Choose a random value of X_i and a 26-bit constant S.

2. Calculate $T1_i$ for all 2^{54} relevant values of $H1_i$ (only the bits that are used in the first half). It is expected that in 2^{28} cases the 26 relevant bits of $LT1_i$ will be equal to S (indeed, 4 parity bits in the first half are ignored and 2 more bits are fixed).

3. Calculate $T2_i$ for all 2^{54} relevant values of $H2_i$. Next, extend $H2_i$ with all possible values for the 10 unused bits, and compute $V1_i$, under the assumption that $LT1_i = S$ (this blocks the influence of $H1_i$ on this calculation). This requires in total $2^{64} + 2^{54}$ DES encryptions, hence one expects to find the correct value of $V1_i$. In this way $H2_i$ is determined.

4. For the 2^{28} cases with $LT1_i = S$, extend $H1_i$ with all possible values for the 10 unused bits, and compute $V2_i$. This requires in total 2^{38} DES encryptions, and the correct value is obtained with probability 2^{-26}.

5. If no match is obtained, one chooses a new value of X or for S; in the latter case, one can avoid recomputing $T1_i$ and $T2_i$ at the cost of more storage.

One can conclude that finding a preimage or a second preimage for compress is computationally infeasible. If we allow 2^n different outputs, the complexity of this attack would decrease by a factor of 2^n.

The best known way to find a collision for the function compress requires $2^{41.5}$ DES encryptions and a storage of $2^{30.5}$ 54-bit quantities (about 10 Gigabyte). This does not lead necessarily to collisions for MDC–4. It is based on a similar observation as the previous attack.

1. Choose a random value of X_i and of $H2_i$ (this can be the specified value).

2. Calculate $T1_i$ for $2^{40.5}$ values of $H1_i$. It is expected that there will be a 26-bit integer S such that in $2^{14.5}$ cases the 26 relevant bits of $LT1_i$ will be equal to S (in fact for 50% of the integers S there will be $2^{14.5}$ cases or more).

3. For these $2^{14.5}$ cases with $LT1_i = S$, extend $H1_i$ with all possible values for the 10 unused bits, and compute $V2_i$ for the $2^{14.5+10} = 2^{24.5}$ different inputs. The probability to find a collision for $V2_i$ is equal to $2^{2 \cdot 24.5}/2^{65} = 2^{-16}$.

4. If no match is obtained, one chooses a new value for S; one can avoid recomputing $T1_i$ if one stores $2^{16} \cdot 2^{14.5} = 2^{30.5}$ 54-bit quantities (about 10 Gigabytes).

5.2.2 One-wayness and Collision Resistance of MDC-4

Finding a (second) preimage for MDC-4 can be done by combining the (second) preimage attack on compress with a so-called meet in the middle attack, see for example [QuDe89b]. Such an attack requires 2^{109} DES encryptions and a storage of 2^{28} 54-bit quantities. If we allow 2^n different hashcodes, the complexity of this attack will decrease to $2^{109-n/2}$ DES encryptions and a storage of $\max(2^{28}, 2^{19+n/2})$ 54-bit quantities. If 2^n becomes larger than 2^{39}, the most efficient attack is a brute force attack which requires $4 \cdot 2^{128-n}$ DES encryptions and a storage of 2^n 64-bit quantities. Of course, the number of operations to find a (second) preimage is also limited by the effective size of the message space, hence this space should not be too small.

In spite of the fact that finding collisions for **compress** is not computationally infeasible, no way has been found to extend these collisions to collisions for MDC-4. This means that currently the best attack to find a pair of message blocks that compress to the same hashcode, given a value for $(H1_i, H2_i)$ is a so-called 'birthday attack', see for example [QuDe89a]. Such an attack will require in the order of $4 \cdot 2^{54}$ DES encryptions and negligible storage. Note that a DES encryption includes the key scheduling. Although $4 \cdot 2^{54}$ operations is for the moment computationally infeasible, it can be expected that this becomes feasible by the end of this decade.

So, currently there seems to be no reason to doubt the security of MDC-4. However, a birthday attack to find collisions for **compress** might become feasible in the future.

6 Performance Evaluation

6.1 Software Implementations

The figures for a very fast software implementation of MDC-4 are given in Table 1. They use the ideas introduced in Section 7 to improve the DES performance as well as the performance of the compression function compress. Both a C and a 80386 Assembly language implementation are considered. The C version has the advantage of being portable (and has been ported, see Appendix A). It is in the configuration described below not much slower than the Assembly language implementation. However, as explained in Section 7, this is not necessarily the case for other configurations. Both versions use the same tables totalling 192K of memory, of which 64K is used to implement the DES encryption operation and 128K for the key scheduling operation. The code of the compression function takes in addition to that about 13K in Assembly language and slightly more in C. The figures of Table 1 are for an IBM-compatible 33 MHz 80386DX based PC with 64K cache memory using WATCOM C/386 9.0 in combination with the DOS/4GW DOS extender. Hence all code runs in protected mode.

	C	Assembly
MDC-4	60 Kbit/s	90 Kbit/s

Table 1. Software performance of MDC-4 on a 33 MHz 80386DX based PC with a 64K memory cache using WATCOM C/386 9.0 in combination with the DOS/4GW DOS extender. Both versions use about 205K of memory.

6.2 Hardware Implementations

The DES algorithm has been designed for hardware implementations. Hence high performance is only attainable in hardware. With current submicron CMOS technology and a clock of 25 MHz a data rate of 90 Mbit/s on chip has been achieved [VHVM88, VHVM91, Cry89, Pij92]. A faster clock of 40 MHz would allow for data rates of up to 150 Mbit/s on chip. However at such speeds the critical path does not run through the DES module, but is situated in the I/O interface. The actual data rates will therefore be lower, but 50 to 60 Mbits/s is achievable.

If used in an MDC-4 implementation, the throughput of the existing chips will be significantly reduced, as for every application of the DES a new key has to be loaded. Moreover this new key is only available at the end of the previous DES operation, which makes it impossible to load the key in advance. It nevertheless is expected that in dedicated hardware the speed mentioned above is attainable. Parallelism can be used to run both halves of MDC-4 simultaneously.

7   Guidelines for Software Implementation

The implementation in the C language given in Appendix A can be used as a guideline for software implementations. It also provides the test values given in Appendix B.

The speed of software implementations will be very low due to the fact that DES, including the (slow) key scheduling, has to be performed four times for each 64-bit message block. Since the the program spends almost all its time in the calls to DES, the speed of a software implementation will be determined by the efficiency of a DES encryption; optimizations other than in DES will not provide significant improvement of the speed.

The software implementation of DES, let alone an efficient implementation, is beyond the scope of this document. Only some guidelines for such an implementation are given. No claim on the completeness or relative importance is made, however.

Note that for each 64-bit block of the expanded message, four applications of DES are needed, each time with a different key. This is where most of the computation time is spent: even a highly optimized key-scheduling will be twice as slow as the encryption operation itself.

The key to an efficient software implementation of the DES will be the use of equivalent representations of the algorithm, see [DDFG83, DDGH84, FeKa89]. This allows a suitable reordering of the bits, the combination of several steps into one (e.g., the P-permutations and the expansion E) and the use of tables instead of the (bit)operations it is described in. Of course there is a time-memory trade-off: the more memory is used for tables, the more instructions can be replaced by table look-ups, and the faster the code will be. Moreover, combination of small tables into larger ones will reduce the number of look-ups, and hence further increase the speed.

However, one must be careful with this analysis. The speed of a computer is (for our purposes) determined by two things: the speed of the central processing unit (CPU) and the speed by which memory can be accessed. On many computers nowadays the speed of the CPU has become so enormous compared to the speed of memory access, that a program with extensive memory access gets significantly slowed down. This means that a program with more instructions but fewer memory access might be faster than a program with less instructions but more memory access. A way around this problem is the use of a (small) amount of very fast (but very expensive) memory, so called cache memory. This way programs with extensive memory access, but that fit in cache memory are significantly faster than programs that only partially can use the benefit of this cache, because the amount of memory they need is larger than the size of the cache. Hence a program that is perfect for one computer (in the sense that it has minimal execution time) is therefore not necessarily optimal for another configuration. That is, there is no such thing as a single program being optimal for every configuration.

References

[BiSh91a]   E. Biham and A. Shamir, "Differential Cryptanalysis of DES-like Cryptosystems," *Journal of Cryptology*, Vol. 4, No. 1, 1991, pp. 3–72.

[BiSh91b]   E. Biham and A. Shamir, "Differential Cryptanalysis of the full 16-round DES," *Technical Report # 708*, Technion - Israel Institute of Technology, Department of Computer Science, December 1991.

[CPMM90]   D. Coppersmith, S. Pilpel, C.H. Meyer, S.M. Matyas, M.M. Hyden, J. Oseas, B. Brachtl, and M. Schilling, *Data Authentication Using Modification Detection Codes Based on a Public One Way Encryption Function*, U.S. Patent No. 4,908,861, March 13, 1990.

[Cry89]   Cryptech, *CRY12C102 DES chip*, 1989.

[DDFG83]   M. Davio, Y. Desmedt, M. Fosseprez, R. Govaerts, J. Hulsbosch, P. Neutjens, P. Piret, J.-J. Quisquater, J. Vandewalle and P. Wouters, "Analytical Characteristics of the DES," *Advances in Cryptology, Proc. Crypto'83*, D. Chaum, Ed., Plenum Press, New York, 1984, pp. 171–202.

[DDGH84]   M. Davio, Y. Desmedt, J. Goubert, F. Hoornaert and J.-J. Quisquater, "Efficient hardware and software implementations of the DES," *Advances in Cryptology, Proc. Crypto'84, LNCS 196*, G.R. Blakley and D. Chaum, Eds., Springer-Verlag, 1985, pp. 144–146.

[FeKa89]   D.C. Feldmeier and P.R. Karn, "UNIX password security – Ten years later," *Advances in Cryptology, Proc. Crypto'89, LNCS 435*, G. Brassard, Ed., Springer-Verlag, 1990, pp. 44–63.

[Mat91]   S.M. Matyas, "Key handling with control vectors," *IBM Systems Journal*, Vol. 30, No. 2, 1991, pp. 151–174.

[Mey89]   C.H. Meyer, "Cryptography - A state of the art review," *Proceedings of COMPEURO'89, Proceedings VLSI and Computer Peripherals*, 3rd Annual European Computer Conference, Hamburg, Germany, May 8-12, 1989, pp. 150–154.

[MeSc88]   C.H. Meyer and M. Schilling, "Secure Program Load with Manipulation Detection Code," *Proceedings of SECURICOM'88*, Paris, France, 1988, pp. 111–130.

[MoSi87]   J.H. Moore and G.J. Simmons, "Cycle structure of the DES for keys having palindromic (or antipalindromic) sequences of round keys," *IEEE Transactions on Software Engineering*, Vol. SE-13, No. 2, 1987, pp. 262–273.

[NBS77]   National Bureau of Standards, *Data Encryption Standard*, Federal Information Processing Standard, Publication 46, US Department of Commerce, January 1977.

[Pij92]   Pijnenburg micro-electronics & software: *PCC100 Data Encryption Device*, 1992.

[QuDe89a]   J.-J. Quisquater and J.-P. Delescaille, "How easy is collision search? Applications to DES," *Advances in Cryptology, Proc. Eurocrypt'89, LNCS 434*, J.-J. Quisquater and J. Vandewalle, Eds., Springer-Verlag, 1990, pp. 429–434.

[QuDe89b]   J.-J. Quisquater and J.-P. Delescaille, "How easy is collision search? New results and applications to DES," *Advances in Cryptology, Proc. Crypto'89, LNCS 435*, G. Brassard, Ed., Springer-Verlag, 1990, pp. 408–413.

[Riv90]   R. L. Rivest, "The MD4 Message Digest Algorithm," *Advances in Cryptology, Proc. Crypto'90, LNCS 537*, S. Vanstone, Ed., Springer-Verlag, 1991, pp. 303–311.

[VHVM88] I. Verbauwhede, J. Hoornaert, J. Vandewalle and H. De Man, "Security and performance optimization of a new DES data encryption chip," *IEEE Journal on Solid-State Circuits*, Vol. 23, No. 3, 1988, pp. 647–656.

[VHVM91] I. Verbauwhede, J. Hoornaert, J. Vandewalle and H. De Man, "ASIC Cryptographic Processor based on DES," *Proceedings of the EuroAsic'91 Conference*, Paris, France, May 1991.

A   C Implementation of the Primitive

This appendix provides an ANSI C-implementation of the primitive MDC-4 and an example program that uses MDC-4 to hash messages. This program can be used for testing purposes as well, as it can provide the test values of Appendix B.

Use of this implementation The file mdc4.c contains the code of the functions MDCinit, compress and MDCfinish. MDCinit performs initialization of $H1$ and $H2$, compress applies compress, MDCfinish pads the message, appends the length and compresses the resulting final blocks. The header file mdc4.h contains the function prototypes.

The test program hashtest can be compiled as follows. First, compile the source files mdc4.c, hashtest.c and a file containing an implementation of DES with an (ANSI) C compiler. Next, link those three files.

This implementation has been tested on a wide variety of environments, so it should be portable or at worst easy to port. The testing environments include MS-DOS (4.2 and 5.0 on 80x86 processors) with several compilers, VAX/VMS, RISC ULTRIX, ConvexOS and Macintosh.

Note that VAX/VMS does not allow the run command to pass arguments to an executable. A patch for this is given in the comment of the main() function in hashtest.c.

A.1   The Header File

```
/*********************************************************************/
/*  file: mdc4.h                                                   */
/*                                                                 */
/*  description: header file for MDC-4, a sample C-implementation  */
/*                                                                 */
/*  copyright (C)                                                  */
/*          Centre for Mathematics and Computer Science, Amsterdam */
/*          Siemens AG                                             */
/*          Philips Crypto BV                                      */
/*          PTT Research, the Netherlands                          */
/*          Katholieke Universiteit Leuven                         */
/*          Aarhus University                                      */
/*  1992, All Rights Reserved                                      */
/*                                                                 */
/*  date:    06/25/92                                              */
/*  version: 1.0                                                   */
/*                                                                 */
/*********************************************************************/

#ifndef  MDC4H                 /* make sure this file is read only once */
#define  MDC4H


/*********************************************************************/

/* typedef 8, 16 and 32 bit types, resp.  */
/* adapt these, if necessary,
   for your operating system and compiler */
typedef    unsigned char        byte;
typedef    unsigned short       word;
typedef    unsigned long        dword;


/*********************************************************************/

/* function prototypes */

byte *DES(byte *input, byte *key);
/*
 * returns output of DES with given input and key.
 * source is not provided by RIPE!
 */

void MDCinit(byte *H1, byte *H2);
/*
 *  initializes H1 and H2
 */

void compress(byte *H1, byte *H2, byte *X);
```

```
/*
 * the compression function.
 * transforms H1, H2 using message bytes X[0] through X[7]
 */

void MDCfinish(byte *H1, byte *H2, byte *strptr,
               dword lswlen, dword mswlen);
/*
 * pads, appends length and compresses the last block(s)
 * note: length in bits == 8 * (lswlen + 2^32 mswlen).
 * note: there are (lswlen mod 8) unprocessed bytes left in strptr.
 */

#endif  /* MDC4H */

/*********************** end of file mdc4.h ***********************/
```

A.2   C Source Code for MDC-4

```
/*********************************************************************/
/*  file: mdc4.c                                                     */
/*                                                                   */
/*  description: A sample C-implementation of the MDC-4              */
/*            hash-function.  The function DES() is external;        */
/*            it is not provided by RIPE.                            */
/*                                                                   */
/*  copyright (C)                                                    */
/*            Centre for Mathematics and Computer Science, Amsterdam */
/*            Siemens AG                                             */
/*            Philips Crypto BV                                     */
/*            PTT Research, the Netherlands                         */
/*            Katholieke Universiteit Leuven                        */
/*            Aarhus University                                     */
/*  1992, All Rights Reserved                                       */
/*                                                                   */
/*  date:    06/25/92                                               */
/*  version: 1.0                                                    */
/*                                                                   */
/*********************************************************************/


/*  header files */
#include <stdio.h>
#include <stdlib.h>
#include <string.h>
#include "mdc4.h"

/*********************************************************************/

void MDCinit(byte *H1, byte *H2)
{
   int   i;

   for (i=0; i<8; i++) {
      H1[i] = 0x52;
      H2[i] = 0x25;
   }

   return;
}

/*********************************************************************/

static void swap(byte *x, byte *y)
{
   byte tmp;
```

```
    tmp = *x;
    *x = *y;
    *y = tmp;

    return;
}

/*****************************************************************/

static void E1xor(byte *input, byte *key, byte *output)
{
    byte        *desres;
    byte         oldbits;
    int          i;

    /* store value of the bits k_1 and k_2 */
    oldbits = key[0] & 96;
    /* set those bits to 1 resp. 0 */
    key[0] ^= oldbits ^ 64;

    /* one-way function: */
    desres = DES(input, key);
    for (i=0; i<8; i++) {
        output[i] = input[i] ^ desres[i];
    }

    if (key != output) {
        /* reset the two bits k_1 and k_2 */
        key[0] ^= oldbits ^ 64;
    }

    return;
}

/*****************************************************************/

static void E2xor(byte *input, byte *key, byte *output)
{
    byte        *desres;
    byte         oldbits;
    int          i;

    /* store value of the bits k_1 and k_2 */
    oldbits = key[0] & 96;
    /* set those bits to 0 resp. 1 */
    key[0] ^= oldbits ^ 32;

    /* one-way function: */
    desres = DES(input, key);
    for (i=0; i<8; i++) {
```

```
         output[i] = input[i] ^ desres[i];
      }

   if (key != output) {
      /* reset the two bits k_1 and k_2 */
      key[0] ^= oldbits ^ 32;
   }

   return;
}

/*******************************************************************/

void compress(byte *H1, byte *H2, byte *X)
{
   byte   temp1[8], temp2[8];
   int    i;

   /* apply E1xor and E2xor to the halves */
   E1xor(X, H1, temp1);
   E2xor(X, H2, temp2);

   /* interchange right halves */
   for (i=4; i<8; i++) {
      swap(temp1+i, temp2+i);
   }

   /* apply E1xor and E2xor to the halves */
   E1xor(H2, temp1, H2);
   E2xor(H1, temp2, H1);
   /* note: H1 and H2 are interchanged, so: */

   /* interchange _left_ halves */
   for (i=0; i<4; i++) {
      swap(H1+i, H2+i);
   }

   return;
}

/*******************************************************************/

void MDCfinish(byte *H1, byte *H2, byte *input,
               dword lswlen, dword mswlen)
{
   int      i;                          /* counter       */
   byte     X[8];                       /* message bytes */

   /* get lswlen mod 8 unprocessed bytes */
   for (i=0; i<(lswlen&7); i++) {
```

```
      X[i] = input[i];
   }

   /* append the bit m_n == 1 */
   X[lswlen&7] = 0x80;
   /* ... and zero bits: */
   for (i=(lswlen&7)+1; i<8; i++) {
      X[i] = 0;
   }

   compress(H1, H2, X);

   /* append length in bits; MSB to LSB */
   X[0] = mswlen >> 21;
   X[1] = mswlen >> 13;
   X[2] = mswlen >> 5;
   X[3] = (mswlen << 3) ^ (lswlen >> 29);
   X[4] = lswlen >> 21;
   X[5] = lswlen >> 13;
   X[6] = lswlen >> 5;
   X[7] = lswlen << 3;

   compress(H1, H2, X);

   return;
}

/*********************** end of file mdc4.c ********************/
```

A.3   An Example Program

This section gives the listing of an example program. By means of command line options, several different tests can be performed (see the top of the file). Test values can be found in Appendix B. The file **test.bin** should contain the string **abc** and nothing else. (Make sure no newline of linefeed is appended by your editor.)

```
/**********************************************************************/
/*  file: hashtest.c                                                  */
/*                                                                    */
/*  description: test file for MDC-4                                  */
/*          DES() is an external function, not provided by RIPE.      */
/*                                                                    */
/*  command line arguments:                                           */
/*          filename  -- compute hash code of file read binary        */
/*          -sstring  -- print string & hashcode                      */
/*          -t        -- perform time trial                           */
/*          -a        -- execute standard test suite, ASCII input     */
/*                       and binary input from file test.bin          */
/*          -x        -- execute standard test suite, hexadecimal     */
/*                       input read from file test.hex                */
/*                                                                    */
/*  copyright (C)                                                     */
/*          Centre for Mathematics and Computer Science, Amsterdam    */
/*          Siemens AG                                                */
/*          Philips Crypto BV                                         */
/*          PTT Research, the Netherlands                             */
/*          Katholieke Universiteit Leuven                            */
/*          Aarhus University                                         */
/*  1992, All Rights Reserved                                         */
/*                                                                    */
/*  date:    06/25/92                                                 */
/*  version: 1.0                                                      */
/*                                                                    */
/**********************************************************************/


#include <stdio.h>
#include <stdlib.h>
#include <time.h>
#include <string.h>
#include "mdc4.h"

/* some compilers do not know CLOCKS_PER_SEC yet */
#ifndef CLOCKS_PER_SEC
#define CLOCKS_PER_SEC   CLK_TCK
#endif

#define TEST_BLOCK_SIZE 100
```

```
#define TEST_BLOCKS 1000

/* number of test bytes = TEST_BLOCK_SIZE * TEST_BLOCKS */
static long TEST_BYTES = (long)TEST_BLOCK_SIZE * (long)TEST_BLOCKS;

/*******************************************************************/

byte *MDC4(byte *message)
/*
 * returns MDC-4(message)
 * message should be a string terminated by '\0'
 */
{
   static byte   H1[16];        /* contains H1_i and H2_i        */
   static byte   *H2 = H1 + 8;  /* points to right half          */
   dword         length;        /* length in bytes of message    */
   dword         nbytes;        /* # of bytes not yet processed  */
   byte          *strptr;       /* points to the current mess. block */

   /* initialize */
   MDCinit(H1, H2);
   strptr = message;                  /* strptr points to first block */
   length = (dword)strlen((char *)message);
   nbytes = length;

   /* process message in 8-byte chunks */
   while (nbytes > 7) {
      compress(H1, H2, strptr);
      strptr += 8;
      nbytes -= 8;                     /* 8 bytes less to process */
   }                                   /* length mod 8 bytes left */

   /* finish: */
   MDCfinish(H1, H2, strptr, length, 0);

   return (byte *)H1;
}

/*******************************************************************/

byte *MDC4binary(char *fname)
/*
 * returns MDC-4(message in file fname)
 * fname is read as binary data.
 */
{
   FILE          *mf;           /* pointer to file <fname>       */
   static byte   H1[16];        /* contains H1_i and H2_i        */
   static byte   *H2 = H1 + 8;  /* points to right half          */
   byte          data[1024];    /* contains current mess. block  */
```

```
    dword           nbytes;         /* length of this block         */
    word            i;              /* counter                      */
    dword           length[2];      /* length in bytes of message   */
    dword           offset;         /* # of bytes unprocessed at    */
                    /* call of MDCfinish */

    /* initialize */
    if ((mf = fopen(fname, "rb")) == NULL) {
        fprintf(stderr, "\nMDC4binary: cannot open \"%s\".\n", fname);
        exit(1);
    }
    MDCinit(H1, H2);
    length[0] = 0;
    length[1] = 0;

    while ((nbytes = fread(data, 1, 1024, mf)) != 0) {
        /* process all complete blocks */
        for (i=0; i<(nbytes>>3); i++) {
            compress(H1, H2, data+(i<<3));
        }

        /* update length[] */
        if (length[0] + nbytes < length[0])
            length[1]++;                 /* overflow to msw of length */
        length[0] += nbytes;
    }

    /* finish: */
    offset = length[0] & 0x3F8;    /* extracts bits 3 to 10 inclusive */
    MDCfinish(H1, H2, data+offset, length[0], length[1]);

    fclose(mf);

    return (byte *)H1;
}

/********************************************************************/


byte *MDC4hex(char *fname)
/*
 * returns MDC-4(message in file fname)
 * fname should contain the message in hex format;
 * first number of bytes, then the bytes in hexadecimal.
 */
{
    FILE        *mf;            /* pointer to file <fname>        */
    static byte H1[16];        /* contains H1_i and H2_i         */
    static byte *H2 = H1 + 8;  /* points to right half           */
    byte        data[8];       /* contains current mess. block   */
```

```
    dword        nbytes;           /* length of the message      */
    word         i, j;             /* counters                   */
    int          val;              /* temp for reading from file */

    /* initialize */
    if ((mf = fopen(fname, "r")) == NULL) {
        fprintf(stderr, "\nMDC4hex: cannot open file \"%s\".\n",
                fname);
        exit(1);
    }
    MDCinit(H1, H2);

    fscanf(mf, "%x", &val);
    nbytes = val;
    i = 0;
    while (nbytes - i > 7) {
        /* read and process complete block */
        for (j=0; j<8; j++) {
            fscanf(mf, "%x", &val);
            data[j] = (byte)val;
        }
        compress(H1, H2, data);
        i += 8;
    }

    /* read last nbytes-i bytes: */
    j = 0;
    while (i<nbytes) {
        fscanf(mf, "%x", &val);
        data[j++] = (byte)val;
        i++;
    }

    /* finish */
    MDCfinish(H1, H2, data, nbytes, 0);

    fclose(mf);

    return (byte *)H1;
}

/*********************************************************************/

void speedtest(void)
/*
 * A time trial routine, to measure the speed of MDC-4.
 * Measures processor time required to process TEST_BLOCKS times
 *   a message of TEST_BLOCK_SIZE characters.
 */
{
```

```
   clock_t        t0, t1;
   static byte    H1[16];            /* contains H1_i and H2_i      */
   static byte    *H2 = H1 + 8;      /* points to right half        */
   byte           data[TEST_BLOCK_SIZE];
   word           i, j;

 /* initialize test data */
 for (i=0; i<TEST_BLOCK_SIZE; i++)
    data[i] = (byte)i;

 printf ("MDC4 time trial. Processing %ld characters...\n", TEST_BYTES);

 /* start timer */
 t0 = clock();

 /* process data */
 MDCinit(H1, H2);
 for (i=0; i<TEST_BLOCKS; i++) {
    for (j=0; j<TEST_BLOCK_SIZE; j+=8) {
       compress(H1, H2, data+(j>>3));
    }
 }
 MDCfinish(H1, H2, data, TEST_BYTES, 0);

 /* stop timer, get time difference */
 t1 = clock();
 printf("\nTest input processed in %g seconds.\n",
        ((double)(t1-t0)/(double)CLOCKS_PER_SEC));
 printf("Characters processed per second: %g\n",
        (double)CLOCKS_PER_SEC*TEST_BYTES/((double)t1-t0));

 printf("\nhashcode: ");
 for (i=0; i<16; i++)
    printf("%02x", H1[i]);

 return;
}

/******************************************************************/

void testascii (void)
/*
 *   standard test suite, ASCII input
 */
{
   int     i;
   byte    *hashcode;

   printf("\nMDC4 test suite results (ASCII):\n");
```

```
   hashcode = MDC4((byte *)"");
   printf("\n\nmessage: \"\"  (empty string)\nhashcode: ");
   for (i=0; i<16; i++)
      printf("%02x", hashcode[i]);

   hashcode = MDC4((byte *)"a");
   printf("\n\nmessage: \"a\"\nhashcode: ");
   for (i=0; i<16; i++)
      printf("%02x", hashcode[i]);

   hashcode = MDC4((byte *)"abc");
   printf("\n\nmessage: \"abc\"\nhashcode: ");
   for (i=0; i<16; i++)
      printf("%02x", hashcode[i]);

   hashcode = MDC4((byte *)"message digest");
   printf("\n\nmessage: \"message digest\"\nhashcode: ");
   for (i=0; i<16; i++)
      printf("%02x", hashcode[i]);

   hashcode = MDC4((byte *)"abcdefghijklmnopqrstuvwxyz");
   printf("\n\nmessage: \"abcdefghijklmnopqrstuvwxyz\"\nhashcode: ");
   for (i=0; i<16; i++)
      printf("%02x", hashcode[i]);

   hashcode = MDC4((byte *)
      "ABCDEFGHIJKLMNOPQRSTUVWXYZabcdefghijklmnopqrstuvwxyz0123456789");
   printf(
      "\n\nmessage: A...Za...z0...9\nhashcode: ");
   for (i=0; i<16; i++)
      printf("%02x", hashcode[i]);

   hashcode = MDC4((byte *)"12345678901234567890123456789012345678901234567890\
1234567890123456789012345678901234567890");
   printf("\n\nmessage: 8 times \"1234567890\"\nhashcode: ");
   for (i=0; i<16; i++)
      printf("%02x", hashcode[i]);

   /* Contents of binary created file test.bin are "abc" */
   printf("\n\nmessagefile (binary): test.bin\nhashcode: ");
   hashcode = MDC4binary("test.bin");
   for (i=0; i<16; i++)
      printf("%02x", hashcode[i]);

   return;
}

/********************************************************************/

void testhex (void)
```

```
/*
 *    standard test suite, hex input, read from files
 */
{
   int i;
   byte *hashcode;

   printf("\nMDC4 test suite results (hex):\n");

   hashcode = MDC4hex("test1.hex");
   printf("\n\nfile test1.hex; hashcode: ");
   for (i=0; i<16; i++)
      printf("%02x", hashcode[i]);

   hashcode = MDC4hex("test2.hex");
   printf("\n\nfile test2.hex; hashcode: ");
   for (i=0; i<16; i++)
      printf("%02x", hashcode[i]);

   hashcode = MDC4hex("test3.hex");
   printf("\n\nfile test3.hex; hashcode: ");
   for (i=0; i<16; i++)
      printf("%02x", hashcode[i]);

   hashcode = MDC4hex("test4.hex");
   printf("\n\nfile test4.hex; hashcode: ");
   for (i=0; i<16; i++)
      printf("%02x", hashcode[i]);

   hashcode = MDC4hex("test5.hex");
   printf("\n\nfile test5.hex; hashcode: ");
   for (i=0; i<16; i++)
      printf("%02x", hashcode[i]);

   hashcode = MDC4hex("test6.hex");
   printf("\n\nfile test6.hex; hashcode: ");
   for (i=0; i<16; i++)
      printf("%02x", hashcode[i]);

   hashcode = MDC4hex("test7.hex");
   printf("\n\nfile test7.hex; hashcode: ");
   for (i=0; i<16; i++)
      printf("%02x", hashcode[i]);

   return;
}

/****************************************************************/

main (int argc, char *argv[])
```

```
/*
 *  main program. calls one or more of the test routines depending
 *  on command line arguments. see the header of this file.
 *
 *  (For VAX/VMS, do: HASHTEST :== $<pathname>HASHTEST.EXE
 *   at the command prompt (or in login.com) first.
 *   (The run command does not allow command line args.)
 *   The <pathname> must include device, e.g., "DSKD:".)
 */
{
  int   i, j;
  byte *hashcode;

  if (argc == 1) {
     fprintf(stderr, "hashtest: no command line arguments supplied.\n");
     exit(1);
  }
  else {
     for (i = 1; i < argc; i++) {
        if (argv[i][0] == '-' && argv[i][1] == 's') {
           printf("\n\nmessage: %s", argv[i]+2);
           hashcode = MDC4((byte *)argv[i] + 2);
           printf("\nhashcode: ");
           for (j=0; j<16; j++)
              printf("%02x", hashcode[j]);
        }
        else if (strcmp (argv[i], "-t") == 0)
           speedtest ();
        else if (strcmp (argv[i], "-a") == 0)
           testascii ();
        else if (strcmp (argv[i], "-x") == 0)
           testhex ();
        else {
           hashcode = MDC4binary (argv[i]);
           printf("\n\nmessagefile (binary): %s", argv[i]);
           printf("\nhashcode: ");
           for (j=0; j<16; j++)
              printf("%02x", hashcode[j]);
        }
     }
  }
  printf("\n");

  return 0;
}

/******************** end of file hashtest.c ********************/
```

B   Test Values

Below, the files **test1.hex** up to **test7.hex** as used by the test **hashtest -x** are listed. The format of those files is as follows. All numbers are hexadecimal; all numbers except possibly the first one are one byte long. The first number represents the number of bytes in the message to be hashed; it is followed by (at least) this number of bytes. For example, **test3.hex** represents the message consisting of the three bytes 0x61, 0x62 and 0x63. This is the string "abc" in ASCII.

test1.hex:

0

test2.hex:

1
61

test3.hex:

3
61 62 63

test4.hex:

e
6d 65 73 73 61 67 65 20 64 69 67 65 73 74

test5.hex:

1a
61 62 63 64 65 66 67 68 69 6a 6b 6c 6d 6e 6f 70
71 72 73 74 75 76 77 78 79 7a

test6.hex:

3e
41 42 43 44 45 46 47 48 49 4a 4b 4c 4d 4e 4f 50
51 52 53 54 55 56 57 58 59 5a 61 62 63 64 65 66
67 68 69 6a 6b 6c 6d 6e 6f 70 71 72 73 74 75 76
77 78 79 7a 30 31 32 33 34 35 36 37 38 39

test7.hex:

50
31 32 33 34 35 36 37 38 39 30
31 32 33 34 35 36 37 38 39 30
31 32 33 34 35 36 37 38 39 30
31 32 33 34 35 36 37 38 39 30
31 32 33 34 35 36 37 38 39 30
31 32 33 34 35 36 37 38 39 30
31 32 33 34 35 36 37 38 39 30
31 32 33 34 35 36 37 38 39 30

The following test values were obtained by running **hashtest -x**. If ASCII encoding is used, **hashtest -a** should provide the same answers, followed by the result of hashing "abc" again. The latter only holds if the file **test.bin** exists and contains nothing but this string.

MDC4 test suite results (hex):

file test1.hex; hashcode: 14131f5dadbc2cc4e4d4c8dcef91d462

file test2.hex; hashcode: f15cc877d7f3c929330f896222410f01

file test3.hex; hashcode: e0abd233a1be9650713609decc1ef62b

file test4.hex; hashcode: 971add04ab1c607dcfa8c855aac15a16

file test5.hex; hashcode: 600cf23bd5eef96472825a34e6bd8236

file test6.hex; hashcode: 7514607cc53c00fb1ef10aeab90cdadf

file test7.hex; hashcode: dee26cddf118817974b89028c7de5999

Chapter 3

RIPEMD

Table of Contents

1 Introduction

This chapter describes the integrity primitive **RIPEMD**. This primitive is a so-called *message-digest algorithm* or *hash function* that compresses messages of arbitrary length to a 128-bit output block, that is called the *fingerprint, hash-code, hash value* or *message-digest* of the message. It is conjectured that it is computationally infeasible to produce two messages having the same hashcode, or to produce any messages having a given prespecified target hashcode. Hash functions with these properties are used in message authentication applications such as the protection of the integrity and the origin of data stored or transmitted using secret-key or public-key techniques (see Section 4 in this chapter and Part II of this report).

RIPEMD is an extension of the MD4 message-digest algorithm [Riv92a]. MD4 consists of two parts: first, the message is expanded slightly to obtain an appropriate length for further processing. Next, a compression function is used iteratively to compress this expanded message to 128 bits. **RIPEMD** has the same structure, but its compression function consists of two parallel copies of MD4's compression function, identical but for some internal constants. The results of both copies are combined to yield the output of **RIPEMD**'s compression function. The reason for this more complicated design lies in the fact that successful attacks exist on two round versions of MD4 [BoBo91, Mer90]. Because of these attacks, the designers of MD4 proposed a modified version, which is called MD5 [Riv92b]. However, there are indications that this redesign has introduced new weaknesses in the algorithm [BoBo93]. The **RIPEMD** extension of MD4 is from [Boe92].

The design of the **RIPEMD** algorithm is such that it is very suitable for software implementation on 32-bit machines. Since no substitution tables are used, the algorithm can be coded quite compactly. The large input block sizes however, do not favor compact hardware realizations.

The structure of this chapter is as follows. In order to avoid any ambiguities in the description of the primitive, the notation and definitions used in this chapter are fixed in Section 2. Section 3 contains a description of the primitive and in Section 4 the possible modes of use of the primitive are considered. The security aspects of the primitive are discussed in Section 5. These include the claimed properties and the results of statistical and algebraic evaluations of the primitive. Finally, in Section 6 the performance aspects of **RIPEMD** are considered, and Section 7 gives some guidelines for software implementation.

This chapter has two appendices. Appendix A contains a straightforward software implementation of **RIPEMD** in the programming language C and in Appendix B test values for the primitive are given.

2   Definitions and Notation

2.1   Introduction

In order to obtain a clear description of the primitive, the notation and definitions used in this chapter are fully described in this section. These include the representation of the numbers in the description, and the operations, functions and constants used by the primitive.

2.2   General

The symbol ":=" is used for the assignment of a value or a meaning to a variable or symbol. That is, $a := b$ either means that the variable a gets the value of the variable b, or it means that a is defined as "b". It will be obvious from the context which meaning is intended.

The equality-sign "=" is used for equality only. That is, it indicates that the two entities on either side are equal.

Note that in C-source code, "=" denotes assignment, while comparison is denoted by "==".

An ellipsis ("...") denotes an implicit enumeration. For example, "$i = 0, 1, \ldots, n$" is meant to represent the sentence "for $i = 0$, $i = 1$, and so on, up to $i = n$".

In pseudo-codes, comment is indicated as in the C-language, viz. by enclosing it between "/*" and "*/".

2.3   Representation of Numbers

In this chapter a *byte* is defined as an 8-bit quantity and a *word* as a 32-bit quantity. A byte is considered to be a nonnegative integer. That is, it can take on the values 0 through $2^8 - 1 = 255$. Likewise, a word is considered to be a nonnegative integer, hence it takes on the values 0 through $2^{32} - 1 = 4294967295$. The value of a word can be given in decimal as well as in hexadecimal form. In the latter case the number is written as '0x' followed immediately by at most 8 hexadecimal digits, the most significant one first. For example, the hexadecimal representation of the 32-bit number 4023233417 is 0xefcdab89.

A sequence of $8n$ bits $b_0, b_1, \ldots, b_{8n-1}$ is interpreted as a sequence of n bytes in the following way. Each group of 8 consecutive bits is considered as a byte B_i, the first bit of such a group being the most significant bit of that byte. Hence,

$$B_i := b_{8i}2^7 + b_{8i+1}2^6 + \cdots + b_{8i+7}, \quad i = 0, 1, \ldots, n - 1. \tag{1}$$

A sequence of $4l$ bytes $B_0, B_1, \ldots, B_{4l-1}$ is interpreted as a sequence of words $W_0, W_1, \ldots, W_{l-1}$ in the following way. Each group of 4 consecutive bytes is considered as a word W_i, the first byte of such a word being the *least* significant byte of that word (!). Hence,

$$W_i := B_{4i+3}(256)^3 + B_{4i+2}(256)^2 + B_{4i+1}(256) + B_{4i}, \quad i = 0, 1, \ldots, l-1. \quad (2)$$

Notice the difference in convention between the notations (1) and (2). This is done for reasons of performance, see [Riv92a] and Section 7.

In accordance with the notations above, the bits of a word W are denoted as

$$W = (w_0, w_1, \ldots, w_{31}), \quad (3)$$

where

$$W = \sum_{i=0}^{3} \sum_{j=0}^{7} w_{8i+j} 2^{8i+(7-j)}. \quad (4)$$

In this chapter words are always denoted by uppercase letters and the bits of this word by the corresponding lowercase letter with indices as in Equation (3). Likewise, bytes are indicated by uppercase letters and the bits that constitute this byte by lowercase letters with indices as in Equation (1). The ordering of bytes in a word is given by Equation (2).

2.4   Definitions and Basic Operations

- A *string* is a sequence of bits. If X is a string consisting of n bits, then those bits are denoted from left to right by x_0, x_1, $\ldots$, x_{n-2}, x_{n-1}.
- The *length* of a string X is the number of bits in the string X. A string of length n is called an n-bit string.
- For two strings X and Y of length n, the $2n$-bit string $W = X \parallel Y$ is defined as the *concatenation* of the strings X and Y. That is, according to the definition of a string above,

$$\begin{aligned} w_i &:= x_i \\ w_{i+n} &:= y_i \end{aligned} \quad i = 0, 1, \ldots, n-1.$$

- Strings of length 32 will also be considered as words according to the representation defined by (4), and vice versa. Hence, if X is a string of length 32, then the corresponding word is equal to

$$X = \sum_{i=0}^{3} \sum_{j=0}^{7} x_{8i+j} 2^{8i+(7-j)}.$$

Note that the same symbol is used for both the string and the corresponding word. It will be clear from the context which representation is intended.

- For an integer N, the *length* of N is defined as the length of the shortest binary representation of N. This is the representation with most significant bit equal to 1. (All "leading zeros" are removed.)

- For a nonnegative integer A and a positive integer B, the numbers A div B and A mod B are defined as the nonnegative integers Q, respectively R, such that

$$A = QB + R \quad \text{and} \quad 0 \leq R < B.$$

That is, A mod B is the *remainder*, and A div B is the *quotient* of an integer division of A by B.

- For two words X and Y, the words $U = X \oplus Y$, $V = X \wedge Y$ and $W = X \vee Y$ are defined as the bitwise *XOR*, *AND* and *OR* of X and Y, respectively. Hence, according to Equation (3):

$$
\begin{aligned}
u_i &:= (x_i + y_i) \bmod 2 \\
v_i &:= x_i y_i \\
w_i &:= (x_i + y_i - x_i y_i) \bmod 2
\end{aligned}
\qquad (i = 0, 1, \ldots, 31).
$$

- For a word X, the word $W = \overline{X}$ is defined as the bitwise *complement* of X, hence

$$W = \overline{X} := X \oplus \texttt{0xffffffff},$$

or according to Equation (3):

$$w_i := (x_i + 1) \bmod 2, \quad i = 0, 1, \ldots, 31.$$

- for a word X and an integer $0 \leq s < 32$, the word $W = X \lll s$ is defined as the result of (cyclicly) rotating X over s bits to the left, hence

$$W = X \lll s := (X2^s + (X \text{ div } 2^{32-s})) \bmod 2^{32}.$$

- The notation "$X \equiv Y \pmod{N}$" (X is equivalent to Y modulo N) is used to indicate that $X \bmod N = Y \bmod N$.

2.5   Functions and Operations used in RIPEMD

RIPEMD uses three basic functions that each map three words onto a word. These functions are defined as follows.

$$
\begin{aligned}
F(X, Y, Z) &:= (X \wedge Y) \vee (\overline{X} \wedge Z) & (5) \\
G(X, Y, Z) &:= (X \wedge Y) \vee (X \wedge Z) \vee (Y \wedge Z) & (6) \\
H(X, Y, Z) &:= X \oplus Y \oplus Z & (7)
\end{aligned}
$$

For each bit of X, the function F *selects* a bit of either Y or Z, depending on the bit of X: if the bit x_i is 1, then the corresponding bit y_i is selected, else z_i is selected ($i = 0, 1, \ldots, 31$).

The function G is the bitwise *majority* of the bits of X, Y and Z: if two or three of the bits x_i, y_i and z_i are 1, then the corresponding bit g_i of $G(X, Y, Z)$ is 1, else $g_i = 0$.

The function H is the bitwise *parity* (or XOR) of X, Y and Z: a bit h_i of $H = H(X, Y, Z)$ is 1 if an odd number of the bits x_i, y_i and z_i is 1, else $h_i = 0$.

Those three functions are used in six other (higher level) operations. These are used to process a message consisting of 16 words $X_0, X_1, \ldots, X_{15}$. For words A, B, C and D, and integers $0 \leq k < 16$ and $0 \leq s < 32$ these operations are defined as follows.

– $FF(A, B, C, D, X_k, s)$ denotes the operation

$$A := ((A + F(B, C, D) + X_k) \bmod 2^{32}) \lll s . \tag{8}$$

– $GG(A, B, C, D, X_k, s)$ denotes the operation

$$A := ((A + G(B, C, D) + X_k + \texttt{0x5a827999}) \bmod 2^{32}) \lll s . \tag{9}$$

– $HH(A, B, C, D, X_k, s)$ denotes the operation

$$A := ((A + H(B, C, D) + X_k + \texttt{0x6ed9eba1}) \bmod 2^{32}) \lll s . \tag{10}$$

– $FFF(A, B, C, D, X_k, s)$ denotes the operation

$$A := ((A + F(B, C, D) + X_k + \texttt{0x50a28be6}) \bmod 2^{32}) \lll s . \tag{11}$$

– $GGG(A, B, C, D, X_k, s)$ denotes the operation

$$A := ((A + G(B, C, D) + X_k) \bmod 2^{32}) \lll s . \tag{12}$$

– $HHH(A, B, C, D, X_k, s)$ denotes the operation

$$A := ((A + H(B, C, D) + X_k + \texttt{0x5c4dd124}) \bmod 2^{32}) \lll s . \tag{13}$$

That is, all six functions add the result of an application of F, G or H to (B, C, D), a message word X_k and possibly a constant to A and rotate the result over s positions to the left.

The four constants used in these operations are not randomly chosen; they are the integer part of $2^{30}\sqrt{2}$, $2^{30}\sqrt{3}$, $2^{30}\sqrt[3]{2}$ respectively $2^{30}\sqrt[3]{3}$. However, there is no specific reason for this choice.

3   Description of the Primitive

3.1   Global Structure of the Primitive

As stated in the introduction of this chapter, RIPEMD is a hash function that maps a message M consisting of an arbitrary number of bits onto a 128-bit block RIPEMD(M). The basis of RIPEMD is the compression function compress. This function compresses a 20-word input to a 4-word output. This function is used in the following way.

First, the message is expanded to an appropriate length and represented by a sequence of words. Then, starting with a 4-word *initial vector*, the resulting sequence of words is compressed by repeatedly appending sixteen message words and compressing the resulting twenty words to four words by applying compress until the message is exhausted. Thus, a 4-word result can be obtained. Below, this is explained in detail.

3.1.1   Outline of compress

The compression function compress accepts an input consisting of four words A, B, C, D and sixteen message words X_0, X_1, ..., X_{15}. It produces four output words denoted as:

$$\text{compress}((A, B, C, D); (X_0, X_1, \ldots, X_{15})) \, . \tag{14}$$

The function compress consists of two separate halves, followed by a final step combining the results of both halves into four words. Each of the halves can be decomposed into three rounds. Each of these rounds consists of sixteen steps. These steps, finally, consist of the application of one of the six operations FF, GG, HH, FFF, GGG and HHH; a different operation for each round. See also Figure 1.

In other words: the input is passed to both halves. Both halves then independently transform, in three rounds of sixteen steps each, a copy of the 4-tuple (A, B, C, D). In a final step, the results of both independent transformations are combined into the result of compress.

3.1.2   Outline of RIPEMD

Let $M = (m_0, m_1, \ldots, m_{n-1})$ be a message consisting of n bits. The hashcode RIPEMD(M) of M is computed as follows, see also Figure 2.

expansion: M is expanded to a message X consisting of $16N$ words X_0, X_1, ..., X_{16N-1}, where $N = ((n + 64) \text{ div } 512) + 1$. That is, the message is expanded such that it becomes a multiple of 512 bits long. This expansion is done even if the message M already is a multiple of 512 bits long.

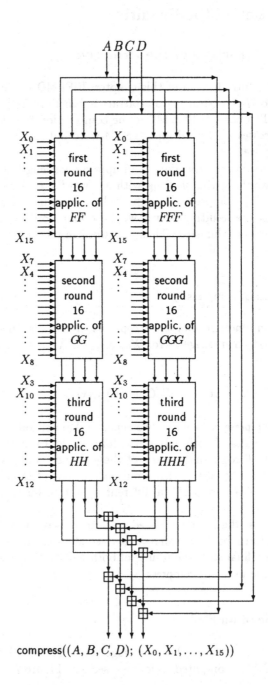

compress$((A, B, C, D); (X_0, X_1, \ldots, X_{15}))$

Fig. 1. Outline of the compression function compress. The input to the right half is identical to that in the left half, only the constants used are different. The symbol ⊞ denotes addition modulo 2^{32}.

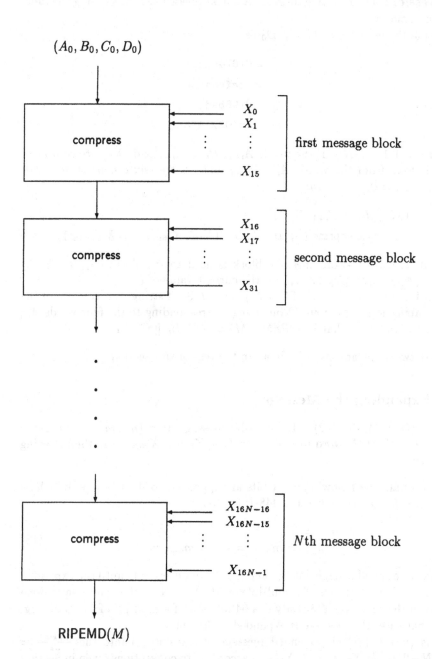

Fig. 2. Outline of RIPEMD. The message M is expanded first to X which is a multiple of 16 words long. Then X is processed as in this picture. The final result is RIPEMD(M).

compression: The resulting message X is compressed as follows using the function compress.

Define the words A_0, B_0, C_0, D_0 as

$$A_0 := \texttt{0x67452301}$$
$$B_0 := \texttt{0xefcdab89}$$
$$C_0 := \texttt{0x98badcfe}$$
$$D_0 := \texttt{0x10325476}$$

For $i = 0, 1, \ldots, N-1$, the words A_{i+1}, B_{i+1}, C_{i+1} and D_{i+1} are computed as follows from the words A_i, B_i, C_i and D_i and sixteen message words X_{16i+j}, $j = 0, 1, \ldots, 15$:

$$(A_{i+1}, B_{i+1}, C_{i+1}, D_{i+1})$$
$$:= \mathsf{compress}((A_i, B_i, C_i, D_i); (X_{16i}, X_{16i+1}, \ldots, X_{16i+15})),$$

That is, each 16-word message block is used to transform (A_i, B_i, C_i, D_i) into $(A_{i+1}, B_{i+1}, C_{i+1}, D_{i+1})$ for the current value of i.

hashcode: The hashcode $\mathsf{RIPEMD}(M)$ is the 128-bit string that consists of the concatenation of the four 32-bit strings corresponding to the four words A_n, B_n, C_n and D_n. That is, $\mathsf{RIPEMD}(M) = A_n \parallel B_n \parallel C_n \parallel D_n$.

The first two steps are given in detail in the rest of this section.

3.2 Expanding the Message

Let $N = ((n + 64) \text{ div } 512) + 1$. The n-bit message $M = (m_0, m_1, \ldots, m_{n-1})$ is expanded to the $16N$-word message $X = (X_0, X_1, \ldots, X_{16N-1})$ in the following three steps.

1. First of all, the following $k + 1$ bits are appended to the message M, where $0 \le k < 512$ and $n + k + 1 \equiv 448 \pmod{512}$:

$$
\begin{aligned}
m_n &:= 1, \\
m_{n+1} &:= m_{n+2} := \cdots := m_{n+k} := 0.
\end{aligned}
\tag{15}
$$

That is, append a single bit "1" and a number of zero bits until the expanded message is 64 bits shy of a multiple of 512 bits. Note that padding is done even if the message M already is a 64 bits shy of a multiple of 512 bits long. In that case, the message is expanded by 512 bits.

2. This $(n + k + 1)$-bit extended message is transformed into the $\frac{n+k+1}{32} = 16N - 2$ words $X_0, X_1, \ldots, X_{16N-3}$ according to conventions given in Section 2.3, hence

$$X_i := \sum_{j=0}^{3} \sum_{l=0}^{7} m_{32i+8j+l} 2^{8j+7-l}, \quad i = 0, 1, \ldots, 16N - 3. \tag{16}$$

3. Finally, the expansion is completed by appending the length n of the original message is in the following way.

$$X_{16N-2} := n \bmod 2^{32},$$
$$X_{16N-1} := (n \bmod 2^{64}) \operatorname{div} 2^{32}.$$

3.3   The Compression Function compress

For the 4-word number (A, B, C, D) and the 16-word message $X_0, X_1, \ldots, X_{15}$, the 4-word function value

$$\mathsf{compress}((A, B, C, D); (X_0, X_1, \ldots, X_{15})) \tag{17}$$

is computed in two parallel sets of three rounds, each round consisting of 16 applications of one of the auxiliary operations defined by Equations (8)–(13).

First, two copies of (A, B, C, D) are made. Next, both halves independently transform those copies in three rounds of sixteen applications of one of the operations FF through HHH. Finally, the results of both halves and the initial values of A, B, C and D are combined into one 4-word output, here denoted as (AA, BB, CC, DD).

In pseudocode:

```
/* copy (A, B, C, D) for both halves */
aa = A;  bb = B;  cc = C;  dd = D;
aaa = A;  bbb = B;  ccc = C;  ddd = D;
```

```
/* Round 1 for both parallel halves */
FF(aa, bb, cc, dd, X_0, 11);        FFF(aaa, bbb, ccc, ddd, X_0, 11);
FF(dd, aa, bb, cc, X_1, 14);        FFF(ddd, aaa, bbb, ccc, X_1, 14);
FF(cc, dd, aa, bb, X_2, 15);        FFF(ccc, ddd, aaa, bbb, X_2, 15);
FF(bb, cc, dd, aa, X_3, 12);        FFF(bbb, ccc, ddd, aaa, X_3, 12);
FF(aa, bb, cc, dd, X_4, 5);         FFF(aaa, bbb, ccc, ddd, X_4, 5);
FF(dd, aa, bb, cc, X_5, 8);         FFF(ddd, aaa, bbb, ccc, X_5, 8);
FF(cc, dd, aa, bb, X_6, 7);         FFF(ccc, ddd, aaa, bbb, X_6, 7);
FF(bb, cc, dd, aa, X_7, 9);         FFF(bbb, ccc, ddd, aaa, X_7, 9);
FF(aa, bb, cc, dd, X_8, 11);        FFF(aaa, bbb, ccc, ddd, X_8, 11);
FF(dd, aa, bb, cc, X_9, 13);        FFF(ddd, aaa, bbb, ccc, X_9, 13);
FF(cc, dd, aa, bb, X_10, 14);       FFF(ccc, ddd, aaa, bbb, X_10, 14);
FF(bb, cc, dd, aa, X_11, 15);       FFF(bbb, ccc, ddd, aaa, X_11, 15);
FF(aa, bb, cc, dd, X_12, 6);        FFF(aaa, bbb, ccc, ddd, X_12, 6);
FF(dd, aa, bb, cc, X_13, 7);        FFF(ddd, aaa, bbb, ccc, X_13, 7);
FF(cc, dd, aa, bb, X_14, 9);        FFF(ccc, ddd, aaa, bbb, X_14, 9);
FF(bb, cc, dd, aa, X_15, 8);        FFF(bbb, ccc, ddd, aaa, X_15, 8);
```

```
/* Round 2 for both parallel halves */
GG(aa, bb, cc, dd, X_7, 7);         GGG(aaa, bbb, ccc, ddd, X_7, 7);
GG(dd, aa, bb, cc, X_4, 6);         GGG(ddd, aaa, bbb, ccc, X_4, 6);
```

$GG(cc, dd, aa, bb, X_{13}, 8)$; $GGG(ccc, ddd, aaa, bbb, X_{13}, 8)$;
$GG(bb, cc, dd, aa, X_1, 13)$; $GGG(bbb, ccc, ddd, aaa, X_1, 13)$;
$GG(aa, bb, cc, dd, X_{10}, 11)$; $GGG(aaa, bbb, ccc, ddd, X_{10}, 11)$;
$GG(dd, aa, bb, cc, X_6, 9)$; $GGG(ddd, aaa, bbb, ccc, X_6, 9)$;
$GG(cc, dd, aa, bb, X_{15}, 7)$; $GGG(ccc, ddd, aaa, bbb, X_{15}, 7)$;
$GG(bb, cc, dd, aa, X_3, 15)$; $GGG(bbb, ccc, ddd, aaa, X_3, 15)$;
$GG(aa, bb, cc, dd, X_{12}, 7)$; $GGG(aaa, bbb, ccc, ddd, X_{12}, 7)$;
$GG(dd, aa, bb, cc, X_0, 12)$; $GGG(ddd, aaa, bbb, ccc, X_0, 12)$;
$GG(cc, dd, aa, bb, X_9, 15)$; $GGG(ccc, ddd, aaa, bbb, X_9, 15)$;
$GG(bb, cc, dd, aa, X_5, 9)$; $GGG(bbb, ccc, ddd, aaa, X_5, 9)$;
$GG(aa, bb, cc, dd, X_{14}, 7)$; $GGG(aaa, bbb, ccc, ddd, X_{14}, 7)$;
$GG(dd, aa, bb, cc, X_2, 11)$; $GGG(ddd, aaa, bbb, ccc, X_2, 11)$;
$GG(cc, dd, aa, bb, X_{11}, 13)$; $GGG(ccc, ddd, aaa, bbb, X_{11}, 13)$;
$GG(bb, cc, dd, aa, X_8, 12)$; $GGG(bbb, ccc, ddd, aaa, X_8, 12)$;

```
/* Round 3 for both parallel halves */
```

$HH(aa, bb, cc, dd, X_3, 11)$; $HHH(aaa, bbb, ccc, ddd, X_3, 11)$;
$HH(dd, aa, bb, cc, X_{10}, 13)$; $HHH(ddd, aaa, bbb, ccc, X_{10}, 13)$;
$HH(cc, dd, aa, bb, X_2, 14)$; $HHH(ccc, ddd, aaa, bbb, X_2, 14)$;
$HH(bb, cc, dd, aa, X_4, 7)$; $HHH(bbb, ccc, ddd, aaa, X_4, 7)$;
$HH(aa, bb, cc, dd, X_9, 14)$; $HHH(aaa, bbb, ccc, ddd, X_9, 14)$;
$HH(dd, aa, bb, cc, X_{15}, 9)$; $HHH(ddd, aaa, bbb, ccc, X_{15}, 9)$;
$HH(cc, dd, aa, bb, X_8, 13)$; $HHH(ccc, ddd, aaa, bbb, X_8, 13)$;
$HH(bb, cc, dd, aa, X_1, 15)$; $HHH(bbb, ccc, ddd, aaa, X_1, 15)$;
$HH(aa, bb, cc, dd, X_{14}, 6)$; $HHH(aaa, bbb, ccc, ddd, X_{14}, 6)$;
$HH(dd, aa, bb, cc, X_7, 8)$; $HHH(ddd, aaa, bbb, ccc, X_7, 8)$;
$HH(cc, dd, aa, bb, X_0, 13)$; $HHH(ccc, ddd, aaa, bbb, X_0, 13)$;
$HH(bb, cc, dd, aa, X_6, 6)$; $HHH(bbb, ccc, ddd, aaa, X_6, 6)$;
$HH(aa, bb, cc, dd, X_{11}, 12)$; $HHH(aaa, bbb, ccc, ddd, X_{11}, 12)$;
$HH(dd, aa, bb, cc, X_{13}, 5)$; $HHH(ddd, aaa, bbb, ccc, X_{13}, 5)$;
$HH(cc, dd, aa, bb, X_5, 7)$; $HHH(ccc, ddd, aaa, bbb, X_5, 7)$;
$HH(bb, cc, dd, aa, X_{12}, 5)$; $HHH(bbb, ccc, ddd, aaa, X_{12}, 5)$;

```
/* combination of results into output */
```

$AA := (B + cc + ddd) \bmod 2^{32}$;
$BB := (C + dd + aaa) \bmod 2^{32}$;
$CC := (D + aa + bbb) \bmod 2^{32}$;
$DD := (A + bb + ccc) \bmod 2^{32}$;

4   Use of the Primitive

The primitive RIPEMD (and any other hash function) can be used in the following ways.

- Firstly, it can be used in a data integrity mechanism, namely for the verification of the authenticity of a message.
- Secondly, it can be used in a signature mechanism, namely to compress a message before signing it.
- Thirdly, it can be used for the generation of publicly accessible password or passphrase files.

These modes of use are explained below.

Use in data integrity mechanisms The primitive RIPEMD can be used for the verification of the authenticity of a message. This is done as follows, and under the following constraints.

After receipt of a message and the corresponding hashcode, one (re)calculates the hashcode of the message. If the calculated hashcode is equal to the value originally received, it is reasonable to assume that the original hashcode is computed from the same message. This holds, as computation of another message with the same hashcode is claimed to be infeasible (see Section 5.1). Therefore, if it can be guaranteed that the hashcode is unmodified, it is reasonable to assume that the message is authentic (unmodified).

So, in order to verify the authenticity of a message, only the hashcode must be protected against modification. For the message itself this is not required. The protection of the hashcode may be achieved by public key methods, such as digital signatures, by secret key methods, such as encryption, or through physical or logical means. For more details, see Part II of this report. An example of a public key primitive that achieves this is RSA that is described in Chapter 7 of this report.

Use in signature mechanisms A digital signature enables the receiver of a message to prove to a third party that the message has been created by a specific entity.

If the message is long, it is much more efficient to sign the hashcode of a message than to sign the message itself. Because of the collision resistance and one-way property, it is infeasible to find two messages with the same hashcode or to find a message resulting in a given hashcode (see Section 5.1). As a consequence, it is infeasible to find two messages with the same signature, or to find a message resulting in a given signature as well.

For a digital signature primitive we refer to Chapter 7 of this report.

Use for readable password files Because of the collision-resistance and the one-way property, RIPEMD can be used for the generation of publicly accessible (readable) password or passphrase files. Instead of storing the password itself in this file, RIPEMD(*password*) is stored. Because of the one-way property, it is infeasible to derive a valid password from an entry in the file. Because of the collision resistance, this holds even if a valid password is known.

5   Security Evaluation

5.1   Claimed Properties

RIPEMD is conjectured to be a one-way collision resistant hash function. That is, it is conjectured to satisfy the following two conditions:

1. It is computationally infeasible to compute two distinct messages M_1 and M_2 that have the same hashcode (message digest), i.e., RIPEMD(M_1) = RIPEMD(M_2). A hash function that satisfies this property is called *collision resistant*.

2. It is computationally infeasible, given a message M and the corresponding hashcode, to compute a different message M' that has the same hashcode. That is, given a message M, it is infeasible to compute a message $M' \neq M$ such that RIPEMD(M') = RIPEMD(M). A hash function that satisfies this property is called *one-way*.

By "computationally infeasible" we mean to express the practical impossibility of computing something with the technology that is currently available or can be foreseen to become available in the near future.

It is hard to give a bound beyond which a computation is infeasible, but currently, a computation requiring 2^{60} (or 10^{18}) operations is computationally infeasible. On the other hand, a computation taking 2^{40} (about 10^{12}) operations is hard, but not impossible.

In view of the past development of computing power and the relatively new possibility of using huge amounts of computing power of for example idle workstations in a network, one should cater for a substantial increase in the bound for computational infeasibility on the longer term.

Since a proof for the conjectured strength of RIPEMD cannot be given, the rest of this section is dedicated to the statistical and algebraic evaluation of the algorithm.

5.2   Statistical Evaluation

It is the general view that in order to avoid possible statistical attacks, a good cryptographic function should behave like a random function. The same holds for the compression function compress used in the hash function RIPEMD. Statistical irregularities in the behavior of this function could be used in finding collisions or messages that produce a given hashcode (see Section 5.1).

In order to determine the statistical properties of compress, three tests were applied to the function. These tests investigate the following properties of a cryptographic function:

1. The dependence of input and output bits of the function.
2. Possible linear relations between input and output bits of the function.
3. The periodicity properties of the function.

Below, these tests and the results of the application of these tests to compress are shortly described.

5.2.1   The Dependence Test

It has been stated in the literature that a good cryptographic function should satisfy the following three properties:

Completeness: a function is said to be *complete* if each output bit depends on all input bits [KaDa79].

Avalanche effect: a function exhibits the *avalanche effect* if for each input bit, a change of this single input bit results in a change of an average of half of the output bits [Fei73].

Strict avalanche criterion: a function satisfies the *strict avalanche criterion* if every output bit changes with probability $\frac{1}{2}$ whenever one input bit is changed [WeTa85].

Obviously, if a function satisfies the strict avalanche criterion, then it will also be complete and exhibit the avalanche effect.

The dependence test determines to what extent a function satisfies these three properties. More precisely, the test computes for a number of randomly chosen inputs the so-called *dependence* and *distance* matrices of the function. These are defined as follows. The (i, j)-th entry of the dependence matrix is defined as the number of inputs for which changing the i-th input bit results in a change of the j-th output bit. The (i, j)-th entry of the distance matrix is defined as the number of inputs for which changing the i-th input bit results in the changing of j output bits. From these matrices the test computes the degree to which the function satisfies the three properties above, and furthermore the test determines whether these matrices differ significantly from what can be expected for a random function.

5.2.2   The Linear Factors Test

A function is said to have a *linear factor* if the modulo 2 sum of a set of input and output bits never changes when a specific input bit is changed. Linear factors indicate a serious problem with the security of a cryptographic function. For example, in [ChEv85] an attack is described on DES with a reduced number of rounds that is based on linear factors.

The linear factors test is a test that determines the linear factors of a function in a very efficient way. Furthermore, this test can also be used to compute *pseudo linear factors*, that is linear factors that hold with a probability significantly larger than one half. However, while the test will always yield all the linear factors of a function, the same does not hold for pseudo linear factors.

5.2.3   The Cycling Test

For any function f that maps n bits onto n bits, and any n-bit number x (the *initial value*), the sequence $x, f(x), f^2(x) = f(f(x)), \ldots$ will ultimately be periodic. More precisely, there exist numbers l and c such that the $l + c$ values

$x, f(x), f^2(x), \ldots, f^{l+c-1}(x)$ are distinct, but $f^{l+c}(x) = f^l(x)$. The number l is called the *leader length* of the sequence, and c the *cycle length*.

The cycling test determines the leader and cycle lengths of sequences of the above form for a number of random values of x, and compares the results with what can be expected for a random function. For more details on the cycling test, see [Knu81, Chapter 3] and [KRS88].

5.2.4 Results of the Tests

The results of the tests are as follows.

1. The dependence test was applied to the three consecutive rounds of the function compress (see Section 3.3). For each application of the test, 25,000 random 128-bit initial values and 512-bit messages were used. After one round of compress each of the 128 output bits depends on each of the 128 bits of the initial values. After two rounds, each of the 128 output bits also depends on each of the 512 message bits. In general, the results of the dependence test applied to two rounds and three rounds (and hence the whole function) of the function compress do not differ significantly from what can be expected for a random function.

2. The function compress does not contain any linear factors. Furthermore, a search for pseudo linear factors yielded no results.

3. The cycling test was applied to a number of 32-bit functions obtained by considering random sets of 32 input bits and 32 output bits of the function compress. Also, for each of these functions, the test was applied for a number of random initial values. The results of these cycling experiments on compress do not differ significantly from what can be expected for a random function.

We can conclude from the results of these tests that there is no indication that the statistical behavior of the function compress used in RIPEMD differs significantly from what can be expected for a random function.

5.3 Algebraic Evaluation

5.3.1 Justification of the Focus on compress

A theorem by Damgård [Dam89] states that a family of hash functions satisfying certain requirements is collision resistant and one-way if the compression function is collision resistant. This implies that a member of such a family with sufficiently large input block size, is collision resistant and one-way with high probability. As RIPEMD can easily be embedded in such a family, Damgård's theorem provides evidence for the fact that RIPEMD is collision resistant and one-way if compress is collision resistant. This justifies the fact that this section focuses on the properties of compress rather than RIPEMD.

5.3.2   Collision Resistance of compress

The fact that compress consists of two independent parallel sets of three rounds makes constructing collisions much harder, as such a construction has to cope with both halves simultaneously: any change in one half has to be cancelled out by the other half.

Moreover, both halves consist of three serial rounds of sixteen steps each. As in both halves each message word is used in all three rounds, a change in one message word results in a cascade of three changes. Because of the choice of the shifts in the different steps, and the order of use of the message words, the effects of such a change are hard to control or restrict. For example, for each message word X_i, three different rotations are used in the three rounds; message words that are used close to each other in one round are far apart in the other two; for each of the four words aa through dd (aaa through ddd) there is at least one round with an odd sum of rotations, the difference of two consecutive rotations is never divisible by 4, etc.

So, finding a collision means simultaneously solving the 'serial' problem per set of three rounds, and the 'parallel' problem of making the results of both halves cancel each other out. This seems infeasible.

Brute force attacks to find a collision are certainly computationally infeasible, as the best known brute force attack, a so-called 'birthday attack' will require 2^{64} steps. Here each step essentially consists of an application of compress.

Thus, the best attack that finds a preimage or a second preimage to compress that yields a prespecified hashcode seems to be a 'brute force' attack.

Similarly, the best attack that finds a preimage that compresses to a prespecified hashcode, given a value for (A_0, B_0, C_0, D_0), seems to be a pure brute force attack. This would take in the order of 2^{127} evaluations of compress. Of course, this number is also limited by the effective size of the message space, hence this space should not be too small.

Finding a different message that compresses to the same hashcode as a given message also requires in the order of 2^{127} evaluations of compress. If we allow n different hashcodes, the complexity of this attack would decrease by a factor of n, but a storage in the order of n message/hashcode pairs is necessary.

Hence, brute force attacks are computationally infeasible.

6 Performance Evaluation

6.1 Software Implementations

The design of the RIPEMD algorithm is oriented towards a fast software implementation on 32-bit architectures: it is based on a simple set of primitive operations on 32-bit words. Moreover, no substitution tables are used. Therefore, the implementation can be quite compact as well. Both a C and a 80386 Assembly language implementation are considered. The C version has the advantage of being portable. The difference in performance between the C and the Assembly language version is mainly due to the inability to efficiently implement a rotation instruction in C. The figures are for an IBM-compatible 33 MHz 80386DX based PC with 64K cache memory using WATCOM C/386 9.0 in combination with the DOS/4GW DOS extender. Hence, both programs use a 32-bit instruction set and are run in protected mode. The codesize entry in Table 1 refers to the size of the compression function code.

	C		Assembly	
	Codesize	Speed	Codesize	Speed
RIPEMD	4125	3.44 Mbit/s	2250	6.80 Mbit/s

Table 1. Software performance of RIPEMD on a 33 MHz 80386DX based PC with a 64K memory cache using WATCOM C/386 9.0 in combination with the DOS/4GW DOS extender. No tables are used.

6.2 Hardware Implementations

The algorithm is specifically designed for software implementations. The large input block size is unfavorable for compact hardware implementations. However, in view of the performance of the software implementations mentioned above, and taking into account that only basic operations like addition modulo 2^{32}, bitwise XOR, AND, rotation and complementation are used, a high speed in hardware is certainly possible. Parallelism can only be used to run both halves of RIPEMD simultaneously, as every register in each half gets updated sequentially.

7   Guidelines for Software Implementation

The C-implementation (and the comments in the code), given in Appendix A can be used as a starting point for an implementation. However, it should be noted that this implementation was written for the sole purpose of documentation. No optimization whatsoever is performed, but only readability and portability were kept in mind. The rest of this section is dedicated to possible optimizations. Since this is to a large extent dependent on the specific architecture on which an implementation is to be performed, only guidelines can be given.

Firstly, the ordering of the bytes in a word enables the following optimization in the conversion of an array of bytes to an array of words on so-called "little endian" architectures. On such architectures, it is not necessary to shift each byte to the left over 0, 8, 16 or 24 positions, and then copy it to a word X_i. (Note that this is done in the macro BYTES_TO_WORD in ripemd.h.) Instead, the array of bytes can be treated as an array of words, as the bytes already are in the correct order.

That is, replace the lines

```
for (i=0; i<16; i++) {
    X[i] = BYTES_TO_WORD(strptr);
    strptr += 4;
}
compress(MDbuf, X);
```

with

```
compress(MDbuf, (dword *)strptr);
strptr += 64;
```

The same thing can be done for the output: the conversion of an array of words to an array of bytes can be done by just returning (byte *)MDbuf.

Those optimizations yield in the order of 20% increase in speed.

The rationale for this ordering of bytes was that "big endian" machines tend to be faster than little endian machines, so they should do the extra work of reordering the bytes into a word [Riv92a].

Secondly, if at all possible, use a 32-bit instruction set. On PC's with a 32-bit architecture (e.g, 80386 and 80486 based IBM-compatibles) this might require another compiler, as many popular compilers only use a 16-bit instruction set. This will increase the speed with a factor in the order of three.

It is worth while to force the buffer variables aa through dd and aaa through ddd in registers.

Some other small optimizations are possible by rewriting the macros G(), ROT() and FF() through HHH().

G() can be optimized by observing that $(X \wedge Y) \vee (X \wedge Z) \vee (Y \wedge Z)$ is equivalent to $(X \wedge (Y \vee Z)) \vee (Y \wedge Z)$.

By using a temporary variable (that should be declared in the calling function) the rotation can be optimized as follows:

```
#define ROT(x, n)     (tmp=(x), (tmp << (n)) | (tmp >> (32-(n))))
```

By doing this, the macros `FF()` through `HHH()` become slightly more efficient (an optimizing compiler will keep `tmp` in a register):

```
#define FF(a, b, c, d, x, n)  (a) = ROT((a)+F((b), (c), (d))+(x), (s))
```

Assembly implementations should incorporate the above ideas. Note that most processors have a rotate instruction, which of course should be used.

References

[Boe92]   B. den Boer, *Personal Communication*, March 1992.

[BoBo91] B. den Boer and A. Bosselaers, "An attack on the last two rounds of MD4," *Advances in Cryptology, Proc. Crypto'91, LNCS 576*, J. Feigenbaum, Ed., Springer-Verlag, 1992, pp. 194–203.

[BoBo93] B. den Boer and A. Bosselaers, "Collisions for the compression function of MD5," *Advances in Cryptology, Proc. Eurocrypt'93, LNCS 765*, T. Helleseth, Ed., Springer-Verlag, 1994, pp. 293–304.

[ChEv85] D. Chaum and J.-H. Evertse, "Cryptanalysis of DES with a reduced number of rounds," *Advances in Cryptology, Proc. Crypto'85, LNCS 218*, H.C. Williams, Ed., Springer-Verlag, 1985, pp. 192–211.

[Dam89]   I.B. Damgård, "A design principle for hash functions," *Advances in Cryptology, Proc. Crypto'89, LNCS 435*, G. Brassard, Ed., Springer-Verlag, 1990, pp. 416–427.

[Fei73]   H. Feistel, "Cryptography and computer privacy," *Scientific American*, Vol. 228, 1973, pp. 15–23.

[NBS77]   National Bureau of Standards, *Data Encryption Standard*, Federal Information Processing Standard, Publication 46, US Department of Commerce, January 1977.

[KRS88]   B.B. Kaliski, R.L. Rivest and A.T. Sherman, "Is the data encryption standard a group? (Results of cycling experiments on DES)," *Journal of Cryptology*, Vol. 1, No. 1, 1988, pp. 3–36.

[KaDa79] J.B. Kam and G.I. Davida, "Structured design of substitution-permutation encryption networks," *IEEE Transactions on Computers*, Vol. C–28, No. 10, 1979, pp. 747–753.

[Knu81]   D.E. Knuth, *The Art of Computer Programming, Vol. 2: Seminumerical Algorithms, 2nd Edition*, Addison-Wesley, Reading Mass., 1981.

[Mer90]   R.C. Merkle, *Personal Communication*, 1990.

[Riv92a] R.L. Rivest, "The MD4 message-digest algorithm," *Request for Comments (RFC) 1320*, Internet Activities Board, Internet Privacy Task Force, April 1992.

[Riv92b] R.L. Rivest, "The MD5 message-digest algorithm," *Request for Comments (RFC) 1321*, Internet Activities Board, Internet Privacy Task Force, April 1992.

[WeTa85] A.F. Webster and S.E. Tavares, "On the design of S-boxes," *Advances in Cryptology, Proc. Crypto'85, LNCS 218*, H.C. Williams, Ed., Springer-Verlag, 1985, pp. 523–534.

A   C Implementation of the Primitive

This appendix provides an ANSI C-implementation of the primitive RIPEMD and an example program that uses RIPEMD to hash messages. This program can be used for testing purposes as well, as it can provide the test values of Appendix B.

Use of this implementation The file ripemd.c contains the code of the functions MDinit, compress and MDfinish. MDinit performs the initialization of (A_0, B_0, C_0, D_0), compress applies compress, MDfinish pads the message, appends the length and compresses the resulting final words. The header file ripemd.h contains the function prototypes and some macros.

The test program hashtest can be compiled as follows. First, compile the source files ripemd.c and hashtest.c with an (ANSI) C compiler. Next, link the resulting object files.

This implementation has been tested on a wide variety of environments, so it should be portable or at worst easy to port. The testing environments include MS-DOS (4.2 and 5.0 on both 80286 and 80386 processors) with several compilers, VAX/VMS, RISC ULTRIX, ConvexOS and Macintosh.

Note that VAX/VMS does not allow the run command to pass arguments to an executable. A patch for this is given in the comment of the main() function in hashtest.c.

A.1   The Header File for RIPEMD

```
/*********************************************************************/
/* file: ripemd.h                                                    */
/*                                                                   */
/* description: header file for RIPEMD, a sample C-implementation    */
/*         This function is derived from the MD4 Message Digest      */
/*         Algorithm from RSA Data Security, Inc.                    */
/*         This implementation was developed by RIPE.                */
/*                                                                   */
/* copyright (C)                                                     */
/*         Centre for Mathematics and Computer Science, Amsterdam    */
/*         Siemens AG                                                */
/*         Philips Crypto BV                                         */
/*         PTT Research, the Netherlands                             */
/*         Katholieke Universiteit Leuven                            */
/*         Aarhus University                                         */
/* 1992, All Rights Reserved                                         */
/*                                                                   */
/* date:    05/06/92                                                 */
/* version: 1.0                                                      */
/*                                                                   */
/*********************************************************************/

#ifndef  RIPEMDH              /* make sure this file is read only once */
#define  RIPEMDH


/*********************************************************************/

/* typedef 8, 16 and 32 bit types, resp.  */
/* adapt these, if necessary,
   for your operating system and compiler */
typedef    unsigned long        dword;
typedef    unsigned short       word;
typedef    unsigned char        byte;



/*********************************************************************/

/* macro definitions */

/* collect four bytes into one word: */
#define BYTES_TO_WORD(strptr)                        \
          (((dword) *((strptr)+3) << 24) | \
           ((dword) *((strptr)+2) << 16) | \
           ((dword) *((strptr)+1) <<  8) | \
           ((dword) *(strptr)))

/* ROL(x, n) cyclically rotates x over n bits to the left */
/* x must be of an unsigned 32 bits type and 0 <= n < 32. */
```

```
#define ROL(x, n)           (((x) << (n)) | ((x) >> (32-(n)))))

/* the three basic functions F(), G() and H() */
#define F(x, y, z)          (((x) & (y)) | ((~x) & (z)))
#define G(x, y, z)          (((x) & (y)) | ((x) & (z)) | ((y) & (z)))
#define H(x, y, z)          ((x) ^ (y) ^ (z))

/* the six basic operations FF() through HHH() */
#define FF(a, b, c, d, x, s)          {\
     (a) += F((b), (c), (d)) + (x);\
     (a) = ROL((a), (s));\
   }
#define GG(a, b, c, d, x, s)          {\
     (a) += G((b), (c), (d)) + (x) + (dword)0x5a827999UL;\
     (a) = ROL((a), (s));\
   }
#define HH(a, b, c, d, x, s)          {\
     (a) += H((b), (c), (d)) + (x) + (dword)0x6ed9eba1UL;\
     (a) = ROL((a), (s));\
   }
#define FFF(a, b, c, d, x, s)          {\
     (a) += F((b), (c), (d)) + (x) + (dword)0x50a28be6UL;\
     (a) = ROL((a), (s));\
   }
#define GGG(a, b, c, d, x, s)          {\
     (a) += G((b), (c), (d)) + (x);\
     (a) = ROL((a), (s));\
   }
#define HHH(a, b, c, d, x, s)          {\
     (a) += H((b), (c), (d)) + (x) + (dword)0x5c4dd124UL;\
     (a) = ROL((a), (s));\
   }

/*******************************************************************/

/* function prototypes */

void MDinit(dword *MDbuf);
/*
 *   initializes MDbuffer to "magic constants"
 */

void compress(dword *MDbuf, dword *X);
/*
 *   the compression function.
 *   transforms MDbuf using message bytes X[0] through X[15]
 */

void MDfinish(dword *MDbuf, byte *strptr, dword lswlen, dword mswlen);
/*
```

```
 *  puts bytes from strptr into X and pad out; appends length
 *  and finally, compresses the last block(s)
 *  note: length in bits == 8 * (lswlen + 2^32 mswlen).
 *  note: there are (lswlen mod 64) bytes left in strptr.
 */

#endif  /* RIPEMDH */

/********************** end of file ripemd.h **********************/
```

A.2   The C Source Code for RIPEMD

```
/***********************************************************************/
/*  file: ripemd.c                                                    */
/*                                                                    */
/*  description: A sample C-implementation of the RIPEMD             */
/*               hash-function. This function is derived from the MD4 */
/*               Message Digest Algorithm from RSA Data Security, Inc. */
/*               This implementation was developed by RIPE.          */
/*                                                                    */
/*  copyright (C)                                                     */
/*               Centre for Mathematics and Computer Science, Amsterdam */
/*               Siemens AG                                           */
/*               Philips Crypto BV                                    */
/*               PTT Research, the Netherlands                        */
/*               Katholieke Universiteit Leuven                       */
/*               Aarhus University                                    */
/*  1992, All Rights Reserved                                         */
/*                                                                    */
/*  date:     05/25/92                                                */
/*  version: 1.0                                                      */
/*                                                                    */
/***********************************************************************/


/*  header files */
#include <stdio.h>
#include <stdlib.h>
#include <string.h>
#include "ripemd.h"

/***********************************************************************/

void MDinit(dword *MDbuf)
{
    MDbuf[0] = 0x67452301UL;
    MDbuf[1] = 0xefcdab89UL;
    MDbuf[2] = 0x98badcfeUL;
    MDbuf[3] = 0x10325476UL;

    return;
}


/***********************************************************************/

void compress(dword *MDbuf, dword *X)
{
    dword aa = MDbuf[0],  bb = MDbuf[1],  cc = MDbuf[2],  dd = MDbuf[3];
    dword aaa = MDbuf[0], bbb = MDbuf[1], ccc = MDbuf[2], ddd = MDbuf[3];
```

```
/* round 1 */
FF(aa, bb, cc, dd, X[0], 11);
FF(dd, aa, bb, cc, X[1], 14);
FF(cc, dd, aa, bb, X[2], 15);
FF(bb, cc, dd, aa, X[3], 12);
FF(aa, bb, cc, dd, X[4],  5);
FF(dd, aa, bb, cc, X[5],  8);
FF(cc, dd, aa, bb, X[6],  7);
FF(bb, cc, dd, aa, X[7],  9);
FF(aa, bb, cc, dd, X[8], 11);
FF(dd, aa, bb, cc, X[9], 13);
FF(cc, dd, aa, bb, X[10],14);
FF(bb, cc, dd, aa, X[11],15);
FF(aa, bb, cc, dd, X[12], 6);
FF(dd, aa, bb, cc, X[13], 7);
FF(cc, dd, aa, bb, X[14], 9);
FF(bb, cc, dd, aa, X[15], 8);

/* round 2 */
GG(aa, bb, cc, dd, X[7],  7);
GG(dd, aa, bb, cc, X[4],  6);
GG(cc, dd, aa, bb, X[13], 8);
GG(bb, cc, dd, aa, X[1], 13);
GG(aa, bb, cc, dd, X[10],11);
GG(dd, aa, bb, cc, X[6],  9);
GG(cc, dd, aa, bb, X[15], 7);
GG(bb, cc, dd, aa, X[3], 15);
GG(aa, bb, cc, dd, X[12], 7);
GG(dd, aa, bb, cc, X[0], 12);
GG(cc, dd, aa, bb, X[9], 15);
GG(bb, cc, dd, aa, X[5],  9);
GG(aa, bb, cc, dd, X[14], 7);
GG(dd, aa, bb, cc, X[2], 11);
GG(cc, dd, aa, bb, X[11],13);
GG(bb, cc, dd, aa, X[8], 12);

/* round 3 */
HH(aa, bb, cc, dd, X[3], 11);
HH(dd, aa, bb, cc, X[10],13);
HH(cc, dd, aa, bb, X[2], 14);
HH(bb, cc, dd, aa, X[4],  7);
HH(aa, bb, cc, dd, X[9], 14);
HH(dd, aa, bb, cc, X[15], 9);
HH(cc, dd, aa, bb, X[8], 13);
HH(bb, cc, dd, aa, X[1], 15);
HH(aa, bb, cc, dd, X[14], 6);
HH(dd, aa, bb, cc, X[7],  8);
HH(cc, dd, aa, bb, X[0], 13);
HH(bb, cc, dd, aa, X[6], 6);
HH(aa, bb, cc, dd, X[11],12);
```

```
HH(dd, aa, bb, cc, X[13], 5);
HH(cc, dd, aa, bb, X[5],  7);
HH(bb, cc, dd, aa, X[12], 5);

/* parallel round 1 */
FFF(aaa, bbb, ccc, ddd, X[0],  11);
FFF(ddd, aaa, bbb, ccc, X[1],  14);
FFF(ccc, ddd, aaa, bbb, X[2],  15);
FFF(bbb, ccc, ddd, aaa, X[3],  12);
FFF(aaa, bbb, ccc, ddd, X[4],  5);
FFF(ddd, aaa, bbb, ccc, X[5],  8);
FFF(ccc, ddd, aaa, bbb, X[6],  7);
FFF(bbb, ccc, ddd, aaa, X[7],  9);
FFF(aaa, bbb, ccc, ddd, X[8],  11);
FFF(ddd, aaa, bbb, ccc, X[9],  13);
FFF(ccc, ddd, aaa, bbb, X[10],14);
FFF(bbb, ccc, ddd, aaa, X[11],15);
FFF(aaa, bbb, ccc, ddd, X[12], 6);
FFF(ddd, aaa, bbb, ccc, X[13], 7);
FFF(ccc, ddd, aaa, bbb, X[14], 9);
FFF(bbb, ccc, ddd, aaa, X[15], 8);

/* parallel round 2 */
GGG(aaa, bbb, ccc, ddd, X[7],  7);
GGG(ddd, aaa, bbb, ccc, X[4],  6);
GGG(ccc, ddd, aaa, bbb, X[13], 8);
GGG(bbb, ccc, ddd, aaa, X[1],  13);
GGG(aaa, bbb, ccc, ddd, X[10],11);
GGG(ddd, aaa, bbb, ccc, X[6],  9);
GGG(ccc, ddd, aaa, bbb, X[15], 7);
GGG(bbb, ccc, ddd, aaa, X[3],  15);
GGG(aaa, bbb, ccc, ddd, X[12], 7);
GGG(ddd, aaa, bbb, ccc, X[0],  12);
GGG(ccc, ddd, aaa, bbb, X[9],  15);
GGG(bbb, ccc, ddd, aaa, X[5],  9);
GGG(aaa, bbb, ccc, ddd, X[14], 7);
GGG(ddd, aaa, bbb, ccc, X[2],  11);
GGG(ccc, ddd, aaa, bbb, X[11],13);
GGG(bbb, ccc, ddd, aaa, X[8],  12);

/* parallel round 3 */
HHH(aaa, bbb, ccc, ddd, X[3],  11);
HHH(ddd, aaa, bbb, ccc, X[10],13);
HHH(ccc, ddd, aaa, bbb, X[2],  14);
HHH(bbb, ccc, ddd, aaa, X[4],  7);
HHH(aaa, bbb, ccc, ddd, X[9],  14);
HHH(ddd, aaa, bbb, ccc, X[15], 9);
HHH(ccc, ddd, aaa, bbb, X[8],  13);
HHH(bbb, ccc, ddd, aaa, X[1],  15);
HHH(aaa, bbb, ccc, ddd, X[14], 6);
```

```
   HHH(ddd, aaa, bbb, ccc, X[7],  8);
   HHH(ccc, ddd, aaa, bbb, X[0], 13);
   HHH(bbb, ccc, ddd, aaa, X[6],  6);
   HHH(aaa, bbb, ccc, ddd, X[11],12);
   HHH(ddd, aaa, bbb, ccc, X[13], 5);
   HHH(ccc, ddd, aaa, bbb, X[5],  7);
   HHH(bbb, ccc, ddd, aaa, X[12], 5);

   /* combine results */
   ddd += cc + MDbuf[1];                    /* final result for MDbuf[0] */
   MDbuf[1] = MDbuf[2] + dd + aaa;
   MDbuf[2] = MDbuf[3] + aa + bbb;
   MDbuf[3] = MDbuf[0] + bb + ccc;
   MDbuf[0] = ddd;

   return;
}

/*********************************************************************/

void MDfinish(dword *MDbuf, byte *strptr, dword lswlen, dword mswlen)
{
   dword        i;                          /* counter        */
   dword        X[16];                      /* message words */

   for (i=0; i<16; i++) {
      X[i] = 0;
   }

   /* put bytes from strptr into X */
   for (i=0; i<(lswlen&63); i++) {
      /* byte i goes into word X[i div 4] at pos.  8*(i mod 4)   */
      X[i>>2] ^= (dword) *(strptr++) << (8 * (i&3));
   }

   /* append the bit m_n == 1 */
   X[(lswlen>>2)&15]  ^= (dword)1 << (8*(lswlen&3) + 7);

   if ((lswlen & 63) > 55) {
      /* length goes to next block */
      compress(MDbuf, X);
      for (i=0; i<16; i++) {
         X[i] = 0;
      }
   }

   /* append length in bits*/
   X[14] = lswlen << 3;
   X[15] = (lswlen >> 29) | (mswlen << 3);
```

```
  compress(MDbuf, X);

  return;
}
```

/*********************** end of file ripemd.c ********************/

A.3   An Example Program

This section gives the listing of an example program. By means of command line options, several different tests can be performed (see the top of the file). Test values can be found in Appendix B. The file **test.bin** used by the test suite **hashtest** -a should contain the string **abc** and nothing else. (Make sure no newline or linefeed character is appended by your editor.)

```
/*******************************************************************/
/*  file: hashtest.c                                               */
/*                                                                 */
/*  description: test file for ripemd.c, a sample C-implementation */
/*          of the RIPEMD hash-function.                           */
/*                                                                 */
/*  command line arguments:                                        */
/*          filename  -- compute hash code of file read binary     */
/*          -sstring  -- print string & hascode                    */
/*          -t        -- perform time trial                        */
/*          -a        -- execute standard test suite, ASCII input  */
/*                       and binary input from file test.bin       */
/*          -x        -- execute standard test suite, hexadecimal  */
/*                       input read from file test.hex             */
/*                                                                 */
/*  copyright (C)                                                  */
/*          Centre for Mathematics and Computer Science, Amsterdam */
/*          Siemens AG                                             */
/*          Philips Crypto BV                                      */
/*          PTT Research, the Netherlands                          */
/*          Katholieke Universiteit Leuven                         */
/*          Aarhus University                                      */
/*  1992, All Rights Reserved                                      */
/*                                                                 */
/*  date:    06/25/92                                              */
/*  version: 1.0                                                   */
/*                                                                 */
/*******************************************************************/

#include <stdio.h>
#include <stdlib.h>
#include <time.h>
#include <string.h>
#include "ripemd.h"

/* some compilers do not know CLOCKS_PER_SEC yet */
#ifndef CLOCKS_PER_SEC
#define CLOCKS_PER_SEC    CLK_TCK
#endif

#define TEST_BLOCK_SIZE 8000
#define TEST_BLOCKS 1250
```

```
/* number of test bytes = TEST_BLOCK_SIZE * TEST_BLOCKS */
static long TEST_BYTES = (long)TEST_BLOCK_SIZE * (long)TEST_BLOCKS;

/********************************************************************/

byte *RIPEMD(byte *message)
/*
 * returns RIPEMD(message)
 * message should be a string terminated by '\0'
 */
{
    dword       MDbuf[4];      /* contains (A, B, C, D)          */
    static byte hashcode[16];  /* for final hash-value           */
    dword       X[16];         /* current 16-word chunk          */
    word        i;             /* counter                        */
    dword       length;        /* length in bytes of message     */
    dword       nbytes;        /* # of bytes not yet processed   */
    byte        *strptr;       /* points to the current mess. chunk */

    /* initialize */
    MDinit(MDbuf);
    strptr = message;                    /* strptr points to first chunk */
    length = (dword)strlen((char *)message);
    nbytes = length;

    /* process message in 16-word chunks */
    while (nbytes > 63) {
        for (i=0; i<16; i++) {
            X[i] = BYTES_TO_WORD(strptr);
            strptr += 4;
        }
        compress(MDbuf, X);
        nbytes -= 64;                    /* 64 bytes less to process */
    }                                    /* length mod 64 bytes left */

    /* finish: */
    MDfinish(MDbuf, strptr, length, 0);

    for (i=0; i<16; i+=4) {
        hashcode[i]   = MDbuf[i>>2];          /* implicit cast to byte */
        hashcode[i+1] = (MDbuf[i>>2] >>  8);  /*  extracts the 8 least */
        hashcode[i+2] = (MDbuf[i>>2] >> 16);  /*  significant bits.    */
        hashcode[i+3] = (MDbuf[i>>2] >> 24);
    }

    return (byte *)hashcode;
}

/********************************************************************/
```

```
byte *RIPEMDbinary(char *fname)
/*
 * returns RIPEMD(message in file fname)
 * fname is read as binary data.
 */
{
    FILE        *mf;            /* pointer to file <fname>        */
    byte         data[1024];    /* contains current mess. block */
    dword        nbytes;        /* length of this block           */
    dword        MDbuf[4];      /* contains (A, B, C, D)          */
    static byte  hashcode[16];  /* for final hash-value           */
    dword        X[16];         /* current 16-word chunk          */
    word         i, j;          /* counters                       */
    dword        length[2];     /* length in bytes of message     */
    dword        offset;        /* # of unprocessed bytes at      */
                                /* call of MDfinish */

    /* initialize */
    if ((mf = fopen(fname, "rb")) == NULL) {
        fprintf(stderr, "\nRIPEMDbinary: cannot open file \"%s\".\n",
                fname);
        exit(1);
    }
    MDinit(MDbuf);
    length[0] = 0;
    length[1] = 0;

    while ((nbytes = fread(data, 1, 1024, mf)) != 0) {
        /* process all complete blocks */
        for (i=0; i<(nbytes>>6); i++) {
            for (j=0; j<16; j++) {
                X[j] = BYTES_TO_WORD(data+64*i+4*j);
            }
            compress(MDbuf, X);
        }
        /* update length[] */
        if (length[0] + nbytes < length[0])
            length[1]++;                    /* overflow to msb of length */
        length[0] += nbytes;
    }

    /* finish: */
    offset = length[0] & 0x3C0;   /* extract bytes 6 to 10 inclusive */
    MDfinish(MDbuf, data+offset, length[0], length[1]);

    for (i=0; i<16; i+=4) {
        hashcode[i]   =  MDbuf[i>>2];
        hashcode[i+1] = (MDbuf[i>>2] >>  8);
        hashcode[i+2] = (MDbuf[i>>2] >> 16);
```

```
      hashcode[i+3] = (MDbuf[i>>2] >> 24);
   }

   fclose(mf);

   return (byte *)hashcode;
}

/****************************************************************/


byte *RIPEMDhex(char *fname)
/*
 * returns RIPEMD(message in file fname)
 * fname should contain the message in hex format;
 * first number of bytes, then the bytes in hexadecimal.
 */
{
   FILE          *mf;            /* pointer to file <fname>    */
   byte          data[64];       /* contains current mess. block */
   dword         nbytes;         /* length of the message      */
   dword         MDbuf[4];       /* contains (A, B, C, D)      */
   static byte   hashcode[16];    /* for final hash-value       */
   dword         X[16];          /* current 16-word chunk      */
   word          i, j;           /* counters                   */
   int           val;            /* temp for reading from file */

   /* initialize */
   if ((mf = fopen(fname, "r")) == NULL) {
      fprintf(stderr, "\nRIPEMDhex: cannot open file \"%s\".\n",
              fname);
      exit(1);
   }
   MDinit(MDbuf);

   fscanf(mf, "%x", &val);
   nbytes = val;
   i = 0;
   while (nbytes - i > 63) {
      /* read and process complete block */
      for (j=0; j<64; j++) {
         fscanf(mf, "%x", &val);
         data[j] = (byte)val;
      }
      for (j=0; j<16; j++) {
         X[j] = BYTES_TO_WORD(data+4*j);
      }
      compress(MDbuf, X);
      i += 64;
   }
```

```
   /* read last nbytes-i bytes: */
   j = 0;
   while (i<nbytes) {
      fscanf(mf, "%x", &val);
      data[j++] = (byte)val;
      i++;
   }

   /* finish */
   MDfinish(MDbuf, data, nbytes, 0);

   for (i=0; i<16; i+=4) {
      hashcode[i]   =  MDbuf[i>>2];
      hashcode[i+1] = (MDbuf[i>>2] >>  8);
      hashcode[i+2] = (MDbuf[i>>2] >> 16);
      hashcode[i+3] = (MDbuf[i>>2] >> 24);
   }

   fclose(mf);

   return (byte *)hashcode;
}

/*********************************************************************/

void speedtest(void)
/*
 * A time trial routine, to measure the speed of ripemd.
 * Measures processor time required to process TEST_BLOCKS times
 *   a message of TEST_BLOCK_SIZE characters.
 */
{
   clock_t   t0, t1;
   byte      data[TEST_BLOCK_SIZE];
   byte      hashcode[64];
   dword     X[16];
   dword     MDbuf[4];
   word      i, j, k;

   /* initialize test data */
   for (i=0; i<TEST_BLOCK_SIZE; i++)
      data[i] = (byte)(i%1000);

   /* start timer */
   printf("RIPEMD time trial. Processing %ld characters...\n",
          TEST_BYTES);
   t0 = clock();

   /* process data */
```

```
  MDinit(MDbuf);
  for (i=0; i<TEST_BLOCKS; i++) {
     for (j=0; j<TEST_BLOCK_SIZE; j+=64) {
        for (k=0; k<16; k++) {
           X[k] = BYTES_TO_WORD(data+j+4*k);
        }
        compress(MDbuf, X);
     }
  }
  MDfinish(MDbuf, data, TEST_BYTES, 0);

  /* stop timer, get time difference */
  t1 = clock();
  printf("\nTest input processed in %g seconds.\n",
         (double)(t1-t0)/(double)CLOCKS_PER_SEC);
  printf("Characters processed per second: %g\n",
         (double)CLOCKS_PER_SEC*TEST_BYTES/((double)t1-t0));

  for (i=0; i<16; i+=4) {
     hashcode[i]   = MDbuf[i>>2];
     hashcode[i+1] = (MDbuf[i>>2] >>  8);
     hashcode[i+2] = (MDbuf[i>>2] >> 16);
     hashcode[i+3] = (MDbuf[i>>2] >> 24);
  }
  printf("\nhashcode: ");
  for (i=0; i<16; i++)
     printf("%02x", hashcode[i]);

  return;
}

/*******************************************************************/

void testascii (void)
/*
 *    standard test suite, ASCII input
 */
{
   int i;
   byte *hashcode;

   printf("\nRIPEMD test suite results (ASCII):\n");

   hashcode = RIPEMD((byte *)"");
   printf("\n\nmessage: \"\"  (empty string)\nhashcode: ");
   for (i=0; i<16; i++)
      printf("%02x", hashcode[i]);

   hashcode = RIPEMD((byte *)"a");
   printf("\n\nmessage: \"a\"\nhashcode: ");
```

```
   for (i=0; i<16; i++)
      printf("%02x", hashcode[i]);

   hashcode = RIPEMD((byte *)"abc");
   printf("\n\nmessage: \"abc\"\nhashcode: ");
   for (i=0; i<16; i++)
      printf("%02x", hashcode[i]);

   hashcode = RIPEMD((byte *)"message digest");
   printf("\n\nmessage: \"message digest\"\nhashcode: ");
   for (i=0; i<16; i++)
      printf("%02x", hashcode[i]);

   hashcode = RIPEMD((byte *)"abcdefghijklmnopqrstuvwxyz");
   printf("\n\nmessage: \"abcdefghijklmnopqrstuvwxyz\"\nhashcode: ");
   for (i=0; i<16; i++)
      printf("%02x", hashcode[i]);

   hashcode = RIPEMD((byte *)
      "ABCDEFGHIJKLMNOPQRSTUVWXYZabcdefghijklmnopqrstuvwxyz0123456789");
   printf("\n\nmessage: A...Za...z0...9\nhashcode: ");
   for (i=0; i<16; i++)
      printf("%02x", hashcode[i]);

   hashcode = RIPEMD((byte *)"12345678901234567890123456789012345678901234567890\
12345678901234567890123456789012345678901234567890");
   printf("\n\nmessage: 8 times \"1234567890\"\nhashcode: ");
   for (i=0; i<16; i++)
      printf("%02x", hashcode[i]);

   /* Contents of binary created file test.bin are "abc" */
   printf("\n\nmessagefile (binary): test.bin\nhashcode: ");
   hashcode = RIPEMDbinary ("test.bin");
   for (i=0; i<16; i++)
      printf("%02x", hashcode[i]);

   return;
}

/***************************************************************/

void testhex (void)
/*
 *    standard test suite, hex input, read from files
 */
{
   int i;
   byte *hashcode;

   printf("\nRIPEMD test suite results (hex):\n");
```

```
      hashcode = RIPEMDhex("test1.hex");
      printf("\n\nfile test1.hex; hashcode: ");
      for (i=0; i<16; i++)
         printf("%02x", hashcode[i]);

      hashcode = RIPEMDhex("test2.hex");
      printf("\n\nfile test2.hex; hashcode: ");
      for (i=0; i<16; i++)
         printf("%02x", hashcode[i]);

      hashcode = RIPEMDhex("test3.hex");
      printf("\n\nfile test3.hex; hashcode: ");
      for (i=0; i<16; i++)
         printf("%02x", hashcode[i]);

      hashcode = RIPEMDhex("test4.hex");
      printf("\n\nfile test4.hex; hashcode: ");
      for (i=0; i<16; i++)
         printf("%02x", hashcode[i]);

      hashcode = RIPEMDhex("test5.hex");
      printf("\n\nfile test5.hex; hashcode: ");
      for (i=0; i<16; i++)
         printf("%02x", hashcode[i]);

      hashcode = RIPEMDhex("test6.hex");
      printf("\n\nfile test6.hex; hashcode: ");
      for (i=0; i<16; i++)
         printf("%02x", hashcode[i]);

      hashcode = RIPEMDhex("test7.hex");
      printf("\n\nfile test7.hex; hashcode: ");
      for (i=0; i<16; i++)
         printf("%02x", hashcode[i]);

      return;
}


/******************************************************************/

main (int argc, char *argv[])
/*
 *  main program. calls one or more of the test routines depending
 *  on command line arguments. see the header of this file.
 *
 *  (For VAX/VMS, do: HASHTEST :== $<pathname>HASHTEST.EXE
 *   at the command prompt (or in login.com) first.
 *   (The run command does not allow command line args.)
 *   The <pathname> must include device, e.g., "DSKD:".)
```

```
*/
{
  int   i, j;
  byte *hashcode;

  if (argc == 1) {
    fprintf(stderr, "hashtest: no command line arguments supplied.\n");
    exit(1);
  }
  else {
    for (i = 1; i < argc; i++) {
      if (argv[i][0] == '-' && argv[i][1] == 's') {
        printf("\n\nmessage: %s", argv[i]+2);
        hashcode = RIPEMD((byte *)argv[i] + 2);
        printf("\nhashcode: ");
        for (j=0; j<16; j++)
          printf("%02x", hashcode[j]);
      }
      else if (strcmp (argv[i], "-t") == 0)
        speedtest ();
      else if (strcmp (argv[i], "-a") == 0)
        testascii ();
      else if (strcmp (argv[i], "-x") == 0)
        testhex ();
      else {
        hashcode = RIPEMDbinary (argv[i]);
        printf("\n\nmessagefile (binary): %s", argv[i]);
        printf("\nhashcode: ");
        for (j=0; j<16; j++)
          printf("%02x", hashcode[j]);
      }
    }
  }
  printf("\n");

  return 0;
}

/********************** end of file hashtest.c **********************/
```

B   Test Values

Below, the files **test1.hex** up to **test7.hex** as used by the test **hashtest -x** are listed. The format of those files is as follows. All numbers are hexadecimal; all numbers except possibly the first one are one byte long. The first number represents the number of bytes in the message to be hashed; it is followed by (at least) this number of bytes. For example, **test3.hex** represents the message consisting of the three bytes 0x61, 0x62 and 0x63. This is the string "abc" in ASCII.

test1.hex:

0

test2.hex:

1
61

test3.hex:

3
61 62 63

test4.hex:

e
6d 65 73 73 61 67 65 20 64 69 67 65 73 74

test5.hex:

1a
61 62 63 64 65 66 67 68 69 6a 6b 6c 6d 6e 6f 70
71 72 73 74 75 76 77 78 79 7a

test6.hex:

3e
41 42 43 44 45 46 47 48 49 4a 4b 4c 4d 4e 4f 50
51 52 53 54 55 56 57 58 59 5a 61 62 63 64 65 66
67 68 69 6a 6b 6c 6d 6e 6f 70 71 72 73 74 75 76
77 78 79 7a 30 31 32 33 34 35 36 37 38 39

test7.hex:

50
31 32 33 34 35 36 37 38 39 30
31 32 33 34 35 36 37 38 39 30
31 32 33 34 35 36 37 38 39 30
31 32 33 34 35 36 37 38 39 30
31 32 33 34 35 36 37 38 39 30
31 32 33 34 35 36 37 38 39 30
31 32 33 34 35 36 37 38 39 30
31 32 33 34 35 36 37 38 39 30

The following test values were obtained by running **hashtest -x**. If ASCII encoding is used, **hashtest -a** should provide the same answers, followed by the result of hashing "abc" again. The latter only holds if the file **test.bin** exists and contains nothing but this string.

RIPEMD test suite results (hex):

file test1.hex; hashcode: 9f73aa9b372a9dacfb86a6108852e2d9

file test2.hex; hashcode: 486f74f790bc95ef7963cd2382b4bbc9

file test3.hex; hashcode: 3f14bad4c2f9b0ea805e5485d3d6882d

file test4.hex; hashcode: 5f5c7ebe1abbb3c7036482942d5f9d49

file test5.hex; hashcode: ff6e1547494251a1cca6f005a6eaa2b4

file test6.hex; hashcode: ff418a5aed3763d8f2ddf88a29e62486

file test7.hex; hashcode: dfd6b45f60fe79bbbde87c6bfc6580a5

Chapter 4

RIPE-MAC

Table of Contents

1 Introduction

This chapter describes the integrity primitives **RIPE-MAC1** and **RIPE-MAC3**, commonly denoted as **RIPE-MAC**. Both are so-called *message authentication codes* (MAC's) or *keyed hash functions* that, under control of a (secret) key, compress messages of arbitrary length to a 64-bit output block, the *hashcode* of the message. **RIPE-MAC1** uses a 56-bit key and **RIPE-MAC3** a 112-bit key. It is conjectured that for someone not in possession of the secret key it is computationally infeasible to produce for a given message the corresponding hashcode, or to produce, given a message and the corresponding hashcode, a different message having the same hashcode (i.e., a second preimage). Moreover it is conjectured that even when a large number of message-hashcode pairs are known, where the messages are selected by the opponent, it is computationally infeasible to determine the key or to produce the hashcode of a message not in this set of selected messages. Keyed hash functions with these properties are used in message authentication applications providing both data integrity and data origin authentication, as well as in identification schemes (see Section 4 of this chapter and Part II of this report).

The **RIPE-MAC** algorithm is based on the ISO/IEC standard 9797 *data integrity mechanism using a cryptographic check function employing a block cipher* [ISO89], but differs from it with respect to the internal structure of the compression function, the padding mechanism and the final processing. It consists of three parts. First, the message is expanded to a length that is a multiple of 64 bits. Next, the expanded message is divided up in blocks of 64 bits. A keyed compression function is used to iteratively compress these blocks under control of the secret key to a single block of 64 bits. For this keyed compression function a keyed one-way function is used based on the DES [NBS77] or a triple encryption mode of the DES, in order to provide a higher security level. The numbers at the end of the names **RIPE-MAC1** and **RIPE-MAC3** refer to the number of DES operations in a single application of this compression function. Finally the output of this iterative compression is subjected to a DES based encryption with a different key, derived from the key used in the compression.

Since the **RIPE-MAC** algorithm uses essentially one or three DES operations per message block, its design is oriented towards implementations using fast DES hardware. The performance of a pure software implementation will suffer from the low software performance of the DES. However, as the same key is used throughout the compression, the slow DES key scheduling has to be done only twice: once for the entire compression and once for the encryption at the end. Moreover, the inverse initial permutation has to be done only once at the end of the MAC calculation. This will help the software speed.

The structure of this chapter is as follows. In order to avoid any ambiguities in the description of the primitive, the notation and definitions in this chapter are fixed in Section 2. Section 3 contains a description of the primitive and in Section 4 the possible modes of use of the primitive are considered. The security aspects of the primitive are discussed in Section 5. These include the claimed properties and the algebraic evaluation of the primitive. Finally, in Section 6 the performance aspects of RIPE-MAC are considered, and Section 7 gives some guidelines for software implementation.

This chapter has two appendices. Appendix A contains a straightforward software implementation of RIPE-MAC in the programming language C and in Appendix B test values for the primitive are given.

2 Definitions and Notation

2.1 Introduction

In order to obtain a clear description of the primitive, the notation and definitions used in this chapter are fully described in this section. These include the representation of the numbers in the description, and the operations, functions and constants used by the primitive.

2.2 General

The symbol ":=" is used for the assignment of a value or a meaning to a variable or symbol. That is, $a := b$ either means that the variable a gets the value of the variable b, or it means that a is defined as "b". It will be obvious from the context which meaning is intended.

The equality-sign "=" is used for equality only. That is, it indicates that the two entities on either side are equal.

Note that in C-source code, "=" denotes assignment, while comparison is denoted by "==".

An ellipsis ("...") denotes an implicit enumeration. For example, "$i = 0, 1, ..., n$" is meant to represent the sentence "for $i = 0$, $i = 1$, and so on, up to $i = n$".

2.3 Representation of Numbers

In this chapter a *word* is defined as a 64-bit quantity. A word is considered to be a nonnegative integer. That is, it can take on the values 0 through $2^{64} - 1 = 18446744073709551615$. Normally the value of a word will be given in hexadecimal form. In that case the number is written as '0x' followed immediately by at most 16 hexadecimal digits, the most significant first. For example, the hexadecimal representation of the 64-bit number 7017280452245743464 is 0x6162636465666768.

A sequence of $64n$ bits $w_0, w_1, \ldots, w_{64n-1}$ is interpreted as a sequence of n words in the following way. Each group of 64 consecutive bits is considered as a word W_i, the first bit of such a group being the most significant bit of that word. Hence,

$$W_i := \sum_{j=0}^{63} w_{64i+j} 2^{63-j}, \qquad i = 0, 1, \ldots, n-1. \tag{1}$$

In this chapter, words are always denoted by uppercase letters and the bits of this word by the corresponding lowercase letter with indices as in Equation (1).

2.4 Definitions and Basic Operations

- A *string* is a sequence of bits. If X is a string consisting of n bits, then those bits are denoted from left to right by $x_0, x_1, \ldots, x_{n-2}, x_{n-1}$.
- The *length* of a string X is the number of bits in the string X. A string of length n is called an n-bit string.
- For two strings X and Y of length n, the $2n$-bit string $W = X \parallel Y$ is defined as the *concatenation* of the strings X and Y. That is, according to the definition of a string above,

$$\begin{aligned} w_i &:= x_i \\ w_{i+n} &:= y_i \end{aligned} \qquad i = 0, 1, \ldots, n - 1 .$$

- Strings of length 64 will also be considered as a word according to the representation defined by Equation (1), and vice versa. Hence, if X is a 64-bit string, then the corresponding word is equal to

$$X = \sum_{i=0}^{63} x_i 2^{63-i} .$$

Note that the same symbol is used for both the string and the corresponding word. It will be clear from the context which representation is intended.
- For a nonnegative integer A and a positive integer B, the numbers A div B and A mod B are defined as the nonnegative integers Q, respectively R, such that

$$A = QB + R \quad \text{and} \quad 0 \leq R < B .$$

That is, A mod B is the *remainder*, and A div B is the *quotient* of an integer division of A by B.
- For two words X and Y, the word $U = X \oplus Y$ is defined as the bitwise *XOR* of X and Y, respectively. Hence, according to Equation (1):

$$u_i := (x_i + y_i) \bmod 2, \qquad i = 0, 1, \ldots, 63 .$$

2.5 Functions used by the Primitive

RIPE-MAC1 uses a single application and RIPE-MAC3 uses three applications of the Data Encryption Standard (DES) [NBS77] to map a word under control of a secret parameter, called the key, onto another word.

A DES encryption operation $E(\cdot)$ will be graphically represented as shown in Figure 1 and mathematically written as

$$Y = E(K, X) .$$

The key K is represented as a word, but the eight parity bits are ignored. That is, the bits k_7, k_{15}, k_{23}, k_{39}, k_{47}, k_{55} and k_{63} of $K = (k_0, k_1, \ldots, k_{63})$ are not used. Hence K has an effective length of only 56 bits. Whenever a reference is made to a 56-bit key K, the length of the string representing K will be 64 bits of which only 56 are used.

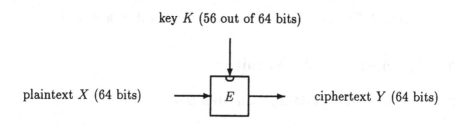

Fig. 1. The basic DES encryption operation.

A DES decryption operation $D(\cdot)$ will be graphically and mathematically represented in the same way as the encryption operation, with E replaced by D. Hence,

$$D(K, E(K, X)) = X \, .$$

RIPE-MAC3 obtains a higher security level than RIPE-MAC1 by replacing the single DES encryption operation with a triple DES operation $E_3(\cdot)$ with two different 56-bit keys K_1 and K_2 [MeMa82]:

$$Y = E_3(K, X) := E(K_1, D(K_2, E(K_1, X))) \, ,$$

where $K = K_1 \parallel K_2$ is a single 112-bit key. Once again both K_1 and K_2 are represented as words, but their parity bits are ignored. Whenever a reference is made to a 112-bit key K, the length of the bit string representing K will be 128 bits of which only 112 are used. This primitive is depicted in Figure 2, together with a shorthand. Note that for $K_1 = K_2$ the result of $E_3(\cdot)$ is reduced to a single DES encryption with that same key:

$$E_3(K \parallel K, X) = E(K, X) \, .$$

Hence an implementation of RIPE-MAC3 can be used to simulate RIPE-MAC1, although it will of course be slower (see Sections 6 and 7).

In the description of the RIPE-MAC scheme, the encryption functions $E(\cdot)$ or $E_3(\cdot)$ can be substituted by other encryption functions. However the security of these new schemes has to be re-evaluated, as they depend on the properties of the new encryption function. In this chapter only the DES-based functions $E(\cdot)$ and $E_3(\cdot)$ are considered.

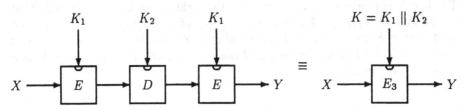

Fig. 2. The triple DES operation, together with a shorthand.

3   Description of the Primitive

3.1   Outline of RIPE-MAC1 and RIPE-MAC3

RIPE-MAC1 is a keyed hash function that maps a message M of arbitrary length under control of a 56-bit K onto a 64-bit block RIPE-MAC1(K, M). The basis of RIPE-MAC1 is the keyed compression function compress1$(\cdot)$. This function compresses a two word input to a single word output under control of the 56-bit key. This function is used in the following way.

First, the message M is expanded to an appropriate length and represented as a sequence of words X. Then, starting with a one-word initial vector, the sequence X is compressed by repeatedly appending a message word and compressing the resulting two words to one by applying compress1$(\cdot)$ until the message is exhausted. Finally, this single word result is encrypted with the function $E(\cdot)$ using a 56-bit K' derived from K. Below this is explained in detail.

Let $M = (m_0, m_1, \ldots, m_{n-1})$ be a message of n bits long. The 64-bit message authentication code RIPE-MAC1(K, M) of M is computed in three steps, see also Figure 4.

expansion: M is expanded to a sequence X consisting of N words $X_0, X_1, \ldots,$
X_{N-1}, where $N = (n \text{ div } 64) + 2$. That is, the message is expanded such that its length becomes a multiple of 64 bits. This expansion is done even if the original message length is a multiple of 64 bits.

compression: Define the word H_0 as the all zero sequence:

$$H_0 := \text{0x0000000000000000}.$$

For $i = 0, 1, \ldots, N - 1$, the words H_{i+1} is computed from the words H_i and the message word X_i under control of the key K as follows:

$$H_{i+1} := \text{compress1}(K, H_i, X_i).$$

hashcode: The hashcode RIPE-MAC1(K, M) is the 64-bit string $E(K', H_N)$, where

$$K' := K \oplus \text{0xf0f0f0f0f0f0f0f0}.$$

That is, every other 4 bits of K are complemented.

RIPE-MAC3 operates in exactly the same way as RIPE-MAC1, except that it uses a 112-bit key. A message M of arbitrary length is compressed to a 64-bit block H_N under control of this 112-bit key K by means of the compression $\mathsf{compress3}(\cdot)$. The hashcode $\mathsf{RIPE\text{-}MAC3}(K, M)$ is equal to the 64-bit string $E_3(K', H_N)$, where $K' = K_1' \,\|\, K_2'$ is derived from $K = K_1 \,\|\, K_2$ by complementing every other 4 bits of K. That is,

$$K_i' := K_i \oplus \mathtt{0xf0f0f0f0f0f0f0f0}, \quad \text{for } i = 1, 2.$$

3.2   Expanding the Message

Let $N = (n \text{ div } 64) + 2$. The n-bit message $M = (m_0, m_1, \ldots, m_{n-1})$ is expanded to the N-word message $X = (X_0, X_1, \ldots, X_{N-1})$ in the following three steps.

1. Append a single 1-bit and $k = 63 - (n \bmod 64)$ 0-bits to the message M:

$$m_n := 1,$$
$$m_{n+1} := m_{n+2} := \cdots := m_{n+k} := 0.$$

   That is, append a single 1-bit and as few (possibly none) 0-bits as necessary to obtain an expanded message that is a multiple of 64 bits. Note that padding is done even if the length of M is already a multiple of 64 bits.

2. Transform this $(n + k + 1)$-bit extended message into the $\frac{n+k+1}{64} = N - 1$ words $X_0, X_1, \ldots, X_{N-2}$ according to the conventions defined in Section 2.3. Hence,

$$X_i := \sum_{j=0}^{63} m_{64i+j} 2^{63-j}, \qquad i = 0, 1, \ldots, N - 2.$$

3. Complete the expansion by appending the length n of the original message:

$$X_{N-1} := n \bmod 2^{64}.$$

3.3   The Compression Functions compress1 and compress3

For the word H_i, the message word X_i and the 56-bit key K the word function value $\mathsf{compress1}(\cdot)$ is defined as (see also Figure 3):

$$\mathsf{compress1}(K, H_i, X_i) := E(K, H_i \oplus X_i) \oplus X_i.$$

Similarly, for the word H_i, the message word X_i and the 112-bit key K the word function value $\mathsf{compress3}(\cdot)$ is defined as:

$$\mathsf{compress3}(K, H_i, X_i) := E_3(K, H_i \oplus X_i) \oplus X_i.$$

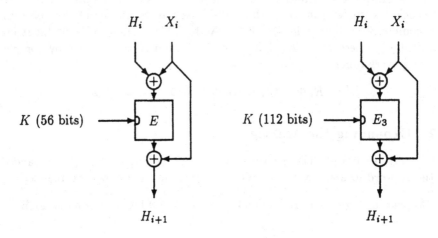

Fig. 3. Outline of the two compression function compress1(·) (left, used in RIPE-MAC1) and compress3(·) (right, used in RIPE-MAC3).

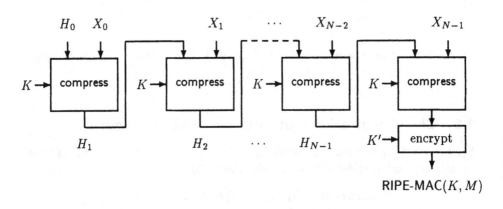

Fig. 4. Outline of RIPE-MAC. The message M is first expanded to X, which is a multiple of 64 bits long. Then the N 64-bit blocks X_i of X are processed as in this picture. The final result is either RIPE-MAC1(K, M) or RIPE-MAC3(K, M), depending on the compression and encryption function used (respectively compress1 and E, or compress3 and E_3). The key K' is derived from the key K.

4   Use of the Primitive

The primitive RIPE-MAC has two intended applications:

- to be used in a data integrity mechanism, to provide both data integrity and data origin authentication,
- to be used in secret key identification schemes.

Below this is explained in detail.

Use in data integrity mechanisms Before a message is sent, the secret key is used to compute a MAC or keyed hashcode from it. This value is sent along with the message and can be checked by the legitimate recipient using the common secret key. If the calculated hashcode is equal to the original, received value, it is reasonable to assume that the original hashcode is computed from the same message. This holds, since computation of another message with the same hashcode is claimed to be infeasible for someone not in possession of the secret key (see Section 5). Moreover, it is reasonable to assume that the message is authentic, as it is infeasible for someone who does not know the secret key to produce a hashcode for a given message (see Section 5). The latter furthermore allows to link the hashcode to the originator of the information. Therefore, the primitive provides both data integrity and data origin authentication (see Part II of this report).

Use in secret key identification schemes Secret key identification schemes allow parties to establish that their secret key sharing counterpart is actually communicating with them at a particular moment. One party supplies the other party a random challenge. The other applies the primitive to the challenge sent and returns the result. The challenging party does the same and compares the calculated hashcode with the returned one. If they are the same, it is reasonable to assume that the other party is in possession of the secret key. Of course the roles can be reversed, so that each party is able to challenge the other. For this unilateral and bilateral authentication it is suggested to use, respectively, the RIPE primitives SKID2 and SKID3, for a description of which we refer to Chapter 6 of this document.

5 Security Evaluation

5.1 Claimed Properties

RIPE-MAC1 and RIPE-MAC3 are both claimed to be keyed one-way hash functions. That is, they should satisfy the following conditions:

1. It is computationally infeasible for someone not in possession of the key K to compute for a given message M the hashcode RIPE-MAC(K, M). Even when a large number of pairs $\{M_i, \text{RIPE-MAC}(K, M_i)\}$ are known, where the M_i have been selected by this opponent, it is computationally infeasible to determine the key K or to compute RIPE-MAC(K, M') for any $M' \neq M_i$. This attack is called an *adaptive chosen text attack*. A function that satisfies this property is called *keyed*.

2. It is computationally infeasible for someone who does not know the key K to compute, given a message and its corresponding hashcode, a second message having the same hashcode. That is, given a message M and its corresponding hashcode RIPE-MAC(K, M) it is infeasible to find a message $M' \neq M$ such that RIPE-MAC$(K, M') = $ RIPE-MAC(K, M). Such a message is called a *second preimage*. A hash function that satisfies this property is called *one-way*.

By "computationally infeasible" we mean to express the impossibility of computing something with the technology that is currently available or can be foreseen to become available in the near future.

It is hard to give a bound beyond which a computation is infeasible, but certainly, a computation requiring 2^{60} (or 10^{18}) operations is computationally infeasible. On the other hand a computation taking 2^{40} (about 10^{12}) operations is hard, but not impossible.

5.2 Algebraic Evaluation

The security of the RIPE-MAC scheme is intimately related with the security of the DES. Up to this point in time there is no reason to doubt it. The most effective known attack on the DES is the so-called 'differential cryptanalysis' [BiSh91a, BiSh91b]. This is a probabilistic attack based on the relation between the XOR of two different inputs and the XOR's of the respective intermediate results and outputs. Note that two message blocks such that their XOR is preserved by the DES yield the same output of the compression function, as the XOR's cancel out. Hence, differential cryptanalysis is in principle applicable to RIPE-MAC.

To obtain the key K of RIPE-MAC1, an adaptive chosen text attack using differential cryptanalysis will require in the order of 2^{47} steps. The best one can do to find the key of RIPE-MAC3 is an exhaustive search requiring 2^{112} steps. The best one can do to obtain the hashcode of a message for RIPE-MAC1 or RIPE-MAC3 is to guess it with a probability of success of 2^{-64}.

The encryption of the hashcode at the end of the compression chain and, to a lesser extent, the expansion of the original message are essential to prevent a chosen text attack on the RIPE-MAC scheme. Without these two steps it is possible, given the hashcodes H_1, H_2 and H_3 of three messages chosen by the user, to calculate the hashcode of a fourth message. Denote by RIPE-MAC' the RIPE-MAC scheme without the encryption and the expansion. Then, given

$$H_1 = \text{RIPE-MAC'}(K, M_1)$$
$$H_2 = \text{RIPE-MAC'}(K, M_2)$$
$$H_3 = \text{RIPE-MAC'}(K, M_1 \parallel M_3),$$

where each of the M_i is a 64-bit message block, the hashcode of the message $M_2 \parallel (M_3 \oplus H_1 \oplus H_2)$ equals

$$\text{RIPE-MAC'}(K, M_2 \parallel (M_3 \oplus H_1 \oplus H_2)) = H_1 \oplus H_2 \oplus H_3.$$

Moreover the compression functions used in this scheme have the advantage that they strengthen the one-way character of the hash function: even for someone in possession of the secret key it requires in the order of 2^{32} steps to find a preimage of a given value. Here each step essentially consists of an application of compress1 or compress3. It is trivial to produce a so called pseudo-preimage, that is, a preimage for an initial value different from the (fixed) proposed one. This follows from the fact that for someone who knows the key K, the scheme is invertible: given H_{i+1}, it is easy to find a pair (H_i, X_i). Hence, he can work his way back through all the stages of the MAC making choices for the message blocks X_i and calculating the corresponding intermediate hash values H_i, until he reaches an initial value H_0. This value will of course be different from the proposed initial value (the zero word). Therefore someone in possession of the secret key can construct a preimage of a given hashcode with a so-called 'meet in the middle attack', that requires in the order of 2^{32} steps and storage.

6   Performance Evaluation

6.1   Software Implementations

The figures for a very fast software implementation of RIPE-MAC1 and RIPE-MAC3 are given in Table 1. They use the ideas introduced in Section 7 to improve the DES performance as well as the performance of the compression functions compress1 and compress3. Both a C and a 80386 Assembly language implementation are considered. The C version has the advantage of being portable (and has been ported, see Appendix A). It is in this configuration only marginally slower than the Assembly language implementation. However, as explained in Section 7, this is not necessarily the case for other configurations. All versions use the same tables totalling 64K of memory, and the same key scheduling, which uses no tables and about 6.5K of code. The figures are for an IBM-compatible 33 MHz 80386DX based PC with 64K cache memory using WATCOM C/386 9.0 in combination with the DOS/4GW DOS extender. Hence all code runs in protected mode. The codesize entry in Table 1 refers to the size of the compression function code.

	C		Assembly language	
	Codesize	Speed	Codesize	Speed
RIPE-MAC1	1383	1.27 Mbit/s	1126	1.50 Mbit/s
RIPE-MAC3	3763	0.50 Mbit/s	3018	0.60 Mbit/s

Table 1. Software performance of RIPE-MAC on a 33 MHz 80386DX based PC with a 64K memory cache using WATCOM C/386 9.0 in combination with the DOS/4GW DOS extender. All versions use 64K of data.

6.2   Hardware Implementations

The DES algorithm has been designed for hardware implementations. Hence high performance is only attainable in hardware. With current submicron CMOS technology and a clock of 25 MHz a data rate of 90 Mbit/s on chip has been achieved [VHVM88, VHVM91, Cry89, Pij92]. A faster clock of 40 MHz would allow for data rates of up to 150 Mbit/s on chip. However at such speeds the critical path does not run through the DES module, but is situated in the I/O interface. The actual data rates will therefore be lower, but 50 to 60 Mbits/s is achievable.

7   Guidelines for Software Implementation

The C-implementation given in Appendix A can be used as a starting point for an implementation. Every application of the compression functions compress1($\cdot$) or compress3($\cdot$) merely involves, respectively, one or three DES applications. Therefore the speed of a software implementation of RIPE-MAC will be determined by the efficiency with which a DES encryption can be performed. In the code of Appendix A both the DES key scheduling and the DES encryption are shown as function calls only. The software implementation of the DES, let alone an efficient implementation, is beyond the scope of this document. Only some rough guidelines for such an implementation are given. As the key scheduling is used only twice for each MAC calculation, or even less if the same key is used for subsequent MAC's, there is no need for an efficient implementation of the key scheduling. Moreover, it is shown how in the implementation of RIPE-MAC one can get rid of all the inverse initial permutations of the DES, except for the last one.

The key to fast software implementation of the DES is the use of equivalent representations of the algorithm [DDFG83, DDGH84, FeKa89]. In general, the implementation of these representations is a time-memory trade-off. The more memory is used for tables, the more instructions can be replaced by a single table lookup, the faster the code will be. The combination of a number of small tables into a fewer number of big tables will reduce the number of these table lookups, and hence will further increase the speed. Moreover, both the initial and inverse initial permutation, as well as the expansion operation contain a lot of structure. A rearrangement of the bit order therefore allows for a very efficient implementation of the expansion operation, while the bit rearrangement can be combined with the already available permutation tables of initial, inverse initial and P permutation. This way typically about 20% of the time for a single DES encryption is spent on the initial and inverse initial permutation, while about 75% is used for running through the 16 rounds. The remaining 5% is spent on the subroutine call and the initialization of some variables. In the case of triple DES the inverse initial permutations at the end of the first two DES applications cancel out against the initial permutations at the beginning of the last two DES applications. This way typically less than 10% of the time for a triple DES application is spent on the initial and inverse initial permutation, while about 90% is used for running through the 48 rounds.

However one must be careful with this analysis. The speed of a computer is (for our purposes) determined by two things: the speed of the central processing unit (CPU) and the speed by which memory can be accessed. On many computers nowadays the speed of the CPU has become so enormous with respect to the speed of memory access, that a program with extensive memory access actually gets slowed down quite significantly. This means that a program with more instructions but less memory access might be faster than a program with less instructions but more memory access. A way around this problem is the use of a (small) amount of very fast (but very expensive) memory, so called cache memory. This way programs with extensive memory access, but which fit in cache memory are significantly faster than programs that only partially can use the benefit of this cache, because the amount of memory they need is larger than the size of the cache. Hence, a program that is perfect for one computer (in the sense that it has minimal execution time) is therefore not necessarily optimal for another configuration. That is, there is no such thing as a single program being optimal for every configuration.

Almost all of the time of RIPE-MAC1 and RIPE-MAC3 spent on the inverse initial permutation can be saved by noting that the initial permutation can be moved upwards over the initial combining XOR towards the inputs H_i and X_i, while similarly the inverse initial permutation can be moved downwards over the final combining XOR towards the output H_{i+1}, see Figure 5. This way the initial permutation of H_i cancels out against the inverse initial permutation at the end of the previous stage. This means that only the message blocks X_i have to be initially permuted, and that only the result at the end of the RIPE-MAC chain has to be inverse initially permuted to obtain the hashcode RIPE-MAC1(K, M) or RIPE-MAC3(K, M).

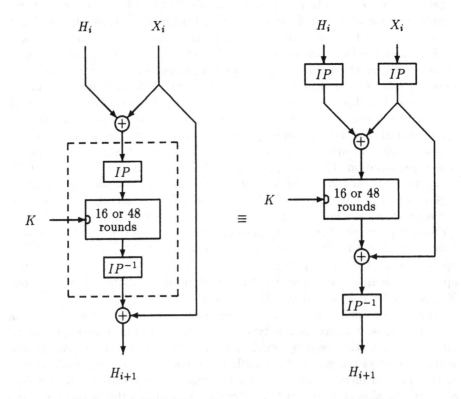

Fig. 5. Equivalent representations of a RIPE-MAC stage.

References

[BiSh91a] E. Biham and A. Shamir, "Differential Cryptanalysis of DES-like Cryptosystems," *Journal of Cryptology*, Vol. 4, No. 1, 1991, pp. 3–72.

[BiSh91b] E. Biham and A. Shamir, "Differential Cryptanalysis of the full 16-round DES," *Technical Report # 708*, Technion - Israel Institute of Technology, Department of Computer Science, December 1991.

[Cry89] Cryptech: *CRY12C102 DES chip*, 1989.

[DDFG83] M. Davio, Y. Desmedt, M. Fosseprez, R. Govaerts, J. Hulsbosch, P. Neutjens, P. Piret, J.-J. Quisquater, J. Vandewalle and P. Wouters, "Analytical Characteristics of the DES," *Advances in Cryptology, Proc. Crypto'83*, D. Chaum, Ed., Plenum Press, New York, 1984, pp. 171–202.

[DDGH84] M. Davio, Y. Desmedt, J. Goubert, J. Hoornaert and J.-J. Quisquater, "Efficient hardware and software implementations of the DES," *Advances in Cryptology, Proc. Crypto'84, LNCS 196*, G.R. Blakley and D. Chaum, Eds., Springer-Verlag, 1985, pp. 144–146.

[FeKa89] D.C. Feldmeier and P.R. Karn, "UNIX password security - Ten years later," *Advances in Cryptology, Proc. Crypto'89, LNCS 435*, G. Brassard, Ed., Springer-Verlag, 1990, pp. 44–63.

[ISO89] ISO/IEC International Standard 9797, *Information technology - Data cryptographic techniques - Data integrity mechanism using a cryptographic check function employing a block cipher algorithm*, 1989.

[MeMa82] C.H. Meyer and S.M. Matyas, *"Cryptography: a new dimension in data security,"* Wiley & Sons, 1982.

[NBS77] National Bureau of Standards, *Data Encryption Standard*, Federal Information Processing Standard, Publication 46, US Department of Commerce, January 1977.

[Pij92] Pijnenburg micro-electronics & software: *PCC100 Data Encryption Device*, 1992.

[VHVM88] I. Verbauwhede, J. Hoornaert, J. Vandewalle and H. De Man, "Security and performance optimization of a new DES data encryption chip," *IEEE Journal on Solid-State Circuits*, Vol. 23, No. 3, 1988, pp. 647–656.

[VHVM91] I. Verbauwhede, J. Hoornaert, J. Vandewalle and H. De Man, "ASIC Cryptographic Processor based on DES," *Proceedings of the EuroAsic'91 Conference*, Paris, France, May 1991.

A   C Implementation of the Primitive

This section provides a C implementation of the primitives RIPE-MAC1 and RIPE-MAC3. It includes an example program that uses these primitives to authenticate messages with a key chosen by the user. This example program can be used for testing purposes as well, as it can provide the test values of Appendix B.

Note that this implementation is designed for readability rather than speed. Moreover both the DES key scheduling and the DES encryption are shown as function calls only. No DES source code is included. Hence the speed of this implementation will mainly be determined by the quality of the DES implementation used with this program. For more details we refer to Section 7.

The functions in this implementation can be used in the following way. Compile the file **ripemac.c** (Appendix A.2) with an (ANSI) C compiler. Furthermore, provide a file that contains the definition of the DES functions **keyinit()** and **endes()** according to the prototypes given in the header file **ripemac.h** (Appendix A.1), taking into account the value of **NBYTES_KEY** defined in the same file. This value is either 8 or 16, and specifies the length in bytes of the data structure containing the key. Hence a value of 8 produces a RIPE-MAC1 implementation (56-bit key), and a value of 16 produces a RIPE-MAC3 implementation (112-bit key) (see comments in **ripemac.h** for more details). Next, provide a file that **#includes** the header file **ripemac.h** and contains a **main()** function calling **RIPEMAC()** or **RIPEMACfile()**. The function **RIPEMAC()** computes the hashcode of a '\0' terminated string, and the function **RIPEMACfile()** computes the hashcode of a binary file. The file **mactest.c**, given in Appendix A.3, can be used for this purpose. Finally link the resulting object files.

This implementation has been tested on a wide variety of environments, so it should be portable or at least easy to port. The testing environments include VAX/VMS, MS-DOS both with 16-bit and 32-bit compilers (Intel 80x86 processor), RISC ULTRIX, Apollo DN3500 Domain/OS (Motorola 68030 processor).

A.1   The Header File for RIPE-MAC

```
/*******************************************************************\
 *                                                                 *
 *      Header file for the Implementation of RIPE-MAC             *
 *                                                                 *
 *      Copyright (c)                                              *
 *         Centre for Mathematics and Computer Science, Amsterdam  *
 *         Siemens AG                                              *
 *         Philips Crypto BV                                       *
 *         PTT Research, the Netherlands                           *
 *         Katholieke Universiteit Leuven                          *
 *         Aarhus University                                       *
 *      1992, All Rights Reserved                                  *
 *                                                                 *
 *      Date    : 05/06/92                                         *
 *      Version : 1.0                                              *
 *                                                                 *
 \*******************************************************************/

/*
   typedef 8, 16, and 32 bit types, respectively.
   adapt these if necessary for your environment
*/
typedef unsigned char  byte;
typedef unsigned short word;
typedef unsigned long  dword;


/*******************************************************************/

/*
   NBYTES_KEY is the length of the key in bytes. It must be either 8 or
   16 bytes, for respectively a 56-bit (RIPE-MAC1) or 112-bit key
   (RIPE-MAC3). The rightmost bit of each byte (parity bit) is ignored.
   The functions keyinit() and endes() should be accordingly adapted.
   That is, for NBYTES_KEY == 8 keyinit() should install a single
   DES-key and endes() should perform a single DES encryption with this
   key. For NBYTES_KEY == 16 keyinit() should install two DES-keys and
   endes() should perform consecutively a DES encryption with the first
   key, a DES decryption with the second key and once again a DES
   encryption with the first key.
*/
#define NBYTES_KEY 8


/*******************************************************************/

/* Data strucure for RIPE-MAC computation */
typedef struct {
   byte  key[NBYTES_KEY]; /* Holds 56/112-bit key of MAC computation */
   byte  buffer[8];       /* Holds 64-bit result of MAC computation */
```

```
    dword count[2];          /* Holds number of blocks processed so far */
    byte  done;              /* Nonzero means computation finished */
} MACstruct, *MACptr;
```

/***/

/* prototypes of DES functions */

```
void keyinit(byte *key);
/*
    installs a single or two new DES key. That is, keyinit() calculates
    the round keys for one or two DES keys. key is a pointer to an
    NBYTES_KEY-byte array. The parity bits are ignored.
*/

void endes(byte *inp, byte *outp);
/*
    a single DES encryption or a triple DES en-/de-/encryption
    operation with the key(s) installed by keyinit(). inp points to an
    8-byte array containing the plaintext, outp points to an 8-byte array
    that will contain the ciphertext.
*/
```

/***/

/* prototypes of RIPE-MAC functions */
```
void MACinit(MACptr MACp);
void MACupdate(MACptr MACp, byte *X, dword nrofblocks);
void MACfinal(MACptr MACp, byte *X, word count);
byte *RIPEMAC(byte *message, byte *key);
byte *RIPEMACfile(char *fname, byte *key);
```

/******************** end of file ripemac.h ************************/

A.2   C Source Code for RIPE-MAC

```
/************************************************************************\
 *                                                                      *
 *      ripe-mac.c                                                      *
 *                                                                      *
 *      A sample C-implementation of the RIPE-MAC message              *
 *      authentication code.                                           *
 *                                                                      *
 *      Copyright (c)                                                  *
 *          Centre for Mathematics and Computer Science, Amsterdam     *
 *          Siemens AG                                                 *
 *          Philips Crypto BV                                          *
 *          PTT Research, the Netherlands                              *
 *          Katholieke Universiteit Leuven                             *
 *          Aarhus University                                          *
 *      1992, All Rights Reserved                                      *
 *                                                                      *
 *      Date    : 05/06/92                                             *
 *      Version : 1.0                                                  *
 *                                                                      *
\************************************************************************/


/* header files */
# include <stdio.h>
# include <stdlib.h>
# include <string.h>
# include "ripemac.h"


/************************************************************************/

void MACinit(MACptr MACp)
/*
   Initialize MAC computation.
*/
{
   int i;

   keyinit(MACp->key);
   for (i=0; i<8; i++)
      MACp->buffer[i] = 0;
   for (i=0; i<2; i++)
      MACp->count[i] = 0;
   MACp->done = 0;
}


/************************************************************************/

void MACupdate(MACptr MACp, byte *X, dword nrofblocks)
/*
```

```
     compresses nrofblocks 8-byte message blocks contained in X.
     The result is returned in MACp->buffer.
     The MAC calculation should be finished up with a call to MACfinal().
*/
{
     register int j;
     dword       i;
     byte        H[8];

     /* Initialize 8-byte buffer H[8] */
     for (i=0; i<8; i++)
        H[i] = MACp->buffer[i];

     for (i=0; i<nrofblocks; i++) {

        /* the compression function */
        for (j=0; j<8; j++)
           H[j] ^= X[j];
        endes(H, H);
        for (j=0; j<8; j++)
           H[j] ^= X[j];

        X += 8;

     }

     for (i=0; i<8; i++)
        MACp->buffer[i] = H[i];

     /* Add count to MACp->count */
     if (nrofblocks + MACp->count[0] < MACp->count[0])
        /* overflow to msdw of MACp->count */
        MACp->count[1]++;
     MACp->count[0] += nrofblocks;

}

/*********************************************************************/

void MACfinal(MACptr MACp, byte *X, word count)
/*
     Put bytes from X into XX and pad out; compress this last block.
     count contains number of message bits in last block (between zero
     63, inclusive).
*/
{
     word  i, cbit, cbyte;
     byte  XX[8], mask;
     dword ls32, ms32;
```

```
if (count == 0 && MACp->done) return;
if (MACp->done) {
  printf("Error: MACfinal already done.\n");
  return;
}

/* Add count to MACp->count */
ms32 = (MACp->count[1] << 6) | (MACp->count[0] >> 26);
ls32 = (MACp->count[0] << 6) + count;
/* Process data */
if (count == 64) {
  /* Full block of data to handle */
  printf("Error: MACupdate should be called.\n");
  return;
} else if (count > 64) {
  /* Check for count too large */
  printf("Error: MACfinal called with illegal count value %d.\n",
         count);
  return;
} else {
  /* partial block -- must be last block so finish up */
  cbyte = count >> 3;
  cbit = count & 7;
  for (i=0; i<=cbyte; i++)
     XX[i] = X[i];
  for (i=cbyte+1; i<8; i++)
     XX[i] = 0;
  mask = 1 << (7 - cbit);
  XX[cbyte] = (XX[cbyte] | mask) & ~(mask - 1);
  MACupdate(MACp, XX, 1UL);

  /* final block with length */
  XX[3] = (byte)ms32;
  XX[2] = (byte)(ms32 >> 8);
  XX[1] = (byte)(ms32 >> 16);
  XX[0] = (byte)(ms32 >> 24);
  XX[7] = (byte)ls32;
  XX[6] = (byte)(ls32 >> 8);
  XX[5] = (byte)(ls32 >> 16);
  XX[4] = (byte)(ls32 >> 24);
  MACupdate(MACp, XX, 1UL);

  /* encrypt final block with different key */
  for (i=0; i<NBYTES_KEY; i++)
     MACp->key[i] ^= 0xF0;
  keyinit(MACp->key);
  endes(MACp->buffer, MACp->buffer);

  MACp->done = 1;
}
```

```
}

/*********************************************************************/

byte *RIPEMAC(byte *message, byte *key)
/*
   computes RIPE-MAC(message,key) and returns the result as
   an array of 8-bytes.
*/
{
   word        i;
   dword       length;
   MACstruct   MAC;
   static byte mac[8];

   length = (dword)strlen((char*)message);
   for (i=0; i<NBYTES_KEY; i++)
      MAC.key[i] = key[i];

   MACinit(&MAC);
   MACupdate(&MAC, message, length >> 3);
   MACfinal(&MAC, message+(length & 0xFFFFFFF8UL), 8*(length & 0x7));

   for (i=0; i<8; i++)
      mac[i] = MAC.buffer[i];
   return mac;
}

/*********************************************************************/

byte *RIPEMACfile(char *fname, byte *key)
/*
   computes RIPE-MAC(contents of file <fname>,key) and
   returns the result as an array of 8-bytes.
   The contents of the file are interpreted as binary data.
*/
{
   word        i;
   dword       length;
   MACstruct   MAC;
   static byte mac[8];
   byte        data[1024];
   FILE        *f;

   if ( (f = fopen(fname,"rb")) == NULL ) {
      fprintf(stderr, "RIPEMACfile: cannot open file \"%s\".\n",fname);
      exit(1);
   }

   for (i=0; i<NBYTES_KEY; i++)
```

```
      MAC.key[i] = key[i];

  MACinit(&MAC);
  do {
    length = fread(data, 1, 1024, f);
    MACupdate(&MAC, data, length >> 3);
  } while ( length && ((length & 0x7) == 0) );
  MACfinal(&MAC, data+(length & 0x7F8UL), 8*(length & 0x7));

  fclose(f);

  for (i=0; i<8; i++)
    mac[i] = MAC.buffer[i];
  return mac;
}

/******************** end of file ripemac.c **************************/
```

A.3   An Example Program

Below an example program is given. It calls both **RIPEMAC** and **RIPEMACfile**.
By means of command line options several different tests can be performed (see
comment to **main()** function). Test values for both RIPE-MAC1 and RIPE-MAC3
can be found in Appendix B.

```
/*****************************************************************************\
 *                                                                           *
 *      mactest.c                                                            *
 *                                                                           *
 *      Test file for ripemac.c, a sample C-implementation of the           *
 *      RIPE-MAC message authentication code.                               *
 *                                                                           *
 *      Copyright (c)                                                        *
 *          Centre for Mathematics and Computer Science, Amsterdam          *
 *          Siemens AG                                                       *
 *          Philips Crypto BV                                               *
 *          PTT Research, the Netherlands                                   *
 *          Katholieke Universiteit Leuven                                  *
 *          Aarhus University                                               *
 *      1992, All Rights Reserved                                           *
 *                                                                           *
 *      Date    : 05/06/92                                                   *
 *      Version : 1.0                                                        *
 *                                                                           *
\*****************************************************************************/

/* header files */
#include <stdio.h>
#include <stdlib.h>
#include <string.h>
#include <time.h>
#include "ripemac.h"

#define TEST_BLOCK_SIZE 4000UL     /* length of buffer, in blocks */
#define TEST_BLOCKS 1000000L       /* maximum number of test blocks */

/* some compilers do not know CLOCKS_PER_SEC yet */
#ifndef CLOCKS_PER_SEC
#define CLOCKS_PER_SEC    CLK_TCK
#endif


/*****************************************************************************/

void MACtimetrial(void)
/*
    A time trial routine, to measure the speed of RIPE-MAC.
    It measures processor time required to authenticate a message
    of nrofblocks (<= TEST_BLOCKS) blocks of 64 bits.
```

```
*/
{
   word      i, j, rounds, remainder;
   byte      *X;
   dword     nrofblocks;
   MACstruct MAC;
   double    time_mac;
   clock_t   t1, t2;

   do {
      printf("\nEnter number of input blocks (<=%lu): ", TEST_BLOCKS);
      scanf("%lu", &nrofblocks);
   } while (nrofblocks > TEST_BLOCKS);
   srand(time(NULL));


   for (i=0; i<NBYTES_KEY; i++)
      MAC.key[i] = (byte)(rand() >> 7);
   MACinit(&MAC);
   printf("\nKey: ");
   for (i=0; i<NBYTES_KEY; i++)
      printf("%02x", MAC.key[i]);
   printf("\n");

   rounds = nrofblocks/TEST_BLOCK_SIZE;
   remainder = nrofblocks % TEST_BLOCK_SIZE;
   i = (rounds ? TEST_BLOCK_SIZE : remainder)*8;
   if ( (X = (byte *) malloc(i)) == NULL ) {
      fprintf(stderr,
        "MACtimetrial: Could not allocate %u bytes - aborting\n", i);
      exit(1);
   }

   time_mac = 0;
   for (j=0; j<rounds; j++) {
      for (i=0; i<8*TEST_BLOCK_SIZE; i++)
         X[i] = (byte)(rand() >> 7);
      t1 = clock();
      MACupdate(&MAC, (byte *)X, TEST_BLOCK_SIZE);
      t2 = clock();
      time_mac += (double)(t2-t1);
   }
   for (i=0; i<8*remainder; i++)
      X[i] = (byte)(rand() >> 7);
   t1 = clock();
   MACupdate(&MAC, (byte *)X, remainder);
   MACfinal(&MAC, (byte *)X, 0);
   t2 = clock();
   time_mac += (double)(t2-t1);
   free(X);
```

```
      time_mac /= (double)CLK_TCK;
      printf("\nRIPE-MAC%1d time trial results:\n", (NBYTES_KEY-4) >> 2);
      printf("Test input processed in %g seconds\n", time_mac);
      time_mac /= nrofblocks;
      printf("Elapsed time per block: %g sec\n", time_mac);
      printf("Characters processed per sec.: %lu.\n", (dword)(8/time_mac));
      printf("mac: ");
      for (i=0; i<8; i++) printf("%02x", MAC.buffer[i]);
      printf("\n");

}


/**********************************************************************/

void MACtestsuite(void)
/*
   standard test suite
*/
{
   byte key[NBYTES_KEY], temp;
   byte *mac;
   int  i;

   printf("\nRIPE-MAC%1d test suite results:\n", (NBYTES_KEY-4) >> 2);

   printf("\nkey: ");
   temp = 0x02;
   for (i=0; i<NBYTES_KEY; i++) {
      key[i] = temp | 0x10;
      printf("%02x", key[i]);
      temp += 0x22;
      if (i == 7)
         temp = 0x8A;
   }
   printf("\n");

   mac = RIPEMAC((byte *)"", key);
   printf("\nmessage: \"\" (empty string)\nmac: ");
   for (i=0; i<8; i++)
      printf("%02x", mac[i]);
   printf("\n");

   mac = RIPEMAC((byte *)"a", key);
   printf("\nmessage: \"a\"\nmac: ");
   for (i=0; i<8; i++)
      printf("%02x", mac[i]);
   printf("\n");

   mac = RIPEMAC((byte *)"abc", key);
```

```
  printf("\nmessage: \"abc\"\nmac: ");
  for (i=0; i<8; i++)
    printf("%02x", mac[i]);
  printf("\n");

  mac = RIPEMAC((byte *)"message authentication code", key);
  printf("\nmessage: \"message authentication code\"\nmac: ");
  for (i=0; i<8; i++)
    printf("%02x", mac[i]);
  printf("\n");

  mac = RIPEMAC((byte *)"abcdefghijklmnopqrstuvwxyz", key);
  printf("\nmessage: \"abcdefghijklmnopqrstuvwxyz\"\nmac: ");
  for (i=0; i<8; i++)
    printf("%02x", mac[i]);
  printf("\n");

  mac = RIPEMAC((byte *)"ABCDEFGHIJKLMNOPQRSTUVWXYZabcdefghijkl\
mnopqrstuvwxyz0123456789", key);
  printf("\nmessage: alphabet in uppercase, in lower case and digits\
 0 through 9\nmac: ");
  for (i=0; i<8; i++)
    printf("%02x", mac[i]);
  printf("\n");

  mac = RIPEMAC((byte *)"12345678901234567890123456789012345678901234567890\
01234567890123456789012345678901234567890", key);
  printf("\nmessage: 8 times \"1234567890\"\nmac: ");
  for (i=0; i<8; i++)
    printf("%02x", mac[i]);
  printf("\n");
}


/********************************************************************/

main(int argc, char *argv[])
/*
   main program. It calls one or more of the test routines depending
   on command line arguments:
       filename  prints filename and mac for key chosen by the user
       -sstring  prints string and mac for key chosen by the user
       -t        performs time trial
       -x        executes a standard suite of test data
*/
{
  word i, j, temp;
  byte *mac, key[NBYTES_KEY];

  if (argc == 1) {
    printf("For each command line argument in turn:\n");
```

```
            printf("  filename prints filename and mac\n");
            printf("  -sstring prints string and mac\n");
            printf("  -t       performs time trial\n");
            printf("  -x       executes a standard suite of test data\n");
    } else {
        for (i=1; i<argc; i++)
            if (argv[i][0] == '-' && argv[i][1] == 's') {
                printf("\nEnter key (%d bytes, in hexadecimal): ",
                        NBYTES_KEY);
                for (j=0; j<NBYTES_KEY; j++) {
                    scanf("%2x", &temp);
                    key[j] = (byte)temp;
                }
                printf("\nkey: ");
                for (j=0; j<NBYTES_KEY; j++)
                    printf("%02x", key[j]);
                printf("\nmessage: %s", argv[i]+2);
                mac = RIPEMAC((byte *)(argv[i]+2), key);
                printf("\nmac: ");
                for (j=0; j<8; j++)
                    printf("%02x", mac[j]);
            }
            else if (strcmp(argv[i],"-t") == 0)
                MACtimetrial();
            else if (strcmp(argv[i],"-x") == 0)
                MACtestsuite();
            else {
                printf("\nEnter key (%d bytes, in hexadecimal): ",
                        NBYTES_KEY);
                for (j=0; j<NBYTES_KEY; j++) {
                    scanf("%2x", &temp);
                    key[j] = (byte)temp;
                }
                printf("\nkey: ");
                for (j=0; j<NBYTES_KEY; j++)
                    printf("%02x", key[j]);
                printf("\nmessagefile (binary): %s", argv[i]);
                mac = RIPEMACfile(argv[i], key);
                printf("\nmac: ");
                for (j=0; j<8; j++)
                    printf("%02x", mac[j]);
            }
    }
    return;
}


/******************* end of file mactest.c *************************/
```

B   Test Values

The following test values were obtained by running `mactest -x`. The first set is for RIPE-MAC1 (56-bit key, `NBYTES_KEY` = 8), while the second set is for RIPE-MAC3 (112-bit key, `NBYTES_KEY` = 16).

```
RIPE-MAC1 test suite results:

key:  123456789abcdef0

message: "" (empty string)
mac: a5c10317dc5aa355

message: "a"
mac: 598298ba39e8265b

message: "abc"
mac: 121db704b52f71aa

message: "message authentication code"
mac: 6288beba08a21bb9

message: "abcdefghijklmnopqrstuvwxyz"
mac: dd7a2a779098ac52

message: alphabet in uppercase, in lower case and digits 0 through 9
mac: 1ed27286699c3ad5

message: 8 times "1234567890"
mac: ce4620b8fd9da619


RIPE-MAC3 test suite results:

key:  123456789abcdef09abcdef012345678

message: "" (empty string)
mac: 25159cb1ec098e62

message: "a"
mac: 55dc3747024f4fad

message: "abc"
mac: ce6d95e85f723caf

message: "message authentication code"
mac: d6661f40954ed8ed

message: "abcdefghijklmnopqrstuvwxyz"
mac: 693181c24ea085ae
```

message: alphabet in uppercase, in lower case and digits 0 through 9
mac: a87d471ba312d3fd

message: 8 times "1234567890"
mac: 6a4c6e7716ef7da3

Chapter 5

IBC-hash

Table of Contents

1   Introduction

This chapter describes the integrity primitive IBC-hash. IBC-hash is a keyed hash function that maps messages to hashcodes. This function is *provably secure*: the probability to find the correct hashcode of a message, without knowing the secret key, is proven to be close to optimal (i.e., exponentially small in the hashcode size), even when the hashcode of one other message is known. Furthermore, this probability is independent of the computing power used.

IBC-hash can be used for message authentication between parties who share a secret key. The party who wants to send a message first computes the hashcode of this message. It then sends both message and hashcode—a so called tagged message—to the other party. The receiver of this tagged message also computes the hashcode of the message and verifies that the outcome equals the received hashcode. If they are equal, he has good reason to believe that the message is genuine, i.e., the message originated from the party with whom he shares the key and was not modified in transit.

The design of the IBC-hash function is such that it is both provably secure and efficient. The basic operation is a simple modular reduction (giving the efficiency) modulo a secret modulus (giving the security). Furthermore, the function is easy to describe and understand.

On the other hand, there are also three disadvantages for IBC-hash, the first of which is inherent in provably secure schemes. As every tagged message reduces the number of possible keys, each key can be used only once. If you only want computational security, you can just generate keys with a pseudo-random number generator.

Also, once the size of the hashcode is fixed, one has implicitly put a maximum to the message size, although it is much larger than the size of the hashcode. The last disadvantage is in the number n of bits in the hashcode. To achieve a security level of say 2^{-64}, n has to be larger than 64. Ideally the probability to find the correct hashcode of a message is 2^{-n} (i.e., one divided by the number of possible hashcodes).

Note that anyone in possession of the key can find messages that hash to a given hashcode; therefore one should trust everyone in possession of the key.

The structure of this chapter is as follows. In order to avoid any ambiguities in the description of the primitive, the notation and definitions in this chapter are fixed in Section 2. Section 3 contains a description of the primitive and in Section 4 the possible modes of use of the primitive are considered. The security aspects of the primitive are discussed in Section 5. These include the claimed properties and the algebraic evaluation of the primitive. Finally, in Section 6 the performance aspects of IBC-hash are considered, and Section 7 gives some guidelines for software implementation.

This chapter has two appendices. Appendix A contains a straightforward software implementation of IBC-hash in the programming language C and in Appendix B test values for the primitive are given.

2 Definitions and Notation

2.1 Introduction

In order to obtain a clear description of the primitive, the notation and definitions used in this document are fully described in this chapter. These include the representation of the numbers in the description, and the operations, functions and constants used by the primitive.

2.2 General

The symbol ":=" is used for the assignment of a value or a meaning to a variable or symbol. That is, $a := b$ either means that the variable a gets the value of the variable b, or it means that a is defined as "b". It will be obvious from the context which meaning is intended.

The equality-sign "=" is used for equality only. That is, it indicates that the two entities on either side are equal.

Note that in C-source code, "=" denotes assignment, while comparison is denoted by "==".

An ellipsis ("...") denotes an implicit enumeration. For example, "$i = 0$, 1, ..., n" is meant to represent the sentence "for $i = 0$, $i = 1$, and so on, up to $i = n$".

2.3 Representation of the Numbers

A sequence of n bits $b_0, b_1, \ldots, b_{n-1}$ corresponds to a nonnegative integer B as follows:

$$B := \sum_{i=0}^{n-1} b_i \, 2^{n-i-1}. \tag{1}$$

Hence the first bit b_0 of the sequence is the most significant bit of B.

2.4 Definitions and Basic Operations

- A *string* is a sequence of bits. If X is a string consisting of n bits, then those bits are denoted from left to right by $x_0, x_1, \ldots, x_{n-2}, x_{n-1}$.
- For a string X the *length* of X is denoted as $|X|$. That is, $|X|$ is the number of bits in the string X. If $|X| = n$, then X is said to be an n-bit string.
- For two strings X and Y of length $|X| = n$ respectively $|Y| = m$, the $(n+m)$-bit string $W = X\|Y$ is defined as the *concatenation* of the strings X and Y. That is,

$$w_i := x_i \qquad i = 0, 1, \ldots, n-1$$
$$w_{i+n} := y_i \qquad i = 0, 1, \ldots, m-1.$$

- For a nonnegative integer A and a positive integer B, the numbers "A div B" and "A mod B" are defined as the nonnegative integers Q, respectively R, such that

$$A = QB + R \quad \text{and} \quad 0 \leq R < B.$$

That is, "A mod B" is the *remainder*, and "A div B" is the *quotient* of an integer division of A by B.
- A *prime* is an integer greater than 1 that is divisible only by 1 and by itself.

2.5 Symbols used by the Primitive

M	message, input for IBC-hash function,
m	message length in bits ($m = |M|$),
$m^\star$	upper bound for m ($m \leq m^\star$),
n	hashcode length in bits, ≥ 64,
X	expanded message ($|X| = $ multiple of n),
r	length of X in n-bit blocks ($|X| = r \cdot n$),
P	n-bit prime greater than 2^{n-1},
V	n-bit number,
$\mathcal{H}_{P,V}$	hashcode, output of IBC-hash function with key (P, V),
$\mathcal{P}_i$, $\mathcal{P}_s$	impersonation and substitution probability, respectively.

3   Description of the Primitive

3.1   Outline of IBC-hash

The IBC-hash function maps messages of variable size to hashcodes of fixed size. Let m and n denote the length in bits of messages and hashcodes, respectively. Let $m^\star$ be the maximum value of m as allowed by the security evaluation (for given n, see Section 5). In order to make programming more efficient, it is recommended that the number n is a multiple of 32.

A key for the hash function is a pair of n-bit numbers (P, V), where P is a prime such that $2^{n-1} < P < 2^n$ and $0 \le V < 2^n$.

Let $M = (b_0, b_1, \ldots, b_{m-1})$ be a message of m bits long. The hashcode $\mathcal{H}_{P,V}(M)$ of M is computed in two steps.

expansion: M is expanded to an $(r \cdot n)$-bit string X, where $r = (m \text{ div } n) + 3$. That is, the message is expanded such that it becomes a multiple of n bits. This expansion is done even if the original message length is a multiple of n bits.

compression: The $(r \cdot n)$-bit string X is transformed into an integer according to Equation 1. The result is reduced modulo P and added to V modulo 2^n:

$$H := ((X \bmod P) + V) \bmod 2^n .$$

hashcode: The hashcode $\mathcal{H}_{P,V}(M)$ is equal to the n-bit string H, where the interpretation of the integer H in terms of an n-bit string is once again given by Equation 1.

3.2   Expanding the Message

Let $r = (m \text{ div } n) + 3$. The m-bit message $M = (b_0, b_1, \ldots, b_{m-1})$ is expanded to the $(r \cdot n)$-bit message X in the following three steps.

1. Append a single "1" and $k = n - 1 - (m \bmod n)$ zero bits to the message M:
$$b_m := 1,$$
$$b_{m+1} := b_{m+2} := \cdots := b_{m+k} := 0 .$$

   This step expands the message M to a message that is a multiple of n bits. Note that padding is done even if the length of M is already a multiple of n bits.

2. Append n bits representing the length m of the original message. That is, if
$$m \bmod 2^n = \sum_{i=0}^{n-1} m_i 2^{n-i-1} ,$$

   append the n-bit string $m_0, m_1, \ldots, m_{n-1}$.

3. Complete the expansion by appending n zero bits.

4   Use of the Primitive

The primitive IBC-hash has two intended applications:

- to provide both data integrity and data origin authentication,
- to be used in identification schemes.

Use in data integrity mechanisms Before a message is sent, the secret key is used to compute a keyed hashcode (sometimes also called MAC or tag) from it. This value is sent along with the message and can be checked by the legitimate recipient using the common secret key. If the calculated hashcode is equal to the received value, it is reasonable to assume that the original hashcode was computed from the same message. This holds, since computation of another message with the same hashcode is *proven* to be infeasible for someone not in possession of the secret key (see next section). Moreover, it is reasonable to assume that the message is authentic, as it is infeasible for someone who does not know the secret key to produce a hashcode for a given message. The latter furthermore allows linking of the hashcode to the originator of the information. Therefore, the primitive provides both data integrity and data origin authentication.

Each key may be used only once however, because two tagged messages made with the same key may reveal this key. Thus each authentication requires its own secret key and before the sender and receiver can communicate with each other, they must agree on the key. Note that the provable security is only guaranteed if such a key exchange is also performed in a provably secure way and not by some way that is only computationally secure. This implies that IBC-hash is better suited for few (long) messages rather than for many (short) messages. Furthermore, the key must be kept secret, because anyone in possession of the key can not only compute the hashcode for any message, but can also compute (many) messages that hash to any given hashcode.

Use in secret key identification schemes Another application for the primitive is identification schemes, which allow parties to establish that their key sharing counterpart is actually communicating with them at a particular moment. One party supplies the other party with a random challenge. The other party applies the primitive to the challenge sent, and returns the result. The challenging party does the same and compares the calculated hashcode with the returned one. If they are equal, it is reasonable to assume that the other party is in possession of the secret key. Of course the roles can be reversed, so that each party is able to challenge the other. For this unilateral and bilateral authentication it is suggested to use, respectively, the RIPE primitives SKID2 and SKID3 (see Chapter 6). However note that in SKID3 the hash function is used twice, and therefore—when using IBC-hash—two different keys must be used.

5   Security Evaluation

5.1   Claimed Properties

In the usual model for authentication there are three parties: a sender, a receiver and a tamperer. The sender wants to communicate some message to the receiver, using a public communication channel; the receiver wants to be sure that the message he receives did come from the sender and was not modified in transit. On the other hand, the tamperer wants to deceive them by getting a message of his own accepted by the receiver. Suppose that the tamperer has the ability to insert messages into the channel and/or to modify existing messages. The first ability is called *impersonation* and the second *substitution*. Let $\mathcal{P}_i$ and $\mathcal{P}_s$ denote the probability that the tamperer can deceive the sender/receiver by impersonation and substitution, respectively.

The IBC-hash function is provably secure: the probabilities for both abilities are exponentially small in n. That is:

$$\mathcal{P}_i = \frac{1}{2^n} \qquad \text{and}$$

$$\mathcal{P}_s < 3 \cdot \frac{m + 3n - m \bmod n}{2^n}, \qquad \text{for } n \geq 64.$$

5.2   Algebraic Evaluation

In [CHB92] it is proven that a necessary and sufficient condition for a tamperer to insert or substitute a message is that he knows a non-zero multiple of the prime number P of the key (P, V) used. Furthermore, for $n \geq 64$ this multiple must also be less than $2^{8(m+3n-m \bmod n)}$ and this gives the equality and inequality of the previous section. Note that the probability to substitute a message is maximal if m is maximal $(m = m^\star)$, but that this probability is much less for small messages. By choosing n and $m^\star$ appropriately, we obtain that large messages can be hashed while keeping the impersonation and substitution probabilities as small as one may require. If $m^\star$ is much larger than $3n - m \bmod n$, which is usually the case when using hash functions, then a simple upper bound for the substitution probability is $\mathcal{P}_s < m^\star \cdot 2^{-(n-2)}$.

Suggested parameter values If $n = 64$ and $m^\star = 2^{32}$, then we have $\mathcal{P}_i < 3 \cdot (2^{32} + 192)/2^{64} < 2^{-30}$. Thus the substitution probability is less than 2^{-30}, while messages can be up to 2^{32} bits (or $2^9 = 512$ Megabytes) long.

The substitution probability can be reduced by increasing n and/or decreasing $m^\star$. Furthermore, increasing n allows that $m^\star$ can be increased significantly: an upper bound of 2^{-60} for the substitution probability is obtained by choosing n and $m^\star$ such that $n - 2 - \log_2 m^\star = 60$. For example $n = 128$, $m^\star = 2^{66}$ and $n = 96$, $m^\star = 2^{34}$ both have $\mathcal{P}_s < 2^{-60}$, while authenticating messages of 2^{43} Megabytes and 2^{11} Megabytes, respectively.

These suggestions are recapitulated in Table 1.

n	$m^\star$	$\mathcal{P}_i$	$\mathcal{P}_s$
64	2^{32}	2^{-64}	$2^{-30.4}$
96	2^{34}	2^{-96}	$2^{-60.4}$
128	2^{66}	2^{-128}	$2^{-60.4}$

Table 1. The lengths (in bits) n and $m^\star$ of respectively the hashcode and the longest message to be hashed and the corresponding impersonation and substitution probabilities $\mathcal{P}_i$ and $\mathcal{P}_s$.

Optimality It was shown in [JKS93] that for a given $\mathcal{P}_s$ and key size, the scheme of [Boe93, MV84] yields an $m^\star$ which is asymptotically optimal. IBC-hash requires a slightly shorter key, but allows a value of $m^\star$ which is about 200 to 400 times smaller for the parameters of Table 1. However, IBC-hash lends itself better to implementations using arithmetic modulo a large prime.

6   Performance Evaluation

6.1   Software Implementations

The basic operation of IBC-hash is a modular reduction. In practical systems the modulus will be 64 or 128 bits long. The argument of the modular reduction is the expanded message and will normally be several orders of magnitude larger than the modulus. The most efficient algorithm will therefore be the classical algorithm as described in [Knu81], see also Chapter 10. The implementation of this modular reduction can be very compact.

Both a C and a 80386 Assembly language implementation are considered. The C version has the advantage of being portable. The difference in performance between the C and the Assembly language version is mainly due to the general nature of the C version and the ability to use 64-bit integers in Assembly. The C version can be used for moduli of arbitrary length, while its Assembly counterpart is restricted to a 64-bit modulus. The figures in Table 2 are for an IBM-compatible 33 MHz 80386DX based PC with 64K cache memory using WATCOM C/386 9.0 in combination with the DOS/4GW DOS extender. Hence all code runs in protected mode. The C version of the compression function uses about 0.5K of memory, while the Assembly version is about half as large. Doubling the modulus will approximately halve the speed.

6.2   Hardware Implementations

The implementation of a modular reduction with a 64-bit or 128-bit modulus can be extremely fast in hardware. It is expected that a speed of up to a 100 Mbit/s is achievable. However it must be borne in mind that at such speeds the critical path is situated in the I/O interface. RSA implementations are existing

	C	Assembly
IBC-hash, $n = 64$	305 Kbit/s	5.27 Mbit/s

Table 2. Software performance of IBC-hash with a 64-bit modulus on a 33 MHz 80386DX based PC with a 64K memory cache using WATCOM C/386 9.0 in combination with the DOS/4GW DOS extender.

alternatives, as they normally provide a modular reduction in their instruction set. The speed will however be reduced with several orders of magnitude.

For a 64-bit modulus the modular reduction can be very efficiently implemented on 32-bit architectures. The modulus is kept in two registers. The message is then reduced as follows. First, the next 32-bit message bits are appended to the 64-bit intermediate reduction result. Next, this 96-bit number is divided by the most significant 32 bits of the modulus. The result of this division is checked by a remultiplication and if necessary adapted. The same ideas can be used to implement a 128-bit reduction.

7   Guidelines for Software Implementation

The implementation in the C language given in Appendix A can be used as a guideline for software implementations. It also provides the test values given in Appendix B.

The basic operation of IBC-hash is a modular reduction of the expanded message modulo an n-bit integer. The value of n will be typically 64 or 128, but other values are possible. As the message will normally be several orders of magnitude larger than the modulus, the most efficient algorithm will be the classical algorithm as described in [Knu81], see also Chapter 10.

References

[Boe93]   B. den Boer, "A simple and key-economical unconditional authentication scheme," *Journal of Computer Security*, Vol. 2, No. 1, 1993, pp. 65–71.

[CHB92]   D. Chaum, M. van der Ham and B. den Boer, "A provably secure and efficient message authentication scheme," available from the authors, April 1992.

[JKS93]   T. Johansson, G. Kabatianskii, and B. Smeets, "On the relation between A-codes and codes correcting independent errors," *Advances in Cryptology, Proc. Eurocrypt'93, LNCS 765*, T. Helleseth, Ed., Springer-Verlag, 1994, pp. 1–11.

[Knu81]   D.E. Knuth, *The Art of Computer Programming, Vol. 2, Seminumerical Algorithms, 2nd Edition*, Addison-Wesley, Reading, Mass., 1981.

[MV84]   K. Mehlhorn and U. Vishkin, "Randomized and deterministic simulations of PRAMs by parallel machines with restricted granularity of parallel memories," *Acta Informatica*, Vol. 21, 1984, pp. 339–374.

A   C Implementation of the Primitive

This appendix provides an ANSI C implementation of the primitive IBC-hash and an example program that uses IBC-hash to hash messages. This program can be used for testing purposes as well, as it can provide the test values of Appendix B.

The IBC-HASH program computes the IBC hashcode of a file. The program imposes two additional restrictions on the value of n: it should be a multiple of 16 and should be at most 256.

The IBC-HASH program ibc-hash.c consists of a single C source file. The full listing is given in Appendix A.1. The program is written in ANSI-C. It uses only standard library routines and should be easily portable. The program accepts the name of the file to compute the hash on as the argument. The key values are read from the file ibc-hash.key. The result is printed on the standard output in hexadecimal format.

The file ibc-hash.key contains 2 lines of text. The first line is the prime P and the second line is V, both in hexadecimal. Three example key files can be found in Appendix A.3.

A separate program ibc-test.c is provided to generate test patterns. The listing is given in Appendix A.2. It takes the length of the required testfile as a command line argument. The testfile is named ibc-test.dat and is generated using a pseudorandom generator and a initial seed. Together with the sample key files of Appendix A.3 the testfile can be used to produce the test values of Appendix B.

A.1   C Source Code for IBC-hash

```
/**************************************************************************\
 *                                                                        *
 *   ibc-hash.c                                                           *
 *                                                                        *
 *   A sample C-implementation of the IBC-HASH message                    *
 *   authentication code                                                  *
 *                                                                        *
 *   Copyright (c)                                                        *
 *      Centre for Mathematics and Computer Science, Amsterdam            *
 *      Siemens AG                                                        *
 *      Philips Crypto BV                                                 *
 *      PTT Research, the Netherlands                                     *
 *      Katholieke Universiteit Leuven                                    *
 *      Aarhus University                                                 *
 *   1992, All Rights Reserved                                            *
 *                                                                        *
 *   Date    : 21/06/92                                                   *
 *   Version : 1.0                                                        *
 *                                                                        *
\**************************************************************************/

/* header files */
#include <stdio.h>
#include <stdlib.h>
#include <stdarg.h>

/*
   Definition of 8, 16, and 32 bit types, respectively.
   Adapt these if necessary.
*/
typedef unsigned char byte;
typedef unsigned short int digit;
typedef unsigned long int ddigit;

/*
   Length in bytes of the buffers for reading from the input file
   and the key file, respectively.
*/
#define BUF_LEN         (1U<<15)
#define MOD_LEN         (16)

/* Data structure for IBC-hash computation */
typedef struct {
    size_t length_P;        /* length of the modulus */
    byte P[MOD_LEN];        /* modulus */
    size_t length_V;        /* length of blinding factor */
    byte V[MOD_LEN];        /* blinding factor */
    byte length[MOD_LEN];   /* #bytes in message */
```

```
    byte buffer[MOD_LEN]; /* result of IBC-hash computation */
} IBCstruct, *IBCptr;

/*
  Constants for the modular reduction functions.
  Do not alter these.
*/
#define DIGIT_MASK      (0xFFFF)
#define MAX_DIGIT       (0xFFFF)
#define DIGIT_LENGTH    (16)
#define DIGIT_MSB_MASK  (0x8000)

/*********************************************************************/
/*  Error Handling and I/O routines */
/*********************************************************************/

void errorexit(char *format, ...)
{
   va_list ap;

   va_start(ap, format);
   fprintf(stderr, "\nFatal Error:\n");
   vfprintf(stderr, format, ap);
   va_end(ap);

   exit(1);
}


/*********************************************************************/

int hexvalue(char c)
/*
  Returns the value of hex digit c or -1 if not legal
*/
{
   if ( c<'0' )  return( -1 );
   if ( c<='9' ) return( c-'0' );
   if ( c<'A' )  return( -1 );
   if ( c<='F' ) return( c-'A'+10 );
   if ( c<'a' )  return( -1 );
   if ( c<='f' ) return( c-'a'+10 );
   return( -1 );
}


/*********************************************************************/

void read_hexnumber(FILE *f, size_t *length, byte *buffer)
/*
  Reads a hexadecimal number from the file f into buffer and
  returns the length in length. All leading white space and
```

```
    everything after the first non-hexadecimal digit character is
    discarded.
*/
{
    int  c;
    char buf[MOD_LEN*2];
    int  len;
    int  i, j;

    c = getc(f);
    while (c==' ' || c == '\t' || c == '\n')
        c = getc(f);

    len = 0;
    while (len<=2*MOD_LEN && c!=EOF && hexvalue(c)>=0) {
        buf[len++] = c;
        c = getc(f);
    }

    if (len == 0)
        errorexit("read_hexnumber: No hex number in file");

    if (len > 2*MOD_LEN)
        errorexit("read_hexnumber: Hex number too long");

    *length = (len + 1)/2;  /* the number of bytes in the number read */

    /* We now convert the ascii to the binary buffer */
    j = 0;
    for (i=0; i<*length; i++) {
        if (i==0 && (len & 1)) {
            buffer[i] = hexvalue(buf[j++]);
        } else {
            buffer[i] = hexvalue(buf[j++]);
            buffer[i] = (buffer[i] << 4) + hexvalue(buf[j++]);
        }
    }
}


/**********************************************************************/
/*  Modular Reduction */
/**********************************************************************/

/* Static globals used by the modular reduction routines */
static int   mod_len;            /* modulus' length, must be >= 2 */
static digit mod_MSd1;           /* MSdigit of modulus */
static digit mod_MSd2;           /* next digit of modulus */
static digit *mod_inv = NULL;    /* 2's complement of modulus */
static digit *mod_buffer = NULL; /* buffer for intermediate result */
```

```
/******************************************************************/

void mod_set_modulus(int length, byte *m)
/*
  Specifies the modulus to be used for subsequent modulo operations
  m points to the modulus (MSbyte first), length is the length in bytes.
*/
{
  digit *p;
  int   i;

  if (length < 4)
     errorexit("set_modulus: length must be at least 4 bytes", length);

  if (length & 1)
     errorexit("set_modulus: length must be even", length);

  mod_len = length/2;
  mod_MSd1 = (m[0]<<8) + m[1];
  mod_MSd2 = (m[2]<<8) + m[3];

  if ((mod_MSd1 & DIGIT_MSB_MASK) == 0)
     errorexit("set_modulus: most significant bit is 0", length);

  if (mod_buffer != NULL)
     free(mod_buffer);
  if ((mod_buffer = malloc((mod_len+1)*sizeof(digit))) == NULL)
     errorexit("mod_set_modulus(1): memory allocation failed");

  if (mod_inv != NULL)
     free(mod_inv);
  if ((mod_inv = malloc(mod_len*sizeof(digit))) == NULL)
     errorexit("mod_set_modulus(2): memory allocation failed");

  /* We now compute the 2's complement of the modulus */
  for (i=0; i<mod_len; i++)
     mod_inv[i] = ~( (m[length-2*i-2] << 8) + m[length-2*i-1] );
  p = mod_inv;
  while (( *p = (*p+1) & DIGIT_MASK ) == 0)
     p++;
}


/******************************************************************/

void mod_init_buffer(void)
/*
  Clear the internal buffer for the intermediate results
*/
{
  int   i;
```

```
    digit *p;

    /* Clear the buffer to 0 */
    for (p = mod_buffer, i = 0; i<mod_len; i++)
        *p++ = 0;
}
```

/***/

```
int mod_read_buffer(int length, byte *buffer)
/*
  Read the contents of the reduced buffer into buffer, MSB first.
  The return value is the length of the result in bytes.
*/
{
    int i;

    if (length < 2*mod_len)
        errorexit(
            "mod_read_buffer: buffer not long enough to contain result");
    for (i=mod_len-1; i>=0; i--) {
        *buffer++ = (mod_buffer[i] >> 8) & 0xff;
        *buffer++ = mod_buffer[i] & 0xff;
    }
    return(2*mod_len);
}
```

/***/

```
void mod_reduce_buffer(void)
/*
  The buffer contains a len+1 sized number which is less than
  2^16 times the modulus. This routine reduces the buffer modulo
  the modulus. For the algorithm of this routine, see Knuth, "The
  art of computer programming", Volume 2, 'Seminumerical Algorithms',
  paragraph 4.3.1, pages 255-263.
*/
{
    int    i;
    digit  q;
    ddigit t;

    /* Step D3 (page 258) */
    t = ((ddigit) mod_buffer[mod_len] << DIGIT_LENGTH)
        + mod_buffer[mod_len-1];

    if (mod_buffer[mod_len] == mod_MSd1)
        q = MAX_DIGIT;
    else
        q = (digit) (t/(ddigit) mod_MSd1);
```

```
    t -= (ddigit)q * mod_MSd1;
    /*
       This is the loop that adjusts q. Note the special case when t is
       larger then MAX_DIGIT. This can occur if q was set to MAX_DIGIT
       instead of t/mod_MSd1. If the second formula had been used, then q
       would have had the value MAX_DIGIT+1, which would give an overflow.
       This special case occurs very infrequently.
       The loop body can also set t to a value larger than MAX_DIGIT.
    */
    while (t <= MAX_DIGIT &&
       mod_MSd2*(ddigit)q > (t<<DIGIT_LENGTH)+mod_buffer[mod_len-2]) {
          q--;
          t += mod_MSd1;
    }

    /* Now we add q times mod_inv to mod_buffer */
    t = 0;
    for (i=0; i<mod_len; i++) {
       t += (ddigit)q * mod_inv[i] + mod_buffer[i];
       mod_buffer[i] = (digit)t & DIGIT_MASK;
       t = (t >> DIGIT_LENGTH) & DIGIT_MASK;  /* shift can be signed! */
    }
    if ( ((digit)t & DIGIT_MASK) + mod_buffer[mod_len] != q ) {
       /*
          A carry occured here, so q was one too large.
          Therefore, we will substract mod_inv once.
          For efficiency reasons we reuse t as the carry variable.
       */
       q = 0;
       for (i=0; i<mod_len; i++) {
           t = (ddigit)mod_buffer[i] - mod_inv[i] - q;
           mod_buffer[i] = (digit)(t & DIGIT_MASK );
           q = (digit)(t >> DIGIT_LENGTH) & 1;
       }
    }
}


/**********************************************************************/

void mod_reduce(size_t length, byte *buffer)
/*
   Takes the data in the buffer as additional data to reduce.
   Several calls of this routine can be used to reduce more data.
   The length of the buffer should be a multiple of 8.
*/
{
   int i;

   if ( (length & 0x7) != 0 )
```

```
        errorexit("mod_reduce(%uld, *): length is not a multiple of 8",
                  (unsigned long) length);
    while (length) {
        /* First we shift the buffer 1 digit and add the new digit */
        for (i=mod_len; i>0; i--)
            mod_buffer[i] = mod_buffer[i-1];
        mod_buffer[0] = (buffer[0] << 8) + buffer[1];

        /* Reduce the buffer modulo the modulus */
        mod_reduce_buffer();

        /* Adjust the loop pointers now */
        buffer += 2;
        length -= 2;
    }
}


/**********************************************************************/
/*  IBC-hash routines */
/**********************************************************************/

void IBCinit(IBCptr IBCp, FILE *f)
/*
  Reads modulus and blinding factor from f.
  Installs modulus for use with modular reduction routines.
*/
{
    size_t i;

    read_hexnumber(f, &IBCp->length_P, IBCp->P);
    mod_set_modulus(IBCp->length_P, IBCp->P);
    read_hexnumber(f, &IBCp->length_V, IBCp->V);
    if (IBCp->length_P != IBCp->length_V)
        errorexit("IBCinit: prime length != blinding factor length");
    for (i=0; i<MOD_LEN; i++)
        IBCp->length[i] = 0;
}


/**********************************************************************/

int IBCreduce(IBCptr IBCp, FILE *f)
/*
  Reads the file f and reduces it modulo the modulus.
  The internal buffer is cleared at the start.
  The file is padded with zeroes so that the length is a multiple
  of 8 bytes, the 64-bit length of the file, and 16 zero bytes.
  The whole sequence of bytes is reduced modulo the modulus.
  The result is returned in the buffer field of the IBCstruct.
  This routine can be speeded up significantly by using a bigger buffer.
*/
```

```
{
    int         i;
    byte        buf[MOD_LEN];
    byte        *data;
    size_t      nbytes, t, u, n, tbytes;

    if ((data = malloc(BUF_LEN)) == NULL)
        errorexit("reduce_file: memory allocation failed");
    mod_init_buffer();

    while ((nbytes = fread(data, 1, BUF_LEN, f)) == BUF_LEN) {
        /* process all complete blocks */
        mod_reduce(BUF_LEN, data);

        /* update length[] */
        for (t=0, i=MOD_LEN-1; i>=0 && nbytes; i--) {
            t += (unsigned)IBCp->length[i] + (nbytes & 0xFF);
            IBCp->length[i] = (byte)t;
            t >>= 8;
            nbytes >>= 8;
        }
        for ( ; i>=0 && t; i--) {
            t += (unsigned)IBCp->length[i];
            IBCp->length[i] = (byte)t;
            t >>= 8;
        }
    }

    tbytes = nbytes;
    /* update length[] */
    for (t=0, i=MOD_LEN-1; i>=0 && nbytes; i--) {
        t += (unsigned)IBCp->length[i] + (nbytes & 0xFF);
        IBCp->length[i] = (byte)t;
        t >>= 8;
        nbytes >>= 8;
    }
    for ( ; i>=0 && t; i--) {
        t += (unsigned)IBCp->length[i];
        IBCp->length[i] = (byte)t;
        t >>= 8;
    }

    n = IBCp->length_P;
    /* append 0x80 and n - 1 - m mod n zero bytes*/
    for (t=0, i=0; i<MOD_LEN; i++) {
        t = (t << 8) + IBCp->length[i];
        u = t / n;
        t -= u * n;
    }
    u = n - 1 - t;
```

```
    data[tbytes++] = 0x80;
    for (i=0; i<u; i++)
        data[tbytes++] = 0;
    mod_reduce(tbytes, data);

    /* append the length in bits in n bytes */
    IBCp->length[0] <<= 3;
    for (i=0; i<MOD_LEN-1; i++) {
        IBCp->length[i] |= (IBCp->length[i+1] >> 5);
        IBCp->length[i+1] <<= 3;
    }
    for (i=0; i<n; i++)
        buf[i] = IBCp->length[MOD_LEN-n+i];
    mod_reduce(n, buf);

    /* add n more zero bytes */
    for (i=0; i<n; i++)
        buf[i] = 0;
    mod_reduce(n, buf);

    free(data);

    return(mod_read_buffer(16, IBCp->buffer));
}

/************************************************************************/

void IBCfinal(IBCptr IBCp)
/*
  Adds the blinding factor to the IBC-hash result
*/
{
    int      i;
    unsigned c;

    c = 0;
    for (i=IBCp->length_V-1; i>=0; i--) {
        c += IBCp->buffer[i] + IBCp->V[i];
        IBCp->buffer[i] = c & 0xFF;
        c >>= 8;
    }
}

/************************************************************************/

void IBChash(FILE *f_mess, FILE *f_key, FILE *f_result)
/*
  Computes ibc_hash of file f_mess using key in file f_key
  result is written in hex to file f_result
*/
```

```
{
    int i;
    IBCstruct IBC;

    IBCinit(&IBC, f_key);
    IBCreduce(&IBC, f_mess);
    IBCfinal(&IBC);

    fprintf(f_result, "IBC-hash mac: ");
    for (i=0; i<IBC.length_P; i++)
        fprintf(f_result, "%02X", IBC.buffer[i]);
    fprintf(f_result, "\n" );
}

/*********************************************************************/
/*  Main routine */
/*********************************************************************/

int main(int argc, char *argv[])
{
    FILE *fi, *fk;

    printf( "IBC-HASH computation program version 1.0\n" );

    if (argc != 2)
        errorexit("Usage: IBC-HASH <filename>\n"
            "Computes hash for file using keys in \"ibc-hash.key\".");
    if ((fi = fopen( argv[1], "rb")) == NULL)
        errorexit( "File \"%s\" could not be opened.", argv[1]);
    if ((fk = fopen("ibc-hash.key", "rt")) == NULL)
        errorexit( "File \"ibc-hash.key\" could not be opened\n");

    IBChash(fi, fk, stdout);

    fclose(fk);
    fclose(fi);
    return( 0 );
}

/********************** end of ibc-hash.c ************************/
```

A.2   Program for Generating Test Programs

```c
/**************************************************************************\
 *                                                                        *
 *    ibc-test.c    A program to generate test files to be used with      *
 *                  ibc-hash.c                                            *
 *                                                                        *
 *    Copyright (c)                                                       *
 *       Centre for Mathematics and Computer Science, Amsterdam           *
 *       Siemens AG                                                       *
 *       Philips Crypto BV                                                *
 *       PTT Research, the Netherlands                                    *
 *       Katholieke Universiteit Leuven                                   *
 *       Aarhus University                                                *
 *    1992, All Rights Reserved                                           *
 *                                                                        *
\**************************************************************************/

#include <stdio.h>
#include <stdlib.h>

int write_testfile(unsigned long l, FILE *f)
{
    unsigned char buf[55]=
       "IBC-HASH test. Copyright (c) 1992 by RIPE consortium   ";
    int  bp= 0;

    while (l--) {
        if (putc(buf[bp], f) != buf[bp]) {
            fprintf(stderr, "\nError while writing output file");
            return(1);
        }
        buf[bp] = (buf[bp] + buf[(bp+55-24)%55]) % 256;
        bp = (bp+1)%55;
    }
    return( 0 );
}

void main(int argc, char *argv[])
{
    FILE *f;

    printf( "IBC-TEST program to generate IBC-HASH test files\n" );

    f = fopen("ibc-test.dat", "wb");
    if (f == NULL)
        fprintf(stderr, "\nCould not create file \"ibc-test.dat\"\n");
    else
        if (argc != 2) {
            fprintf(stderr, "Usage: IBC-TEST <size>");
```

```
    } else {
        long l = atol(argv[1]);
        if (l<0 || l>16777216L)
            fprintf(stderr, "\nIllegal size paramter\n");
        else
            write_testfile(l, f);
    }
}

/*********************** end of ibc-test.c ************************/
```

A.3 Sample Key Files

The following three files are sample key files. They all contain 2 lines. The first line is a 64-bit prime P and the second is V, both in hexadecimal.

IBC-HASH.KE1:

8537366B9856CCE7
7589024781647928

IBC-HASH.KE2:

AEC5E2D5F4BAA261
FF0055AAFF0055AA

IBC-HASH.KE3:

FFAEF21A73E83E3F
4782901478657483

B Test Values

The following table gives the hashcodes of 4 different files produced by the program of Appendix A.2 for the 3 keys given in Appendix A.3.

Size	Key1	Key2	Key3
0	77145977EAC3C538	661501D1C6279EB5	81929D2A02519A69
55	8FD0E942435F23A7	97148596A09CFF4E	A68E1E8CB51C348B
100000	F753F3CD683FD476	4968CB77400DD516	6B66CB784BDDC2D1
1048575	8F1C4E0E133D2EF7	9A3AB79CCBB50F55	1D10FEB3ECF77D62

Chapter 6

SKID

Table of Contents

1   Introduction

The secret key identification protocols SKID2 and SKID3 provide entity authentication between a user Alice and a user Bob.

SKID2 provides unilateral authentication after two passes. That means after having sent out a challenge to her communication partner Bob and having received the correct reply, Alice has good reason to assume that she is communicating with whom she thinks.

Using SKID2, the authentication is unilateral, the authenticity of Alice is not checked. However, an extension of the protocol, SKID3, which provides authentication of Alice as well by an additional pass, is also described.

Both SKID2 and SKID3 are based on a secret key only known to the two parties involved, and the application of a keyed hash function using this key. The keyed hash function to use is not specified, but it is suggested to use **RIPE-MAC** described in Chapter 4 of this report. Random numbers are used so that with high probability in different invocations of the protocol different values are exchanged.

These protocols have been used as a contribution to ISO-standardization and are to be incorporated in future versions of the proposed set of entity authentication standards specified in ISO/IEC 9798 [ISO93a, ISO93b, ISO93c]. The SKID primitives are not the result of a submission but have been selected and enhanced by Markus Dichtl and Walter Fumy.

It should be noted that entity authentication can also be achieved by using asymmetric cryptographic algorithms. Examples are the primitives RSA and COMSET described in respectively Chapter 7 and Chapter 8 of this report.

The structure of this description of SKID2 and SKID3 is as follows. In order to avoid any ambiguities in the description, the notation and definitions used are fixed in Section 2. In Section 3 the primitive is described and in Section 4 its purpose is explained. In Section 5 security aspects of the primitive are discussed. This includes claimed properties and the results of the algebraic evaluation of the primitive. Finally, in Section 6 the performance of the protocol is considered.

2 Definitions and Notation

2.1 Introduction

In order to obtain a clear description of the primitive, the notation and definitions used in this chapter are fully described in this section. These include the representation of the numbers in the description, and the operations, functions and constants used by the primitive.

2.2 General

The symbol ":=" is used for the assignment of a value or a meaning to a variable or symbol. That is, $a := b$ either means that the variable a gets the value of the variable b, or it means that a is defined as "b". It will be obvious from the context which meaning is intended.

The equality-sign "=" is used for equality only. That is, it indicates that the two entities on either side are equal.

An ellipsis ("...") denotes an implicit enumeration. For example, "$i = 0, 1, \ldots, n$" is meant to represent the sentence "for $i = 0$, $i = 1$, and so on, up to $i = n$".

2.3 Representation of the Numbers

In this chapter a *word* is defined as a 64-bit quantity. A word is considered to be a nonnegative integer. That is, it can take on the values 0 through $2^{64} - 1 = 18446744073709551615$.

A sequence of $64n$ bits $w_0, w_1, \ldots, w_{64n-1}$ is interpreted as a sequence of n words in the following way. Each group of 64 consecutive bits is considered as a word, the first bit of such a group being the most significant bit of that word. Hence,

$$W_i := \sum_{j=0}^{63} w_{64i+j} 2^{63-j}, \qquad i = 0, 1, \ldots, n-1. \tag{1}$$

In this chapter, words are always denoted by uppercase letters and the bits of this word by the corresponding lowercase letter with indices as in Equation (1).

2.4 Definitions and Basic Operations

- A *string* is a sequence of bits. If X is a string consisting of n bits, then those bits are denoted from left to right by $x_0, x_1, \ldots, x_{n-2}, x_{n-1}$.
- The *length* of a string X is the number of bits in the string X. A string of length n is called an n-bit string.

- For two strings $X = x_0, x_1, \ldots, x_{n-2}, x_{n-1}$ of length n and $Y = y_0,$ $y_1, \ldots, y_{n-2}, y_{m-1}$ of length m the $(n+m)$-bit string $W = w_0, w_1, \ldots,$ $w_{n+m-1} = X \parallel Y$ is defined as the *concatenation* of the strings X and Y. That is, according to the definition of a string above,

$$w_i := x_i \qquad i = 0, 1, \ldots, n-1$$
$$w_{i+n} := y_i \qquad i = 0, 1, \ldots, m-1.$$

- Strings of length 64 will also be considered as a word according to the representation defined by Equation (1), and vice versa. Hence, if X is a 64-bit string, then the corresponding word is equal to

$$X = \sum_{i=0}^{63} x_i 2^{63-i}.$$

Note that the same symbol is used for both the string and the corresponding word. It will be clear from the context which representation is intended.

- The *keyed hash function* $\mathcal{H}_K()$ compresses messages M of arbitrary length, under control of a secret key K, to an output block $\mathcal{H}_K(M)$ of fixed length, the *hashcode* of the message. More details can be found in Part II of this report.

3 Description of the Primitive

SKID2 and SKID3 are secret key identification protocols. The participants in the protocol are called Alice and Bob. SKID2 provides unilateral entity authentication of Bob to Alice, SKID3 provides mutual entity authentication of Alice and Bob.

The SKID2 protocol for participants Alice and Bob is based on the following requirements:

- The secret key K is only known to Alice and Bob.
- Alice wants to communicate with Bob and knows his distinguished name B. This distinguished name must identify Bob uniquely.
- The keyed hash function $\mathcal{H}_K()$ to be used must be specified. The requirements for this function are discussed in Section 5.2 of this chapter. It is suggested to use the primitive RIPE-MAC described in Chapter 4 of this report.

The protocol SKID2 consists of the following steps:

1. Alice chooses a random 64-bit word R_A. Each of the possible 2^{64} words should be selected with equal probability. This random word is also the first message $M_1 := R_A$. Alice sends M_1 to Bob.
2. Bob chooses a random 64-bit word R_B. Each of the possible 2^{64} words should be selected with equal probability. Bob calculates $H := \mathcal{H}_K(R_B \parallel R_A \parallel A)$ and sends $M_2 := R_B \parallel H$ to Alice
3. Alice extracts the 64-bit word R_B from M_2, computes $\mathcal{H}_K(R_B \parallel R_A \parallel A)$ and checks whether the result is the same as the corresponding part H of the message M_2 she received. If it is, she has good reason to assume that she is communicating with Bob, otherwise the entity authentication of Bob to Alice failed and the protocol is aborted.

These are also the first steps of the protocol SKID3, but, if everything went well so far, SKID3 consists of two more steps:

4. Alice computes message M_3 defined by $M_3 := \mathcal{H}_K(R_A \parallel R_B \parallel B)$ and sends it to Bob.
5. Bob computes $\mathcal{H}_K(R_A \parallel R_B \parallel B)$ and checks whether the result is equal to the received M_3. If it is, he has good reason to assume that he is communicating with Alice, otherwise the entity authentication of Alice to Bob failed and the protocol is aborted.

For SKID3, in addition to the requirements given for SKID2, Bob should want to communicate with Alice and know her distinguished name A.

The descriptions of the protocols can be summarized in the bird's eye views of Figures 1 and 2.

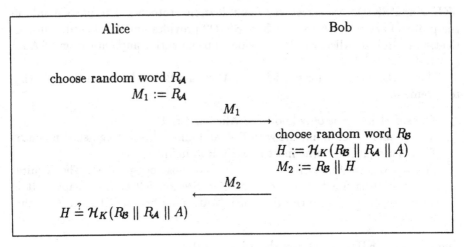

Fig. 1. The SKID2 protocol

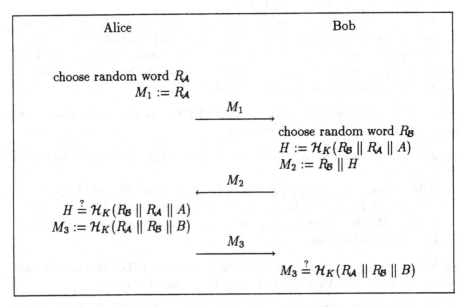

Fig. 2. The SKID3 protocol

4   Use of the Protocol

SKID2 provides unilateral entity authentication of Bob to Alice. This means that Alice has, after having completed the protocol successfully, good reason to believe that she is communicating with Bob.

Note that for SKID2 Bob has no reason to believe that he is communicating with Alice. If this is desired as well, SKID3 can be used, which additionally provides entity authentication of Alice to Bob.

5   Security

5.1   Claimed Properties

If initially the key K is known to users Alice and Bob only, the SKID2 and SKID3 protocols are expected to satisfy the following:

- If the users share the same key, and both follow the instructions, both SKID2 and SKID3 will always complete successfully.
- Even after watching a large number of conversations between Alice and Bob, or having taken part in a number of conversations with Bob, it is computationally infeasible for any third party on his own to execute SKID2 successfully with Alice. This remains true, even if different instances of the protocol are allowed to take place simultaneously.
- Even after watching a large number of conversations between Alice and Bob, or having taken part in a number of conversations with Alice and Bob, it is infeasible for any third party on his own to execute SKID3 successfully with Alice or with Bob. This remains true, even if different instances of the protocol are allowed to take place simultaneously.

Here, and in what follows, by "computationally infeasible" we mean to express the impossibility of computing something with the technology that is currently available or can be foreseen to become available in the near future.

It is hard to give a bound beyond which a computation is infeasible, but certainly, a computation requiring 2^{60} (or 10^{18}) operations is computationally infeasible. On the other hand a computation taking 2^{40} (about 10^{12}) operations is hard, but not impossible.

5.2   Algebraic Evaluation

The properties claimed rely on the following property, which we assume is satisfied by the keyed hash function $\mathcal{H}_K()$:

If the key K is not known, the following problem is infeasible to solve: first choose some inputs $R_1, R_2, \ldots$ and receive $\mathcal{H}_K(R_1'), \mathcal{H}_K(R_2'), \ldots$, where R_i is a prefix of R_i'. This is precisely the situation an attacker will find himself in by eavesdropping previous SKID protocols. Now compute some R_0 and $\mathcal{H}_K(R_0)$, such that R_0 is not equal to any of $R_1', R_2', \ldots$.

Consider an enemy trying to impersonate Bob when talking to Alice in the SKID2 protocol. If the inputs to $\mathcal{H}_K()$ are chosen at random, there is only a negligible probability that the current random input received from Alice has been used before. The assumption above on $\mathcal{H}_K()$ therefore implies that the enemy cannot on his own compute the $\mathcal{H}_K()$ value he needs to complete the protocol.

Hence the only remaining possibility is to fool a user that knows K (i.e., Alice or Bob) into computing the value needed. This must be done while the current instance of the protocol is still running.

The only way to get answers from Alice or Bob is of course to start an instance of the protocol with them. Doing this with Bob would mean that the enemy would merely act as a relay between Alice and Bob. However this is not a successful attack for the enemy: the purpose of the protocol is to prove to Alice that Bob is active in the current protocol-instance, and this would in fact be the case here. The only remaining possibility is to start a simultaneous protocol instance with Alice, set up such that Alice is the party supplying the $\mathcal{H}_K()$-output. However, any $\mathcal{H}_K()$-input used here will have the name of the enemy and not of Alice inserted into it. Therefore the output will be useless to the enemy because his original purpose was to impersonate Bob.

A similar argument can be made for SKID3: the enemy cannot impersonate Bob for the same reasons as above (the first part of SKID3 equals SKID2). If the enemy is trying to impersonate Alice, starting a parallel session with Alice as above does not make sense. Likewise, a parallel session with Bob will be useless because of the names inserted on the $\mathcal{H}_K()$-inputs, and by the property of $\mathcal{H}_K()$, the value he receives from Bob in the second protocol message will not help him either.

Finally, we mention some general security aspects related to implementing systems based on identification protocols of the kind presented here. The claimed properties ensure that the party being authenticated is in fact active and taking part in the protocol. They do not, however, imply anything about the physical location of that party. In particular, the existence of an intermediate person who simply forwards the messages (acts as a relay) is not ruled out. This is also known as the mafia attack [BBDGQ91]. When implementing systems based on such identification protocols, potential problems arising from the mafia attack should be taken into account. In some cases the problem is of no consequence, but with for example access control or other kinds of physical identification systems, it may be necessary to take precautions such as ensuring by physical means that the device being verified cannot easily get "external" help to complete the protocol.

It should also be mentioned that if communication subsequent to the identification protocol is not being authenticated in any way, the identification protocol of course cannot protect against modification of such communication by a third party. If the only protection required is against passive eavesdropping, this is no problem. Otherwise, it is necessary to authenticate the communication using for example RIPE-MAC or RSA signatures.

6   Performance Evaluation

SKID2 requires 2 passes of communication. The computations required in total are: the generation of two 64-bit random integers, and two applications of the keyed one-way function. SKID3 requires 3 passes of communication. The computations required in total are: the generation of two 64-bit random integers, and four applications of the keyed one-way function. The computational effort is equally balanced between Alice and Bob. The actual performance depends on the choice and implementation of the function $\mathcal{H}_K()$. If, as is suggested, the primitive RIPE-MAC is used for $\mathcal{H}_K()$, we refer to Section 6 of Chapter 4 for the actual performance figures.

References

[BBDGQ91] S. Bengio, G. Brassard, Y. Desmedt, C. Goutier, and J.-J. Quisquater, "Secure Implementation of Identification Systems," *Journal of Cryptology*, Vol. 4, No. 3, 1991, pp. 175–183.

[ISO93a]   ISO/IEC Draft International Standard 9798-2, *Information technology - Security techniques - Entity authentication mechanisms, Part 2: Entity authentication using symmetric techniques*, 1993.

[ISO93b]   ISO/IEC International Standard 9798-3, *Information technology - Security techniques - Entity authentication mechanisms, Part 3: Entity authentication using a public key algorithm*, 1993.

[ISO93c]   ISO/IEC Committee Draft 9798-4, *Information technology - Security techniques - Entity authentication mechanisms, Part 4: Entity authentication using non-reversible functions*, 1993.

Chapter 7

RSA

Table of Contents

1   Introduction

This chapter describes the integrity primitive RSA.

RSA in its basic form is a so called public key system, where each user has a private key, known only to him. Corresponding to this private key, there exists a public key, which may be known to anyone. Data processed by one key can be recovered using the other key. Yet, there is no feasible way known by which the private key can be found from the public key. In the case of RSA, the difficulty of finding the secret key is based on the difficulty of factoring large numbers.

Using proper modes of use, RSA can be used for digital signatures, and for distributing keys for authentication systems.

The name RSA is derived from the inventors of the algorithm: Rivest, Shamir and Adleman, who presented the algorithm in [RSA78].

In Section 2 of this chapter, we present the definitions and notation used, in order to avoid ambiguities in the description. Section 3 describes the primitive proper, Section 4 gives the recommended modes of use. Section 5 contains results of the algebraic evaluation of the primitive, while Section 6 contains the results of the performance evaluation. Finally, Section 7 gives some guidelines to software implementation of the primitive, and there is an appendix containing some test values.

2   Definitions and Notation

2.1   Introduction

In order to obtain a clear description of the primitive, the notation and definitions used in this chapter are fully described in this section. These include the representation of the numbers in the description, and the operations, functions and constants used by the primitive.

2.2   General

The symbol ":=" is used for the assignment of a value or a meaning to a variable or symbol. That is, $a := b$ either means that the variable a gets the value of the variable b, or it means that a is defined as "b". It will be obvious from the context which meaning is intended.

The equality-sign "=" is used for equality only. That is, it indicates that the two entities on either side are equal.

An ellipsis ("...") denotes an implicit enumeration. For example, "$i = 0, 1, \ldots, n$" is meant to represent the sentence "for $i = 0$, $i = 1$, and so on, up to $i = n$".

2.3   Representation of the Numbers

In this chapter a *byte* is defined as an 8-bit quantity. A byte is considered to be a nonnegative integer. That is, it can take on the values 0 through $2^8 - 1 = 255$.

A sequence of n bits $b_0, b_1, \ldots, b_{n-1}$ is interpreted as a nonnegative integer B in the following way. The bits are considered as the binary representation of B, the most significant bits being first in the sequence. That is,

$$B := \sum_{i=0}^{n-1} b_i 2^{n-i-1}.$$

Conversely, an interpretation of a number as a sequence of bits is defined by this equation, if a bit length for this number is fixed.

A sequence of $8n$ bits $b_0, b_1, \ldots, b_{8n-1}$ is interpreted as a sequence of n bytes in the following way. Each group of 8 consecutive bits is considered as a byte B_i, the first bit of such a group being the most significant bit of that byte. Hence,

$$B_i := b_{8i} 2^7 + b_{8i+1} 2^6 + \cdots + b_{8i+7}, \quad i = 0, 1, \ldots, n - 1.$$

2.4   Definitions and Basic Operations

- A *string* is a sequence of bits.
- For a string X the *length* of X is denoted as $|X|$. That is, $|X|$ is the number of bits in the string X. If $|X| = n$, then X is said to be an n-bit string.
- For an integer N, the *length* of N is defined as the length of the shortest binary representation of N. The length of N is denoted as $|N|$.
- For two strings $X = x_0, x_1, \ldots, x_{n-1}$ and $Y = y_0, y_1, \ldots, y_{m-1}$, the $(n+m)$-bit string $W = X \parallel Y$ is defined as the *concatenation* of the strings X and Y. That is,

$$w_i := x_i \qquad i = 0, 1, \ldots, n - 1$$
$$w_{i+n} := y_i \qquad i = 0, 1, \ldots, m - 1.$$

- For a nonnegative integer A and a positive integer B, the numbers A div B and A mod B are defined as the nonnegative integers Q, respectively R, such that

$$A = QB + R \quad \text{and} \quad 0 \le R < B.$$

That is, A mod B is the *remainder*, and A div B is the *quotient* of an integer division of A by B.
- For two strings $X = x_0, x_1, \ldots, x_{n-1}$ and $Y = y_0, y_1, \ldots, y_{m-1}$, the string $U = X \oplus Y$, is defined as the bitwise *XOR* of X and Y, where, if the strings are of different length, the shorter of the two is preceded by 0-bits in order to make the lengths equal. For two bits x and y the *XOR* is defined as $(x + y) \bmod 2$. This notation is also used for nonnegative integers. In this case its shortest binary representation as described above is used.

- The notation "$X \equiv Y$ (mod N)" (X is equivalent to Y modulo N) is used to indicate that $X \bmod N = Y \bmod N$.
- For two nonzero integers X and Y we say that X *divides* Y if $Y \bmod X = 0$. That is, if Y is a multiple of X.
- For two nonnegative integers X and Y, not both zero, the *greatest common divisor* $\gcd(X, Y)$ is defined as the greatest positive integer that divides both X and Y.
- For two nonnegative integers X and Y, not both zero, the *least common multiple* $\mathrm{lcm}(X, Y)$ is defined as the least positive integer that is a multiple of both X and Y. That is, $\mathrm{lcm}(X, Y) = (X \cdot Y)/\gcd(X, Y)$.
- An integer X is *invertible modulo N* if $\gcd(X, N) = 1$.
- An integer X that is invertible modulo N is said to be a *quadratic residue modulo N* if there is an integer Y such that $X \equiv Y^2$ (mod N). Otherwise X is said to be a *quadratic nonresidue modulo N*.
- A *prime* is an integer greater than 1 that is divisible only by 1 and by itself.
- A *composite* is an integer greater than 1 that is not a prime. A composite can uniquely be written as the product of at least two (not necessarily different) primes.
- When a is invertible modulo n, we let $\left(\frac{a}{n}\right)$ denote the *Jacobi symbol* of a modulo n (see [Kob87]). When $n = pq$, where p and q are primes, the Jacobi symbol of a modulo n can be defined as

$$\left(\frac{a}{n}\right) = \left(\frac{a}{p}\right)\left(\frac{a}{q}\right),$$

where $\left(\frac{a}{p}\right)$ is defined to be 1 if a is a quadratic residue modulo p, and -1 if a is a quadratic nonresidue modulo p, and similarly for $\left(\frac{a}{q}\right)$. Note that this number is always 1 or -1. See [Kob87] for the mathematical background.

2.5   Symbols

In what follows we also use lower case letters for numbers to facilitate the reading of formulas.

- p, q will denote prime numbers.
- n will be the *modulus*, the product of p and q.
- $\lambda(n)$ will denote the least common multiple of $p - 1$ and $q - 1$.
- k will denote $|n|$, the bit length of n.
- e, d will denote the public, respectively the secret exponent.
- P, S denote the operation with the public, respectively the secret key in the RSA system.
- $\mathcal{H}()$ denotes a hash function.
- $RR(x)$ denotes the representative element for the hashcode x, computed as defined below in this section.
- $SIG_S(M)$ is the digital signature of M, computed using secret key S.
- l denotes the length of an authentication key to be exchanged.

2.6   The Redundancy Function RR

In both modes of use of the RSA primitive a redundancy function RR is needed to prevent certain attacks (see Section 5.2 for the details). The ISO/IEC standard 9796 [ISO91] describes such a redundancy function RR. The scheme described in the standard works for any input length, in this chapter only the special case of input lengths which are multiples of 8 bits is given. In our case, the input will always be a hashcode.

Let the hashcode H be the concatenation of z bytes h_i

$$H = h_0 \parallel h_1 \parallel \cdots \parallel h_{z-1}.$$

The redundancy scheme requires that the inequality $16z \le k + 2$ holds. This should be no problem for the value $z = 16$, as suggested in this report, since RSA moduli should be larger anyway.

A number t is determined from k by

$$t := (k + 14) \text{ div } 16.$$

Now t bytes w_i $(0 \le i < t)$ are determined from the hashcode by

$$w_i := h_{z-1-((t-1-i) \bmod z)}.$$

Basically this just means that the bytes of H are repeatedly inserted at the beginning of the string until a length of t bytes is reached.

For $0 \le i < 2t$ the byte u_i is determined by

$$u_i := \begin{cases} w_{(i-1)\text{div}2} & \text{if } i \text{ is odd} \\ Sh(w_{(i-1)\text{div}2}) & \text{if } i \text{ is even}, \end{cases}$$

where for nonnegative integers a and b less than 16

$$Sh(16a + b) := 16\Pi(a) + \Pi(b)$$

and the values of the function $\Pi()$ are determined by the following table:

x	0	1	2	3	4	5	6	7	8	9	10	11	12	13	14	15
$\Pi(x)$	14	3	5	8	9	4	2	15	0	13	11	6	7	10	12	1

The bytes u_i are concatenated to form a string

$$U = u_0 \parallel u_1 \parallel \cdots \parallel u_{2t-2} \parallel u_{2t-1}.$$

The bits of U are denoted by b_i

$$U = b_0, b_1, \ldots, b_{16t-2}, b_{16t-1}.$$

The $(k-1)$-bit number I is defined by

$$I := \sum_{i=0}^{k-2} v_{k-2-i}\, 2^i,$$

where the bits v_i are

$$
v_i = \begin{cases}
1 & \text{if } i = 0 \\
b_i & \text{if } 0 < i < k + 6 - 16z \\
1 - b_i & \text{if } i = k + 6 - 16z \\
b_i & \text{if } k + 6 - 16z < i \le k - 10 \\
b_{i+4} & \text{if } k - 10 < i \le k - 6 \\
0 & \text{if } i = k - 5 \\
1 & \text{if } i = k - 4 \\
1 & \text{if } i = k - 3 \\
0 & \text{if } i = k - 2.
\end{cases}
$$

In the case of plain RSA (see Section 3.1) the redundancy scheme is finished, so we define

$$
RR(H) = I.
$$

In the case of the Rabin variant of RSA (see Section 3.2) the result $RR(H)$ of the redundancy function is defined by

$$
RR(H) = \begin{cases}
I & \text{if } \left(\frac{I}{n}\right) = +1 \\
I/2 & \text{if } \left(\frac{I}{n}\right) = -1.
\end{cases}
$$

For the Rabin variant we therefore need to compute the Jacobi symbol, or equivalent information. To this end, any of the following 3 methods can be used:

1. If the prime factors of n are available (which will often be the case due to optimization of arithmetic modulo n), one can simply use the definition

$$
\left(\frac{I}{n}\right) = \left(\frac{I}{p}\right)\left(\frac{I}{q}\right),
$$

   where $\left(\frac{I}{p}\right) \equiv (I^{(p-1)/2} \pmod p)$ and $\left(\frac{I}{q}\right) \equiv (I^{(q-1)/2} \pmod q)$. However this is not very effective, so the following two methods are preferable.

2. Without knowledge of the factors of n one can calculate the value of the Jacobi symbol as described in Chapter 10 of this report.

3. This final method does not require explicit computation of the Jacobi symbol, and is particularly efficient if the public exponent e is small. For maximum efficiency, it requires that the number $T := 2^{-d} \bmod n$ has been precomputed and stored as part of the secret key.
   The goal is to compute directly $S(RR(H))$. To do this, we first compute $V := I^d \bmod n$ and $V^e \bmod n$. Then,

$$
S(RR(H)) = \begin{cases}
V & \text{if } V^e \bmod n = I \text{ or } V^e \bmod n = n - I \\
VT \bmod n & \text{otherwise.}
\end{cases}
$$

3   Description of the Primitive

3.1   Plain RSA

Any user of the RSA system must generate a pair of keys, a secret and a public one. This is done by first choosing at random two large primes p, q. The number n is defined to be $n = pq$ and is called the modulus. Let

$$\lambda(n) = \mathrm{lcm}(p - 1, q - 1) = \frac{(p - 1)(q - 1)}{gcd(p - 1, q - 1)}.$$

Next choose the public exponent e such that

$$\gcd(e, \lambda(n)) = 1.$$

The secret exponent d is defined to be the smallest non-negative integer satisfying

$$ed \bmod \lambda(n) = 1.$$

See Chapter 9 for detailed information on how to generate these numbers and for possible refinements. It is recommended to choose p, q such that k, the bit length of n, is between 512 and 1024. See Chapter 9 for details.

We can now define the public and secret keys:

- Public key P: $n = pq$ and e.
- Secret key S: n, d, and optionally p, q.

The operations with the public and secret key can take any number m as input, that satisfies $0 \le m < n$. They produce as output a number in the same range. The public key operation is defined as follows (for notational convenience we shall reuse the symbols P and S. It will be clear from the context exactly which meaning is intended):

$$P(m) := m^e \bmod n$$

and the secret key operation is defined by:

$$S(m) := m^d \bmod n.$$

It is shown in [RSA78] that P and S are inverses of each other, i.e.,

$$P(S(m)) = S(P(m)) = m$$

for all m in the range.

3.2   The Rabin Variant

A variant of RSA is known as the Rabin system [Rab79, Wil80]. In this variant, p, q are chosen such that

$$p \bmod 8 = 3 \quad \text{and} \quad q \bmod 8 = 7.$$

Chapter 9 contains guidelines for generating p, q to satisfy this. The public exponent e is always 2, while the secret exponent d is defined to be

$$d := \frac{(p-1)(q-1)+4}{8}.$$

The definitions of P and S are the same as for RSA. Using similar methods as in [RSA78] it can be shown that $P(S(m)) = S(P(m)) = m$ if $0 \le m < n$ and m is a quadratic residue modulo n.

4   Use of the Primitive

4.1   Digital Signatures

We describe here a mode of use for RSA that allows generation of a digital signature on a binary string M of arbitrary length. Let $\mathcal{H}()$ denote one of the hash functions recommended in this report. Then $\mathcal{H}(M)$, i.e., the hashcode of M, is a binary string of length 128 bits, independently of the length of M.

The other ingredient we need is the ISO/IEC standard 9796 [ISO91], which contains the description of a *redundancy function* which takes a binary string as input and produces an output at least twice as long. We denote the final result of these operations by $RR(X)$ where X was the original input to the redundancy function. This number is known in the terminology of the standard as the *representative element*. In Section 2.6 we give details on how to compute the RR function. We now define the digital signature on M using secret key operation S as:

$$SIG_S(M) := \text{the smallest of } S(RR(\mathcal{H}(M))) \text{ and } n - S(RR(\mathcal{H}(M)))\,.$$

A digital signature may be checked as follows: given the message M, the signature $SIG_S(M)$, and the public key operation P corresponding to S, we define the signature to be valid, if and only if

$$P(SIG_S(M)) = RR(\mathcal{H}(M)) \quad \text{or} \quad P(SIG_S(M)) = n - RR(\mathcal{H}(M))\,.$$

This holds for both plain RSA and for the Rabin variant ($e = 2$).

4.2   Forwarding of Authentication Keys

This mode of use enables user B to send a message to user A, such that after A has processed the message, the two users share a key to a system for conventional message authentication, such as RIPE-MAC described in Chapter 4 of this report.

We assume that both A and B have generated a pair of RSA keys, (P_A, S_A) and (P_B, S_B), and that each knows the public key of the other. This can be accomplished using a public key directory or public key certificates. Let n_A be the modulus used by A, of length k_A, and let n_B be the modulus used by B, of length k_B.

We let l denote the length in bits of the key to be shared. In general, l will depend on the message authentication system where the key will be used. But we require that l is at most $k_A/2$.

B will now execute the following:

1. Choose at random a number r, such that $0 \leq r < n_A$ and the length of r is at least $k_A/2$ (see Chapter 9 for a discussion of random numbers). If P_A is a key for the Rabin variant of RSA, i.e., public exponent 2, then put $x := r^2 \bmod n_A$. Otherwise, put $x := r$.
2. Compute $y := P_A(x)$, and let the key K be the least significant l bits of y.

3. Compute the digital signature $SIG_{S_B}(x)$. Put $c := SIG_{S_B}(x) \oplus RR(\mathcal{H}(x))$. Also compute $z := P_A(y)$. Send c, z to A.

After receiving c, z, A does the following:

4. Put $x := S_A(S_A(z))$.
5. Put $\sigma := c \oplus RR(\mathcal{H}(x))$. Using P_B, test whether $\sigma = SIG_{S_B}(x)$. If not, reject the message and stop (in practice, more may have to be done, depending on the application — such as notifying B that the message was rejected). Otherwise continue.
6. Compute the key K as the least significant l bits of $P_A(x)$.

The description of this protocol can be summarized in the bird's eye view of Figure 1.

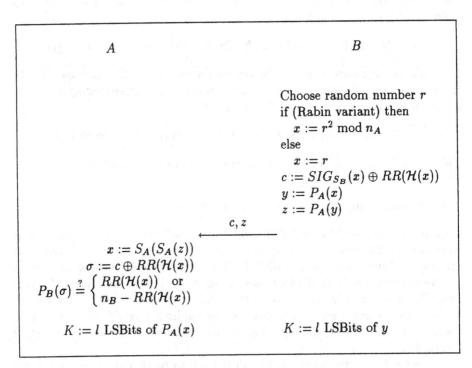

Fig. 1. The forwarding of authentication keys

The above description of A's algorithm has been optimized for the case where a small public exponent is used, so that the P-operation is much faster than the S-operation: if $d^2 \bmod \lambda(n)$ has been precomputed and stored as part of the secret key, x can be computed in one exponentiation as $x = z^{d^2 \bmod \lambda(n)} \bmod n$. The subsequent cost of computing $P_A(x)$ is negligible if e is small. If e is as large as d, the intermediate result $S_A(z) = P_A(x)$ of step 1 should be saved.

5 Security

5.1 Claimed Properties

The signature mode is expected to have the following property:

- given a public key P, and valid signatures on messages in a set M, it is infeasible to come up with a message m not in M and a valid signature on m. This remains true, even if the attacker gets to choose the messages in M.

The forward authentication key mode is expected to satisfy the following:

- If A accepts the message he gets, the owners of S_A and S_B are both capable of computing the same K, and it is infeasible for any third party to compute K.
- For large key lengths (which in practice means $l \geq 56$), the key resulting from an execution of B's algorithm is not easily controllable. More precisely, let K_0 be an l-bit key selected by some efficient method. Then the following is infeasible: given K_0, choose the initial input x such that the resulting message c, z will be accepted by A, and such that the key associated with c, z equals K_0 with probability significantly larger than 2^{-l}.

Remark: one reason for considering the second property is that it gives some extra protection against the case where B's source of random bits is fallacious, and outputs for example a highly patterned string of bits (the all-1 string is an extreme example). This situation will always be problematic because the number of possible keys will be limited. However, direct use of such a bitstring as a key in subsequent authentication could be particularly dangerous, because some authentication algorithms are weaker when such keys are used. The second property ensures that no such pattern is likely to show up in the key produced.

5.2 Algebraic Evaluation

The security of the use of RSA is based on the belief that factoring is a hard problem, i.e., that computing p, q from $n = pq$ is infeasible for large n. This is the problem one needs to solve to find a secret RSA key from the corresponding public one. From current state of the art in factoring algorithms, and the previous development, there is no indication that factoring will become feasible in general. At present, factorization of 512-bit numbers with two primes factors of comparable size is out of reach, even with the most efficient methods. From what is known today, the hardness of the problem increases quickly with increasing bit size, and it will therefore be easy to defend against developments in computing equipment that are unknown at present. Factoring of 1024-bit numbers is generally thought to be totally out of the question in any foreseeable future. More details on this can be found in Chapter 9.

Breaking RSA is at most as hard as factoring the modulus used, and is in fact precisely as hard as finding the secret key from the public one. Whether inverting the P-function is also equivalent to factoring is an open problem, however, as far as ordinary RSA is concerned. The P-function of the Rabin variant, however, is provably equivalent to factoring, as long as one uses the algorithm in its pure form, i.e., without a mode of use. This, on the other hand, means that the system is open to a chosen message attack when used for signatures. Using the mode of use recommended here solves this problem, but also means that the equivalence to factoring is not provable anymore. Hence, ordinary RSA and Rabin are on equal footing as far as this aspect is concerned.

5.2.1   Security of the Signature Mode

If RSA is used directly for digital signatures, it is possible to use knowledge of legitimately signed messages to generate new, signed messages, without knowing the secret key. For example, it always holds that

$$S(M_1) \cdot S(M_2) \bmod n = S(M_1 \cdot M_2 \bmod n),$$

and so if signatures on M_1 and M_2 are known, an enemy can always sign the "message" $M_1 \cdot M_2 \bmod n$. Another attack puts $M := P(R)$ for some number R which then becomes a valid signature of M. Although such new messages are unlikely to be meaningful, the security of this system is clearly not optimal.

It is the purpose of the redundancy function RR to defend against these attacks. The properties of RR were analyzed in [GQWL91], and the evaluation in RIPE has revealed nothing that goes against the results obtained there. Using the hash function before RR serves as an extra precaution, and adds the benefit that messages can be of arbitrary lengths.

Note, however, that the hash function must be secure, i.e., it should be hard to find different messages with the same hashcode. It is therefore recommended to use a carefully analyzed hash function, such as MDC-4 or RIPEMD described respectively in Chapter 2 and Chapter 3 of this report.

5.2.2   Security of the Forward Authentication Key Mode

For the first property of this mode, note that given a message c, z, it is clear that A can compute a key with the right connection to z. On the other hand, no one else can do this efficiently, since first z is an RSA ciphertext that requires knowledge of the secret key for decryption, and second c's only connection to x is that it depends on $\mathcal{H}(x)$ — the security of the hash function implies that x cannot be computed efficiently from $\mathcal{H}(x)$.

Assume now that A accepts the message c, z as having originated from B, i.e., the signature he checks turns out to be valid. We claim that this means that B must have generated the message, and is the only other party capable of computing the key. Since the processes leading from x to z and from x to c are both one-way functions, assuming security of RSA, it is a reasonable conjecture (supported in part by the conjecture from [MiSc91]) that a valid pair c, z can only be generated by first choosing x and then computing the pair. Hence the fact that A accepts the pair is evidence that *some* other user knows x and therefore the key. Moreover, because $RR(\mathcal{H}(x))$ is XORed onto the signature to produce c, $\mathcal{H}(x)$ is difficult to compute from c. Therefore, once the pair is generated, the signature hidden in c cannot be easily replaced by the signature of another party, and so A can conclude that the other party capable of computing the key must be B.

For the second property, note that the key K is extracted from the output of a one-way function that B cannot easily invert, namely P_A, and that B must know the input value x in order to be able to sign it (A would not accept the message without the signature). So to control the value of K, only three possibilities seem to be open to B:

- Invert P_A on a random output value producing the desired key. This is infeasible because B does not know S_A.
- Choose carefully an input value such that the intermediate results and the output can be controlled. The obvious way to do this is to choose a small input value so that no modular reductions will take place during the computation of P_A. But this is prevented by the conditions on the choice of x.
- Generate many keys with randomly chosen input, and hope that one will equal the desired key value. With current state of the art, this is infeasible if the key has length at least 56.

It therefore seems reasonable to conjecture that B cannot control the value of K.

6 Performance Evaluation

6.1 Software Implementations

Both the P and S operations in plain RSA (see Section 3.1) are modular exponentiations, where the modulus is the product of two large primes. In practical systems both primes are either 256, 384 or 512 bits long, resulting in, respectively a 512, 768 or 1024-bit modulus. The basic multiprecision operations needed to implement such a modular exponentiation are the multiplication of two integers, the squaring of an integer and the modular reduction of a integer (see Chapter 10 for an algorithm). For the multiplication and squaring optimized versions of the classical algorithms are used, as described in [Knu81]. The modular reduction is implemented according to a method due to P.L. Montgomery, allowing a reduction in almost the same time as a multiplication [Mon85].

Using knowledge of the prime factors of the modulus, the S operation can be speeded up with a factor 3 to 4. That is, using the so-called Chinese Remainder Theorem (CRT) the S operation is basically reduced to two exponentiations modulo the two prime factors, being only half the length of the modulus, see [QuCo82]. To improve the performance of the P operation of plain RSA a small public exponent can be chosen in the key generation, such as $2^{16} + 1$. Since the public exponent of the Rabin variant is always 2, its P operation is just a modular squaring.

Both a C and a 80386 Assembly language implementation are considered. The C version has the advantage of being portable. The considerable difference in performance between the C and the Assembly language version is due to the general nature of the C code: it can be used for integers of arbitrary length, whereas the Assembly versions use different code for each length, which has been optimized for that particular length. All figures of Table 1 are for an IBM-compatible 33 MHz 80386DX based PC with 64K cache memory. The C version was compiled with the WATCOM C/386 9.0 and run with the DOS/4GW DOS extender (i.e., in protected mode). The Assembly language implementation was assembled with Turbo Assembler 2.5 and run in real mode.

	speed in bit/s					
	C			Assembly		
	512	768	1024	512	768	1024
General exponentiation	191	90	52	1045	485	280
P (plain RSA, $2^{16} + 1$)	4447	3126	2405	34K	24K	18K
P (Rabin variant)	120K	85K	66K	662K	473K	356K
S (with CRT)	653	322	190	3460	1688	1042

Table 1. Software performance of the public key and secret key operations in plain RSA and its Rabin variant on a 33 MHz 80386DX based PC with a 64K memory cache using WATCOM C/386 9.0 in combination with the DOS/4GW DOS extender.

An interesting alternative to custom hardware is the implementation of RSA on a digital signal processor (DSP) providing hardware speed yet software flexibility. The figures of Table 2 were obtained on a 20 MHz Motorola DSP56001.

	speed in bit/s
	512 bits
General exponentiation	5K
P (plain RSA, $2^{16} + 1$)	184K
S (with CRT)	15K

Table 2. Software performance of the public key and secret key operations in plain RSA on a 20 MHz Motorola DSP56001.

6.2   Hardware Implementations

The figures of Table 3 are for a general exponentiation on the fastest RSA chip yet available [Pij92]. It uses a 25 MHz clock frequency. The speed of the S operation can be improved as in the software case, but here the factor of improvement is only about 1.5.

	speed in bit/s		
	512	768	1024
General exponentiation	40K	30K	25K
S (with CRT)	60K	45K	40K

Table 3. Hardware performance of a general modular exponentiation on the PCC200 RSA Encryption Device.

7   Guidelines to Software Implementation

For generating keys for RSA, we refer to Chapter 9. For implementation of the multiprecision arithmetic needed for RSA itself, we refer to Chapter 10. Implementing the modes of use is straightforward, given an implementation of RSA.

References

[FiSh86]   A. Fiat and A. Shamir, "How to prove yourself: practical solutions of identification and signature problems," *Advances in Cryptology, Proc. Crypto'88,
LNCS 403*, S. Goldwasser, Ed., Springer-Verlag, 1990, pp. 186–194.

[GQWL91]   L. Guillou, J.-J. Quisquater, M. Walker, P. Landrock and C. Shaer, "Precautions taken against various potential attacks in ISO/IEC 9796," *Advances in Cryptology, Proc. Eurocrypt'90, LNCS 473*, I.B. Damgård, Ed.,
Springer-Verlag, 1991, pp. 465–473.

[ISO91]   ISO/IEC International Standard 9796, *Information technology - Security
techniques - Digital signature scheme giving message recovery*, 1991.

[Knu81]   D.E. Knuth, *The Art of Computer Programming, Vol. 2: Seminumerical
Algorithms, 2nd Edition*, Addison-Wesley, Reading Mass., 1981.

[Kob87]   N. Koblitz, *A Course in Number Theory and Cryptography*, Springer-
Verlag, Berlin-Heidelberg-New York, 1987.

[MiSc91]   S. Micali and C.P. Schnorr, "Efficient perfect polynomial random number
generators," *Journal of Cryptology*, Vol. 3, No. 3, 1991, pp. 157–172.

[Mon85]   P.L. Montgomery, "Modular multiplication without trial division," *Mathematics of Computation*, Vol. 44, 1985, pp. 519–521.

[Pij92]   Pijnenburg micro-electronics & software: *PCC200 RSA Encryption Device*,
1992.

[QuCo82]   J.-J. Quisquater, C. Couvreur, "Fast decipherment algorithm for RSA
public-key cryptosystems," *Electronic Letters*, Vol. 18, 1982, pp. 905–907.

[Rab79]   M.O. Rabin, *Digital Signatures and Public Key Functions as Intractable
as Factoring*, Technical Memo TM-212, Laboratory of Computer Science,
Massachusetts Inst. of Technology, 1979.

[RSA78]   R.L. Rivest, A. Shamir and L. Adleman, "A method for obtaining digital
signature and public key cryptosystems," *Communications of the ACM*,
Vol. 21, 1978, pp. 120–126.

[Wil80]   H.C. Williams, "A Modification of the RSA Public-Key Encryption Procedure," *IEEE Trans. on Information Theory*, Vol. IT–26, No. 6, 1980,
pp. 726–729.

A   Test Values for Signature Mode

The following shows some an example of the computation of a signature. The example starts from the hashcode, which has size 128 bits in this example. To facilitate reference to ISO/IEC 9796, we use the terminology from that standard but also refer to the notation from Section 2.6.

```
9796 TEST
Data in HEX notation and ordinary number format:
most significant digit first


modulus:
9FFC F9B7 B211 3D86 B214 4A07 6047 D24F EB78 2369 63F6 3653
3D24 4BA1 6AEF 4812 8D3A FE8B 1626 3E62 E02F 1260 1BC5 176F
F0C6 01E4 744D 000E 13C8 0178 46C9 98B1 9F


public exponent:
10001


secret exponent:
232C 329A 3803 A24B 228B 635B 0BC7 BE6C E38F 9DF9 6588 9398
E930 3990 5B3A 0FD6 3EA9 B7DB B667 B8DF 86C8 CA96 3991 2438
B5A0 A1E6 2F89 50ED CFF9 A505 B347 56EB 81


hashcode:
FFEEDDCCBBAA99887766554433221100


Padded and extended message
(only bytes in non-redundant positions shown)
00.. FF.. EE.. DD.. CC.. BB.. AA.. 99.. 88.. 77.. 66.. 55..
44.. 33.. 22.. 11.. 00.. FF.. EE.. DD.. CC.. BB.. AA.. 99..
88.. 77.. 66.. 55.. 44.. 33.. 22.. 11.. 00


Message with redundancy bytes (U)
0011 FFCC EEAA DD77 CC66 BBBB AADD 9900 88FF 7722 6644 5599
4488 3355 2233 11EE 0010 FFCC EEAA DD77 CC66 BBBB AADD 9900
88FF 7722 6644 5599 4488 3355 2233 11EE 00


After truncate and force least sig. byte (I)
4011 FFCC EEAA DD77 CC66 BBBB AADD 9900 88FF 7722 6644 5599
4488 3355 2233 11EE 0010 FFCC EEAA DD77 CC66 BBBB AADD 9900
88FF 7722 6644 5599 4488 3355 2233 11EE 06
```

Representative element (RR)
4011 FFCC EEAA DD77 CC66 BBBB AADD 9900 88FF 7722 6644 5599
4488 3355 2233 11EE 0010 FFCC EEAA DD77 CC66 BBBB AADD 9900
88FF 7722 6644 5599 4488 3355 2233 11EE 06

Signature
3F84 1031 166A 4EA9 E956 C80A 6B57 CF9A F3B0 ADC8 AD9B 6E7F
AD93 313C 844D B12F F8C2 26DB 00B4 0F28 A0DA 7E9B B559 40EB
8FCA 25BA 7C20 2804 1521 8605 59D0 3FC8 15

Chapter 8

COMSET

Table of Contents

1   Introduction

COMSET is a cryptographic protocol that allows any two users to identify themselves to each other, and also to exchange a secret key that they use for subsequent data origin authentication. Such interaction will typically occur at the beginning of a session, and this led to the acronym

COMSET for COMmunication SETup.

The essential idea of the protocol is that in order to identify a user in a system with public key cryptography, it is sufficient to establish authenticity of his public key and subsequently to be convinced that the user is in possession of the corresponding secret key. The first task can be solved by a public key directory, or by certificates (cf. [CCI89]); this is not part of COMSET. COMSET concentrates on the second task: how can A (Alice) convince B (Bob) that she possesses the corresponding secret key, if B knows the public key of A? Furthermore, COMSET provides the two users with a secret key known only to them. In many situations this is desirable for subsequent data origin authentication using a symmetric cryptosystem. These concepts are explained in Part II of this report.

The underlying mathematical principle of COMSET is the Rabin variant [Rab79, Wil80] of the RSA scheme [RSA78], which is a primitive described in Chapter 7 of this report.

Originally COMSET was suggested by J. Brandt, I. Damgård, P. Landrock and T. Pedersen in [BDLP88].

The structure of this description of COMSET is as follows. In order to avoid any ambiguities in the description, the notation and definitions used are fixed in Section 2. In Section 3 the primitive is described and in Section 4 its use is explained. In Section 5 security aspects of the primitive are discussed. This includes claimed properties and the results of the algebraic evaluation of the primitive. Finally, in Section 6 the performance of the protocol is considered. Section 7 refers the reader to the Chapter 10 "Implementation Guidelines for Arithmetic Computation".

2   Definitions and Notation

2.1   Introduction

In order to obtain a clear description of the primitive, the notation and definitions used in this chapter are fully described in this section. These include the representation of the numbers in the description as well as the operations, functions and constants used by the primitive.

2.2   General

The symbol ":=" is used for the assignment of a value or a meaning to a variable or symbol. That is, $a := b$ either means that the variable a gets the value of the variable b, or it means that a is defined as "b". It will be obvious from the context which meaning is intended.

The equality-sign "=" is used for equality only. That is, it indicates that the two entities on either side are equal.

An ellipsis ("...") denotes an implicit enumeration. For example, "$i = 0$, 1, ..., n" is meant to represent the sentence "for $i = 0$, $i = 1$, and so on, up to $i = n$".

2.3   Representation of the Numbers

A sequence of n bits b_0, b_1, ..., b_{n-1} is interpreted as an nonnegative integer B in the following way. The bits are considered as the binary representation of B, the most significant bits being first in the sequence. That is,

$$B := \sum_{i=0}^{n-1} b_i 2^{n-i-1}.$$

Conversely, an interpretation of a number as a sequence of bits is defined by this equation, if a bit length for this number is fixed. In this chapter only the bit length L of the modulus is used.

2.4   Definitions and Basic Operations

- A string is a sequence of bits.
- For a bit string X the *length* of X is denoted as $|X|$. That is, $|X|$ is the number of bits in the string X. If $|X| = n$, then X is said to be an n-bit string.
- For an nonnegative integer N, the *length* of N is defined as the length of the shortest binary representation of N. This is the representation with most significant bit equal to 1. (All "leading zeros" are removed.) The length of N is denoted as $|N|$.

- For a string $X = x_0, x_1, \ldots, x_{n-1}$, the string $x_i, x_{i+1}, \ldots, x_j$ with $0 \le i \le j < |X|$, is denoted as $X_{i,j}$. This notation is also used for nonnegative integers. In this case its binary representation as an L-bit number is used to take the substring from.
- For a nonnegative integer A and a positive integer B, the numbers A div B and A mod B are defined as the nonnegative integers Q, respectively R, such that

$$A = QB + R \quad \text{and} \quad 0 \le R < B.$$

That is, A mod B is the *remainder*, and A div B is the *quotient* of an integer division of A by B.
- The notation "$X \equiv Y \pmod{N}$" (X is equivalent to Y modulo N) is used to indicate that X mod $N = Y$ mod N.
- For two nonzero integers X and Y we say that X *divides* Y if Y mod $X = 0$. That is, if Y is a multiple of X.
- For two nonnegative integers X and Y, not both zero, the *greatest common divisor* $\gcd(X, Y)$ is defined as the greatest positive integer that divides both X and Y.
- An integer X is *invertible modulo* N if $\gcd(X, N) = 1$, see [Kob87].
- An integer X that is invertible modulo N is said to be a *quadratic residue modulo* N if there is an integer Y such that $X \equiv Y^2 \pmod{N}$.
- A *prime* is an integer greater than 1 that is divisible only by 1 and by itself.

2.5   Functions and Symbols used by the Primitive

- The users of the protocol are denoted by $\mathcal{A}$ (for Alice) and $\mathcal{B}$ (for Bob).
- $p_\mathcal{A}$ and $q_\mathcal{A}$ are the secret prime factors of the modulus $n_\mathcal{A}$ of $\mathcal{A}$.
- L is the bit length of $n_\mathcal{A}$.
- The public encryption function of $\mathcal{A}$ is denoted by $P_\mathcal{A}()$. It is defined by $P_\mathcal{A}(m) = m^2 \bmod n_\mathcal{A}$
- The secret decryption function of $\mathcal{A}$ is denoted by $S_\mathcal{A}()$. It is defined by $S_\mathcal{A}(c) = c^{d_\mathcal{A}} \bmod n_\mathcal{A}$, where

$$d_\mathcal{A} = \frac{(p_\mathcal{A} - 1)(q_\mathcal{A} - 1) + 4}{8}.$$

- m, c, v and k denote respectively the message, challenge, challenge validator and secret key exchanged in the protocol.

3   Description of the Primitive

COMSET is a public key identification protocol. It provides entity authentication of its user A. It also provides exchange of secret keys between A and B.

Each potential participant A of the protocol must have secretly selected two primes p_A and q_A with $p_A \equiv 3 \pmod 8$ and $q_A \equiv 7 \pmod 8$. It is recommended that L, the length of the modulus $n_A = p_A q_A$, is at least 512, see Chapter 9 for details. Note that for security reasons p_A and q_A have to meet additional conditions which are also described in Chapter 9.

A publishes the product $n_A = p_A q_A$ as her public key P_A. She must keep the prime factors p_A and q_A secret.

The public encryption function of A is given by $P_A(m) = m^2 \bmod n_A$. It is only used for quadratic residues m modulo n_A.

Only A knows her secret decryption function $S_A(c) = c^{d_A} \bmod n_A$, where

$$d_A = \frac{(p_A - 1)(q_A - 1) + 4}{8}.$$

An explanation of why this Rabin variant of the RSA scheme (cf. [RSA78] and Chapter 7 of this report) works may be found in [Wil80].

The COMSET protocol for participants A and B is as follows.

1. B chooses a random integer x with $2 \leq x < n_A$. Each number in this interval should be selected with equal probability. The message m is determined by the equation $m := x^2 \bmod n_A$. He encrypts m to the *challenge* $c := P_A(m)$ using the public key P_A of A. He sends the challenge c together with a *challenge validator* $v := m_{L-64, L-1}$ (i.e., the 64 least significant bits of m) to A.

2. A decrypts c into $m' := S_A(c)$ and compares $m'_{L-64, L-1}$ with v. If equality holds, she sends the *answer* $w := m'_{L-128, L-65}$ to B. Otherwise she compares $(n_A - m')_{L-64, L-1}$ with v and, if equality holds, she sends the *answer* $w := (n_A - m')_{L-128, L-65}$ to B. If this check also fails, A sends the message "stop" to B, and the execution of the protocol is aborted.

3. B compares w with $m_{L-128, L-65}$; if equality holds, the authentication of A has been successful.

4. Finally, both A and B determine their shared secret key. Let l be the bit length of the key to be used for symmetrical message authentication. B takes as secret key $k := m_{L-128-l, L-129}$. A finds the (same) secret key $k := m'_{L-128-l, L-129}$, if $m'_{L-64, L-1} = v$ holds, or $k := (n_A - m')_{L-128-l, L-129}$, if $(n_A - m')_{L-64, L-1} = v$.

The description can be summarized in the bird's eye view of the protocol in Figure 1.

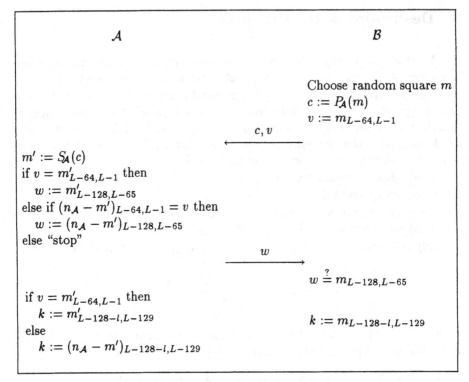

Fig. 1. The COMSET protocol

4   Use of the Primitive

COMSET provides entity authentication of A, where the entity A is identified by her knowledge of the factorization of an L-bit public number, combined with the exchange of a secret key that can be used for subsequent message authentication. This means that B has good reason to believe that he is communicating with A, and that the secret key exchanged is only known to him and A.

Note that A has no reason to believe that she is communicating with B, or that the one she shares the secret key with is indeed B. If this is desired as well, the protocol has also to be executed with the roles of A and B interchanged. Both authentication processes can be executed at essentially the same time. This means that while B is computing in the first step of the protocol message and challenge validator, A executes the first step of the protocol as well (of course she uses the public key of B to determine the challenge validator). Then A and B exchange their c and v values. After that both can execute the second step of the protocol at essentially the same time, and so on. At the end, each user has two keys. The bitwise exclusive or of these is used as the common secret key of A and B.

Note that B must establish the authenticity of the public key of A. This is not achieved by the COMSET protocol, but can be realized using a public key directory or certificates (cf. [CCI89]).

5 Security

5.1 Claimed Properties

The COMSET protocol is claimed to satisfy the following:

- If both parties follow the protocol, all checks will be satisfied, and the protocol will complete successfully.
- It is infeasible for any user $\mathcal{X}$ to claim he is $\mathcal{A}$ and on his own complete the protocol successfully with $\mathcal{B}$, unless $\mathcal{X}$ possesses the secret key of $\mathcal{A}$.
- COMSET is a zero-knowledge protocol (see [GMR89] for a formal definition), i.e., after completing the protocol with $\mathcal{A}$, $\mathcal{B}$ has obtained no information that he could not have computed efficiently by himself. In particular, he has learnt nothing that could help him to impersonate $\mathcal{A}$ later.
- If $\mathcal{A}$ and $\mathcal{B}$ complete the protocol successfully, $\mathcal{B}$ can assume that the key k has been received by $\mathcal{A}$. Moreover, it is infeasible for any third party observing the communication to guess the value of k essentially better than at random.

Here, and in what follows, by "computationally infeasible" we mean to express the impossibility of computing something with the technology that is currently available or can be foreseen to become available in the near future.

It is hard to give a bound beyond which a computation is infeasible, but certainly, a computation requiring 2^{60} (or 10^{18}) operations is computationally infeasible. On the other hand a computation taking 2^{40} (about 10^{12}) operations is hard, but not impossible.

5.2 Algebraic Evaluation

The properties claimed rely on the following two assumptions:

1. Given only $m^2 \bmod n_{\mathcal{A}}$ and $n_{\mathcal{A}}$, the least significant half of the bits of m are simultaneously secure, i.e., even if some of the bits are revealed, it is infeasible to guess any of the remaining bits essentially better than at random. In particular, this means that from only n and (c, v) it is infeasible to guess m or w, and also that from n, (c, v) and w it is infeasible to guess any bit of k.
2. Given only $n_{\mathcal{A}}$, it is infeasible to compute a pair (c, v) such that v equals the least significant 64 bits of a square root m of c, without also being able to compute all the bits of m. A number m is a square root of c if $m^2 = c \bmod n_{\mathcal{A}}$.

The first assumption made is a special case of the conjecture made by Micali and Schnorr in [MiSc91], this conjecture is in turn based on the assumption that modular squaring is a one-way function, in other words that RSA and Rabin's variant of RSA are secure. Therefore the first assumption is reasonable.

The second assumption is also supported in part by [MiSc91]: their conjecture says that the least significant bits of a modular square root are simultaneously secure (see explanation above). This implies that the most obvious way of trying to break the assumption, namely by selecting a random number and trying to compute the least significant bits of a square root, will not be feasible. It is therefore conjectured that essentially the only feasible way of computing a valid pair (c, v) is by first selecting m and then computing the pair, and this is just the content of the second assumption.

While it is relatively easy to see why the first, second and fourth of the claimed properties follow from assumptions 1 and 2, the third property may be less obvious. We offer here some intuitive reasoning that may help the reader to see why the design of the protocol and assumption 2 ensures that the protocol is zero-knowledge. First of all, what zero-knowledge means is that B learns nothing from the protocol that he could not have computed himself just as easily. The significance of this is that A can be sure that he does leak information to B that may later help B to impersonate A.

It may be helpful to think of the m chosen by B as a message, and $c = P_A(m)$ as an encryption of m. Recall that v, which is sent along with c is supposed to contain some of the bits of m and therefore shows (if correctly computed) that B already knows a large part of the message.

There is one complicating factor, we have to mention, however: given some ciphertext c, there is not just 1, but in fact 4 different "plaintexts" with the property that when you apply A's public key, i.e., square them modulo n_A, you get c as result (these are in fact square roots of c). One of these is $S_A(c)$. It is special among the 4 by being the only one that is a square, i.e., it is of the form $x^2 \bmod n_A$ for some x. The other 3 are of the form $n_A - S_A(c)$ and y, $n_A - y$ for some y. We will call y and $n_A - y$ illegal plaintext. By computing the so called Jacobi symbol (see Chapter 7), it is easy for both A and B to distinguish between legal and illegal plaintexts, but only A can tell whether a given legal plaintext m is actually $S_A(c)$ for some c or $n_A - S_A(c)$.

Suppose now that B has some arbitrary strategy for trying to get nontrivial knowledge from A. There are only 2 possible cases:

1. The pair (c, v) sent by B is such that v equals the least significant 64 bits of one of the 4 square roots of c. Call this root m. Assumption 2 tells us that B can in fact compute all of the bits of m. But then he can also test whether m is illegal or not. If m is illegal, B knows that A will return "stop", since A only tests v against legal plaintexts. If m is legal, B knows that A will return the 64 bits of m just "above" v (i.e., preceding the bits that make up v in significance).

2. The pair (c, v) sent by B is such that v is not the least significant 64 bits of any of the 4 square roots of c. B knows that by assumption 2, there is a method by which he should be able to compute a square root of c, if we were in case 1 above. Hence if this method fails, B knows we are in case 2, and that A will therefore always return "stop".

Note that, in case 1 when the m found by $\mathcal{B}$ is legal, $\mathcal{B}$ may not know whether m is equal to $S_{\mathcal{A}}(c)$ or $n_{\mathcal{A}} - S_{\mathcal{A}}(c)$. This is because there is no guarantee that $\mathcal{B}$ has followed the protocol and has chosen $m = x^2 \bmod n_{\mathcal{A}}$ for some x. But since $\mathcal{A}$ tests v against both $S_{\mathcal{A}}(c)$ and $n_{\mathcal{A}} - S_{\mathcal{A}}(c)$, this is not a problem.

If, however, $\mathcal{A}$ had insisted that v always be the least significant 64 bits of $S_{\mathcal{A}}(c)$, the protocol would not be zero-knowledge. $\mathcal{B}$ could use $\mathcal{A}$ to test if a given m was of the form $S_{\mathcal{A}}(c)$ or not, since then sending $P_{\mathcal{A}}(m)$ and the least significant 64 bits of m would cause $\mathcal{A}$ to return "stop" precisely if m was not of the form $S_{\mathcal{A}}(c)$.

In summary, what the reasoning in case 1 and 2 shows, is that no matter how $\mathcal{B}$ behaves, he *always knows in advance* what $\mathcal{A}$ is going to say, and therefore he learns nothing from the protocol that he could not compute himself.

Finally we mention some general security aspects related to implementing systems based on identification protocols of the kind presented here. The claimed properties ensure that the party being authenticated is in fact active and taking part in the protocol. They do not, however, imply anything about the physical location of that party. In particular, the existence of an intermediate person who simply forwards the messages (acts as a relay) is not ruled out. This is also known as the mafia attack. When implementing systems based on such identification protocols, potential problems arising from the mafia attack should be taken into account. In some cases the problem is of no consequence, but with for example access control or other kinds of physical identification systems, it may be necessary to take precautions such as ensuring by physical means that the device being verified cannot easily get "external" help to complete the protocol.

It should also be mentioned that if communication subsequent to the identification protocol is not being authenticated in any way, the identification protocol of course cannot protect against modification of such communication by a third party. If the only protection required is against passive eavesdropping, this is no problem. Otherwise, it is necessary to authenticate the communication using for example RIPE-MAC or RSA signatures.

6 Performance Evaluation

In the protocol B has to perform only two modular squarings, i.e., one squaring to choose m and one squaring to compute c. This is negligible compared to the general modular exponentiation A has to perform: the length of the exponent e is about the same as that of the modulus n_A. Therefore, the performance of COMSET is completely determined by the time needed to perform *one* general modular exponentiation. This still holds if both A and B have to prove themselves to each other, because in that case the two general exponentiations can be done simultaneously.

6.1 Software Implementations

In practical systems both primes of the modulus are either 256, 384 or 512 bits long, resulting in, respectively a 512, 768 or 1024-bit modulus. The basic multiprecision operations needed to implement such a modular exponentiation are the multiplication of two integers, the squaring of an integer and the modular reduction of a integer (see Chapter 10 for an algorithm). For the multiplication and squaring optimized versions of the classical algorithms are used, as described in [Knu81]. The modular reduction is implemented according to a method due to P.L. Montgomery, allowing a reduction in almost the same time as a multiplication [Mon85].

Using knowledge of the prime factors of the modulus, the S_A operation can be speeded up with a factor 3 to 4. That is, using the so-called Chinese Remainder Theorem (CRT) the S_A operation can be reduced to basically two general exponentiations modulo the two prime factors, being only half the length of the modulus, see [QuCo82].

Both a C and a 80386 Assembly language implementation are considered. The C version has the advantage of being portable. The considerable difference in performance between the C and the Assembly language version is due to the general nature of the C code: it can be used for integers of arbitrary length, whereas the Assembly versions use different code for each length, which has been optimized for that particular length. All figures of Table 1 are for an IBM-compatible 33 MHz 80386DX based PC with 64K cache memory. The C version was compiled with the WATCOM C/386 9.0 and run with the DOS/4GW DOS extender (i.e., in protected mode). The Assembly language implementation was assembled with Turbo Assembler 2.5 and run in real mode.

An interesting alternative to custom hardware is the implementation of a modular exponentiation on a digital signal processor (DSP) providing hardware speed yet software flexibility. The figures of Table 2 were obtained on a 20 MHz Motorola DSP56001.

6.2 Hardware Implementations

The figures of Table 3 are for a general exponentiation on the fastest RSA chip yet available [Pij92]. It uses a 25 MHz clock frequency. The speed of the S_A operation can be improved as in the software case, but here the factor of improvement is only about 1.5.

	speed in bit/s					
	C			Assembly		
	512	768	1024	512	768	1024
General exponentiation	191	90	52	1045	485	280
S_A (with CRT)	653	322	190	3460	1688	1042

Table 1. Software performance of the secret key operation S_A on a 33 MHz 80386DX based PC with a 64K memory cache using WATCOM C/386 9.0 in combination with the DOS/4GW DOS extender.

	speed in bit/s
	512 bits
General exponentiation	5K
S_A (with CRT)	15K

Table 2. Software performance of the secret key operation S_A on a 20 MHz Motorola DSP56001.

	speed in bit/s		
	512	768	1024
General exponentiation	40K	30K	25K
S_A (with CRT)	60K	45K	40K

Table 3. Hardware performance of a general modular exponentiation on the PCC200 RSA Encryption Device.

7   Guidelines for Implementation

The implementation of the protocol is straightforward. For multiprecision arithmetic which is needed for the computations required by the protocol we refer to Chapter 10.

References

[BDLP88] J. Brandt, I.B. Damgård, P. Landrock and T. Pedersen, "Zero-knowledge authentication scheme with secret key exchange," *Advances in Cryptology, Proc. Crypto'88, LNCS 403*, S. Goldwasser, Ed., Springer-Verlag, 1990, pp. 583–588.

[CCI89]   CCITT Recommendation X.509, *The Directory–Authentication Framework*, 1989, (same as ISO 9594-8, 1989).

[GMR89]   S. Goldwasser, S. Micali and C. Rackoff, "The knowledge complexity of interactive proof systems," *SIAM Journal on Computing*, Vol. 18, No. 1, 1989, pp. 186–208.

[Knu81]   D.E. Knuth, *The Art of Computer Programming, Vol. 2: Seminumerical Algorithms, 2nd Edition*, Addison-Wesley, Reading Mass., 1981.

[Kob87]   N. Koblitz, *A Course in Number Theory and Cryptography*, Springer-Verlag, Berlin-Heidelberg-New York, 1987.

[MiSc91] S. Micali and C.P. Schnorr, "Efficient perfect polynomial random number generators," *Journal of Cryptology*, Vol. 3, No. 3, 1991, pp. 157–172.

[Mon85]   P.L. Montgomery, "Modular multiplication without trial division," *Mathematics of Computation*, Vol. 44, 1985, pp. 519–521.

[Pij92]   Pijnenburg micro-electronics & software: *PCC200 RSA Encryption Device*, 1992.

[QuCo82] J.-J. Quisquater, C. Couvreur, "Fast decipherment algorithm for RSA public-key cryptosystems," *Electronic Letters*, Vol. 18, 1982, pp. 905–907.

[Rab79]   M.O. Rabin, *Digital Signatures and Public Key Functions as Intractable as Factoring*, Technical Memo TM-212, Laboratory of Computer Science, Massachusetts Institute of Technology, 1979.

[RSA78]   R.L. Rivest, A. Shamir and L. Adleman, "A method for obtaining digital signature and public key cryptosystems," *Communications of the ACM*, Vol. 21, 1978, pp. 120–126.

[Wil80]   H.C. Williams, "A Modification of the RSA Public-Key Encryption Procedure," *IEEE Trans. on Information Theory*, Vol. IT–26, No. 6, 1980, pp. 726–729.

Chapter 9

RSA Key Generation

Table of Contents

1   Introduction

This chapter gives an overview of the state-of-the-art of key generation for the RSA public key cryptosystem (see Chapter 7). It contains a minimum of theoretical background, and a maximum of practically oriented information.

The chapter treats RSA key generation by a top-down approach, and ends with a conclusion on which methods are preferable in various situations.

All the definitions and the notation from the RSA-chapter 7 of this report are also used in this chapter. Let us recall the most important symbols. RSA uses the following key data:

Public Key: Modulus n, Public exponent e.
Secret Key: Prime numbers p, q such that $pq = n$. Secret exponent d, such that $ed \equiv 1 \bmod \operatorname{lcm}(p - 1, q - 1)$[1].

The public key operation P is defined by $P(m) = m^e \bmod n$ for any $0 \leq m < n$, while the secret key operation S is defined by $S(c) = c^d \bmod n$ for any $0 \leq c < n$. The choice of e, d ensures that P and S are the inverses of each other.

The primes are not really needed to execute the S-operation, except for some optimized versions of it. Nevertheless, they need to be computed during the key generation phase, in order to correctly generate the rest of the key data.

The chapter is structured as follows: Section 2 describes a generic algorithm for key generation, and Section 3 discusses the security constraints needed to ensure that the RSA key is sufficiently protected against the known attacks. Section 4 then explains different ways of generating primes for use in RSA, probable as well as provable. Section 5 briefly mentions the problem of randomness, and finally Section 6 discusses the cryptographic aspects of the choice of algorithm.

2   High Level Algorithm

This section describes a generic algorithm *keygen* for RSA key generation. We will assume that it is given a public exponent e as input, such that the goal is to generate the rest of the key material to fit e. This is because some applications of RSA need the public exponent to be a constant which is the same for all users. Moreover, one may wish to choose a small public exponent since this makes the P-operation more efficient. We will also assume that *keygen* is given an exact bit length k for the modulus produced, and random seeds s_p, s_q from which the two primes are to be generated.

keygen assumes the existence of two procedures:

- *generateprime*(s, I, e), which returns a random prime p in the interval I, generated from random seed (bit string) s, such that e and $p - 1$ have greatest common divisor 1. The last condition is necessary to ensure that we can

---

[1] $(p - 1)(q - 1)$ could be used instead and results in slightly larger exponents

find a suitable secret exponent. Section 4.1 shows one concrete implementation, *strongprime* and some simpler methods *probprime* and *probprimeinc*. Another alternative is the procedure *hybridprime* from Section 4.3 or methods derived from Section 4.2. Section 6 gives a discussion on the choice of method.

- *inverse*(a, m), which returns a number b, such that $ab \equiv 1 \bmod m$. A standard algorithm for implementing it is an extension of the algorithm for calculating the greatest common divisor *gcd* of two numbers, and can be found in any textbook on numerical algorithms (e.g., [Knu81] and Chapter 10). The *gcd* function will be needed in the implementation of *generateprime*.

The input parameters to *keygen* leave open a choice for the interval in which to generate the primes. The only constraint is that they must multiply together to a number of the right length. For security reasons (see Section 3.1.1 for details) the primes should be of approximately the same bit length. We take a simple approach, and let the lengths of the primes be as close as possible, and ensure simultaneously that the modulus will have exact bit length k.

An example: suppose $k = 512$. Then we will let each prime be of length 256, and choose the interval such that both p and q have the two most significant bits set, i.e., p, q are in the open interval $]2^{254} + 2^{255} \ldots 2^{256}[$. This will ensure that $n = pq$ is in the open interval $]2^{511} \ldots 2^{512}[$, i.e., has bit length exactly 512. Generalizing this, we have the following notation:

$$I_p(k) = \begin{cases}]2^{k/2-1} + 2^{k/2-2} \ldots 2^{k/2}[& \text{if } k \text{ is even} \\ ]2^{(k+1)/2-1} + 2^{(k+1)/2-2} \ldots 2^{(k+1)/2}[& \text{otherwise,} \end{cases}$$

$$I_q(k) = \begin{cases}]2^{k/2-1} + 2^{k/2-2} \ldots 2^{k/2}[& \text{if } k \text{ is even} \\ ]2^{(k-1)/2-1} + 2^{(k-1)/2-2} \ldots 2^{(k-1)/2}[& \text{otherwise.} \end{cases}$$

With this in mind, we can describe the algorithm itself. Below follow subsections explaining how to choose the input parameters:

PROCEDURE KEYGEN(seed s_p, s_q, integer k, exponent e)

output: RSA key set (with public exponent e) consisting of
    n (k bits),
    p, q (about $k/2$ bits each),
    d (k bits)

1. $p := generateprime(s_p, I_p(k), e)$
2. $q := generateprime(s_q, I_q(k), e)$
3. $d := inverse(e, \mathrm{lcm}(p - 1, q - 1))$
4. $n := pq$
5. return n, p, q, d

2.1 Management of Secret Data

Although physical security is not a main subject of this chapter, we point out that some of the data handled by *keygen* are of course to be kept secret, and should be treated accordingly by the implementation.

It is important to realize that this is true, not only for the secret key, i.e., p, q, d, but also for the random seeds s_p, s_q: with knowledge of the seeds, the entire RSA key can be reconstructed. All the numbers s_p, s_q, p, q, d should therefore be treated at the same level of security.

2.2 Choice of Public Exponent *e*

The definition of the secret key implies that e must be an odd number (there is a variant of RSA that uses $e = 2$, the so called Rabin system — see Section 2.5 for a description of the changes needed in the key generation to support this system).

Hence *keygen* should be called with an odd number e as input. It should have at most k bits, but as mentioned above, a small e gives a much more efficient P-operation (but does not affect the time for the S-operation). In general, the time to compute $m^e \bmod n$ is directly proportional to the bit length of e.

There is nothing known to suggest that there is any difference in security between a small e and a randomly chosen one, although it should be mentioned that when using RSA for secrecy with very small values of e, one should not send messages that are numerically extremely small, or send exactly the same message to many different users. No such problems occur with the modes of use suggested in this report.

The smallest possible value of e is of course 3. Another popular value is $e = 2^{16} + 1$. It has only two 1's in its binary representation which makes the square-and-multiply algorithm very efficient for this exponent compared to other 17 bit numbers (see Chapter 10).

2.3 Choice of the Bitlength *k*

The parameter k controls the size of the modulus generated. To attack the key generated, one may try to find p, q from n, i.e., factor the modulus. It is necessary that k is large enough to make this a difficult task. State of the art suggests that $k = 512$ is the absolutely smallest value one should consider. At the other extreme, all experts agree that it is not even remotely possible to factor a 1024-bit number in any foreseeable future. Already 600 bits is way out of reach currently. See Section 3.1.1 for details.

There is a trade-off here between security and performance. In practice, doubling the length of the modulus will make the P and S operations 3-4 times slower in software, and about 2 times slower in hardware.

2.4　Choice of the Seeds s_p, s_q

As mentioned above, the random seeds must be treated as secret data. This also means that they must be hard to predict for an outsider. Therefore one should not rely only on approaches that are good enough in other contexts, like e.g., taking the system time, or using the standard random number generator of the programming language used. It is advisable to take at least some random input from the user, and of course a hardware source of really random bits is preferable, if available.

To prevent an outsider from simply guessing the seeds, they should be at least 64 bits each, but $k/2$ bits each are required to ensure maximal diversity of the primes generated.

2.5　Rabin's RSA Variant

This system works essentially like RSA, except that we use $e = 2$. This means that the E operation maps 4 different inputs to one output, while the D operation reconstructs exactly 1 of these inputs. The problems caused by this can be solved in various ways, and we will not give any details here, but refer to for instance [Wil80].

The most commonly used version of the Rabin system can be described as follows:

Public Key: Modulus n.
Secret Key: Prime numbers p, q such that $pq = n$ and p is congruent to 3 modulo 8, and q is congruent to 7 modulo 8.
　　Secret exponent $d = ((p - 1)(q - 1) + 4)/8$.

The procedures described in the sequel can be made to generate primes suitable for this system, by calling *generateprime* with $e = 1$, and inside this procedure, whenever a number is considered as a candidate prime, discard it immediately, if it is not congruent to 3 modulo 8, respectively 7 modulo 8.

3　Security Constraints

Before we go into the actual algorithms for generating primes, we have to describe some constraints that are necessary in order to ensure that the RSA key we generate will in fact be hard to break with the known algorithms. It should be noted that the example parameters given represent acceptable security today, but that higher values might be needed in the future.

3.1　Precautions against Factoring Algorithms

It is clear that an enemy should not be able to find the prime factors p, q from the RSA modulus n, i.e., it should be hard to factor n. There are a large number of factoring algorithms known, out of which some are particularly efficient against numbers of various special forms. We should make sure that the numbers we generate are not of this kind. The subsections below list the relevant factoring algorithms, and the constraints they imply.

3.1.1   General Factoring Algorithms

These are algorithms that can be used against numbers that do not have properties to make them vulnerable to special methods (see below). The best algorithm of this type is currently the quadratic sieve algorithm. It may eventually be outperformed by a variant known as the number field sieve [LLMP90]. The largest numbers without special properties that can be factored using this type of algorithm are of length about 120 decimal digits. The factorization can be found in about 60 days real time, using a large number of computers in parallel [LeMa90]. It seems likely that the number field sieve algorithm will turn out to be faster than the quadratic sieve for general numbers larger than 120 digits, but at the time of writing, no practical experiments have been completed.

It is generally accepted that the hardest input for such algorithms are randomly chosen numbers with two prime factors of approximately the same size. This is the motivation for letting p and q have the same bit length. It should be mentioned that if $p - q$ is relatively small (less than 2^{75}, say), there is an easy and elementary way of factoring $n = pq$. However, for all the methods described below for prime number generation, the diversity of the primes generated is large enough to make the probability of having such a small $p - q$ completely negligible.

3.1.2   The $p - 1$ and the Elliptic Curve Method

The $p - 1$ method is a factoring method suggested by Pollard, which will work if $p - 1$ has only small prime factors (which is called a "smooth" number), where p is some prime factor in n. Lenstra found a generalization of this method that will work, if one can find a so called elliptic curve over p, whose order is a smooth number. The orders that are possible can be expected to be in the interval $[p - \sqrt{p} \ldots p + \sqrt{p}]$.

Although it is completely infeasible to check all possible orders of elliptic curves for smoothness, it may still be a good idea to pay special attention to smoothness of $p - 1$ since if $p - 1$ is indeed smooth, Pollard's algorithm will be much more efficient than the elliptic curve method, even if we get a smooth order curve for free.

Thus, we should ensure that the p, q generated for RSA are such that none of $p - 1$, $q - 1$ are smooth. More concretely, with the current state of the art, this means that $p - 1$ and $q - 1$ should have at least one prime factor of at least 75 bits. If we look for large enough numbers (about 350-400 bits), a randomly chosen prime will satisfy the condition with very large probability. For smaller numbers, however, a special algorithm is needed.

3.1.3 The Cyclotomic Polynomial Method

This is a factoring method suggested by Bach and Shallit [BaSh89]. It will be efficient if n has a prime factor p, such that a particular function of p produces a smooth number. There are several choices for this function. One possibility is $p+1$, others are $p-1$ and p^2+p+1, and there are many others involving p^2 or larger powers of p.

Out of these possibilities, $p-1$ has already been considered, and those involving p^2 or larger powers can be neglected, because the function values will be much larger than p (at least 512 bits) and will therefore have negligible probability of being smooth.

As far as $p+1$ is concerned, it can be as small as 256 bits in practice, and a random number this size has a small, but non-negligible probability of being smooth. Therefore the RSA key generation should make sure that $p+1$ and $q+1$ are not smooth, at least if the modulus is less than 600-700 bits.

3.2 Precautions against Iterated Encryption

One potential way of breaking RSA without factoring is by repeated encryption, i.e., given ciphertext C, one encrypts C m times to get $P(P(\cdots P(C)\cdots)) = P^m(C)$, for increasing values of m, until we get to a point where for some m, $C = P^m(C)$. Then the corresponding plaintext will in fact be $P^{m-1}(C)$.

For any instance of the RSA system, there is an m with this property. However, it will almost always be the case that m is so large that the attack is infeasible.

If one knows a relatively large prime factor t_p of r_p-1, where r_p is a prime that divides $p-1$ and similar primes t_q, r_q for q, it is possible to check that the value of m is not too small: if the public exponent e satisfies that $e^{(r_p-1)/t_p} \neq 1 \bmod r_p$ and $e^{(r_q-1)/t_q} \neq 1 \bmod r_q$, then m is divisible by both t_p and t_q, so it is at least $t_p t_q$, if $t_p \neq t_q$.

3.3 Summary of Constraints

In summary, we have the following demands to RSA key material of good quality:

1. p, q should be of approximately the same bit length, but $p - q$ must not be less than 2^{75}.
2. $p-1, q-1, p+1, q+1$ should have prime factors respectively r_p, r_q, s_p, s_q, all of which should be of length at least 75 bits.
3. The multiplicative order of e modulo $\mathrm{lcm}(p-1, q-1)$ must be large. This is satisfied if $r_p - 1$ and $r_q - 1$ have prime factors t_p, resp. t_q such that $e^{(r_p-1)/t_p} \neq 1 \bmod r_p$ and $e^{(r_q-1)/t_q} \neq 1 \bmod r_q$; such that $t_p \neq t_q$; and such that $t_p t_q$ is of length at least 75 bits.

Of these constraints, the first part of 1 has been taken care of by the construction of *keygen* above. The second part is satisfied with overwhelming probability, if one uses the methods described below for generating the primes. Of course, one may also check it directly, if absolute certainty is desired.

Conditions 2 and 3 may be taken care of by integrating them in the method for generating p and q. Details will be given below.

4   Generation of Primes

This section explains in detail ways of generating primes for use in RSA-keys. There are several possibilities: One can use numbers generated such that it can only be asserted with some (large) probability that they are primes, one can use numbers generated in such a way that it can be proven that they are primes, or one can combine the two methods in various ways. The following subsections contain technical considerations dealing with these aspects. For a conclusion see Section 6.

4.1   Probable Primes

Probable primes are numbers generated such that we can only assert with some (large) probability that they are primes. Later we will look at other methods that provide absolute certainty, and produce so called provable primes. In practice, however, probable primes are sometimes preferable because they often can be generated more efficiently, and nearly always lead to smaller program sizes than provable primes.

4.1.1   The Rabin Test

The Rabin test is a procedure that is called with an integer n as input. It will test whether n is a prime and will accordingly return "fail" or "pass" as output. As we shall see, the answer is not always correct, but we can gain larger certainty by repeating the test.

rabintest works as follows:

PROCEDURE RABINTEST(integer n)
Output: "fail" or "pass"
1. define h, a by: $n - 1 = a2^h$, and a is odd.
2. choose b uniformly at random from the interval $]1 \ldots n - 1[$
3. $b := b^a \bmod n$
4. if $b = 1$, return(pass)
5. if there is an i, such that $0 \leq i < h$ and $b^{2^i} \bmod n = n - 1$ then
       return(pass)
   else
       return(fail)

The number b is called the "base". Note that the numbers $b^{2^i} \bmod n$ can be computed easily by repeated squaring of b.

The basic facts about this test are:

- If n is a prime, then $rabintest(n) = $ "pass" always.
- If n is a composite, then $rabintest(n) = $ "pass" with probability at most $1/4$.

Note that these basic facts do not necessarily imply that a method for prime number generation using t iterations of the test will have an error probability less than $(1/4)^t$. The error probability depends on the distribution with which candidate primes are chosen. More details are given below.

4.1.2   Uniform Probable Primes

We describe here one possible procedure, *probprime*, for generating a random prime number in an interval. To facilitate the description of procedures later in this report, we also give *probprime* the ability to ensure that the prime p generated satisfies that some given integer v divides $p-1$ and that p can be used with a given public exponent e, i.e., $gcd(p-1, e) = 1$. A totally random prime is obtained by setting $e = v = 1$.

It assumes the existence of the procedure *randomchoice*, which is called with an interval I as input and returns a random odd number chosen from I. We will return later to how this procedure will be realized in practice (see Section 5).

Also, a table is assumed that contains all odd primes less than some upper limit r, where r is a constant chosen once and for all. Since dividing a candidate number by a small prime is much faster than doing a Rabin test, the overall time to find a prime will be smaller, if we subject candidates to the Rabin test only if they are not divisible by the small primes in the table. Maurer [Mau89] has shown that the optimal value of r is R/D, where R is the time needed to do one Rabin test, and D is the time needed to divide a candidate prime number by one prime less than r.

Finally, we assume a function *gcd* for computing the greatest common divisor of two integers. The algorithm can be found in e.g., [Knu81] and in Chapter 10. If I is the interval $[a \ldots b]$, we let cI denote the interval $[ca \ldots cb]$.

The procedure guarantees that if *randomchoice* returns uniformly distributed numbers, and $v = e = 1$ then the primes produced by *probprime* will be uniformly distributed in the interval specified as input.

PROCEDURE PROBPRIME(interval I, divisor v, exponent e)

Output: a probable prime number p chosen at random from I, such that $p-1$ is divisible by v and $gcd(p-1, e) = 1$. Remark that $gcd(v, e)$ must be 1 in order for such a prime p to exist.

1. $n := 2v \cdot randomchoice(1/(2v)I) + 1$
2. if n is divisible by a prime less than r, or $gcd(n-1, e) \neq 1$, go to 1.
3. for $count = 1 \ldots t$ do:
      if $rabintest(n) = $ "fail" go to 1
4. return(n)

In [DLP93], the probability that this procedure outputs a composite number is analyzed, in the cases where the interval specified is of the form $[2^{k-1} \ldots 2^k]$ for some k, and $e = v = 1$. Upper bounds for the probability are given in Table 1. The numbers given are $-\log_2$ of the bound for the probability. For example, if we look for 250-bit primes and use $t = 6$, the error probability is less than 2^{-60}.

$k \backslash t$	1	2	3	4	5	6	7	8	9	10
100	5	14	20	25	29	33	36	39	41	44
150	8	20	28	34	39	43	47	51	54	57
200	11	25	34	41	47	52	57	61	65	69
250	14	29	39	47	54	60	65	70	75	79
300	19	33	44	53	60	67	73	78	83	88
400	37	46	55	63	72	80	87	93	99	105
500	56	63	70	78	85	92	99	106	113	119
600	75	82	88	95	102	108	115	121	127	133

Table 1. $-\log_2$ of the bound on the error probability of *probprime*, with $e = v = 1$.

4.1.3   Incremental Search

An alternative to *probprime*, which is more economical in its use of random bits, is to choose at random only some odd starting point n_0, and then do an incremental search for the smallest prime larger than n_0, i.e., we look at $n_0, n_0 + 2, \ldots$.

If we want the same enhancement as for *probprime*, i.e., ensuring that the result minus 1 is divisible by a given v, we make sure that $n_0 - 1$ is divisible by v, and examine $n_0, n_0 + 2v, \ldots$.

One advantage of this approach is that the testdivision by small primes can be done much more efficiently: first compute the residue of n_0 modulo each small prime in the table. Each time we add $2v$ to the current current candidate, add $2v$ to each residue modulo the small primes, and test that no residue becomes 0. In [BDL91] it is shown that the optimal limit r for the small primes in this case is $r = \frac{R}{D \cdot log(R/D)}$.

We have the following implementation of this idea:

PROCEDURE PROBPRIMEINC(interval I, divisor v, exponent e)

Output: a probable prime number p chosen at random from I by incremental search, such that v divides $p - 1$ and $gcd(p - 1, e) = 1$. Remark that $gcd(v, e)$ must be 1 in order for such a prime p to exist.

1. $n := 2v \cdot randomchoice(1/(2v)I) + 1$, initialize testdivision.

2. $n := n + 2v$, if n is now not in I, go to 1.
3. if n is divisible by a prime less than r (use optimized test division),
   or $gcd(n - 1, e) \neq 1$, go to 2.
4. for $count = 1 \ldots t$ do:
      if $rabintest(n) =$ "fail" go to 2.
5. return(n).

In [BrDa92], it is shown that if one accepts an upper limit on the number of candidates to be examined (and therefore a small probability that the algorithm fails altogether), one can estimate the error probability of *probprimeinc* in the case where $v = e = 1$. One takes the numbers in Table 2 as the point of departure. If the maximal number of candidates is $c \cdot log(2^k)$, then almost all numbers in the table should be decreased by $log(c^2)$, except those in the upper left corner, which are decreased by less (see [BrDa92] for more details). The algorithm will fail with probability $exp(-2c)$.

$k \backslash t$	1	2	3	4	5	6	7	8	9	10
100	0	7	13	18	22	26	29	32	34	36
150	3	12	20	26	31	35	39	43	46	49
200	5	17	25	33	39	44	49	53	57	61
250	7	21	31	39	45	51	57	62	66	70
300	9	24	35	44	51	58	64	70	75	79
400	13	31	44	54	63	70	77	84	90	95
500	17	37	51	63	72	81	89	96	103	110
600	20	42	58	70	81	91	100	108	115	123

Table 2. $-\log_2$ of the bound on the error probability of *probprimeinc*, when the maximal number of candidates is $\log(2^k)$ and $e = v = 1$.

4.1.4   Satisfying Security Constraints

In this section, we will discuss ways to ensure that the primes we produce will satisfy constraints 2 and 3 mentioned in Section 3.3.

To fix some notation, let p be the prime to be produced, such that r divides $p - 1$, s divides $p + 1$, and t divides $r - 1$, where r, s, t are prime numbers.

We show here a variant of an algorithm of Gordon [Gor84], which works by first constructing t, s from scratch, then r from t, and finally p from r, s [Gan90].

If I is the interval $[a \ldots b]$, we let $\sqrt{I}$ denote the interval $[\sqrt{a} \ldots \sqrt{b}]$.

We assume the existence of a procedure *initrand*, which will initialize a scheme for generation of random or nearly random bits (see Section 5), using a random seed which is passed as a parameter. All subsequent calls to *randomchoice* will refer to the seed used with *initrand*.

A concrete implementation will have to choose fixed functions c_1, c_2 which are used in the procedure *strongprime* to control the size of the prime factors generated for $p \pm 1$ and $r - 1$. Below we discuss how to choose these functions.

PROCEDURE STRONGPRIME(seed se, interval I, exponent e)

Output: a prime p chosen at random from interval I based on seed s, such that it can be used in RSA with public exponent e. Security conditions from Section 3.3 are satisfied.

1. $initrand(se)$
2. $t := probprime(c_1(I)\sqrt{I}, 1, 1)$
3. $s := probprime(c_2(I)\sqrt{I}, 1, 1)$
4. $r := probprime(c_2(I)\sqrt{I}, t, 1)$
5. $p_0 := 2s \cdot inverse(s, r) - 1$
6. Search through numbers of the form $p = 2krs + p_0$, k chosen such that p is in I and $gcd(p - 1, e) = 1$, until p is probably prime.
7. $return(p)$.

When the interval I is $[a \ldots b]$, one possible choice for the functions c_1, c_2 is

$$c_1(I) = \frac{1}{2 \cdot bitlength(a)}, \quad c_2(I) = \frac{1}{2 \cdot bitlength(\sqrt{a})}$$

This choice allows the maximum possible size of r, s, t such that we still have a good chance of finding a prime in the interval I with the right properties. At the other extreme, one can replace the constant 2 in the formulas for c_1, c_2 by a larger number, chosen such that r, s, t will be of the minimum required size (see Section 3.3). This will give a larger number of primes to choose from in the interval I.

An even more advanced idea is to choose c_1, c_2 at random between the two extremes each time these values are needed. This will make it possible to generate virtually every existing prime that satisfies the security constraints.

If absolute certainty that demand 3 of Section 3.3 is satisfied is required, one directly test it after step 4 of the above algorithm.

The calls to *probprime* in the procedure may of course be replaced by calls to *probprimeinc*, which will give an efficiency improvement.

4.2   Provable Primes

Provable primes are numbers generated in such a way that one can prove with certainty that they are primes. Even though primality tests that always give correct answers are quite complicated and inefficient, it is possible to generate provable primes quite efficiently. The reason for this is that when we generate a number from scratch, we may know some side information which can help us in proving the number to be prime.

4.2.1   Maurer's Algorithm

Maurer [Mau89] has proposed a recursive algorithm for generating provable primes, based on the following number theoretic result by Pocklington:

Let $n - 1 := FR$, and let $q_1, \ldots q_t$ be the distinct prime factors of F. Suppose there exists a number a such that

$$a^{n-1} \equiv 1 \bmod n$$

and for all $i = 1 \ldots t$,

$$gcd(a^{(n-1)/q_i} - 1, n) = 1,$$

then if $F > \sqrt{n}$, n is a prime.

This suggests a straightforward algorithm for generating a random prime in some interval $[low \ldots high]$: first generate recursively $q_1, q_2, \ldots$, where $q_1 \geq q_2 \geq \ldots$. This goes on until F, the product of the q's is larger than $\sqrt{high}$. Then choose random even R-values such that $n = FR + 1$ is in $[low \ldots high]$, until an n-value can be proven prime.

Maurer shows that if the q's are large, nearly any choice of a will suffice for proving primality of n (provided n really is prime!), so we are not likely to miss any primes, even if we only try once for each candidate. Furthermore, it is shown that if the number e is used to prove primality of the prime factors of $p - 1$ and $q - 1$, then the resulting RSA system with e as public exponent will not be easy to break by repeated encryption.

If the goal is to generate a prime uniformly chosen from the interval, then we should know something about the distribution of the prime factors of $n - 1$, in particular about the distribution of their sizes. Fortunately, the distribution of the size of the largest prime factor of a number is well known. More precisely, for large N, one can compute $\rho(\alpha)$, the fraction of numbers x less than N whose largest prime factor is less than $x^{1/\alpha}$. In Table 3, sample values of this function are given. From heuristic arguments, this distribution function seems to be applicable as well, if we add the condition that the number we are looking at is a prime minus 1.

Finally, we note that by the recursive nature of the algorithm, it is of course necessary to have some lower limit for the primes generated, below which one generates a prime, simply by exhaustive search and test division.

4.2.2   Various Tricks for Optimization

What can be done to speed up this algorithm? First of all, we should of course use test division by small primes on a candidate before going into expensive exponentiations. Maurer suggests that since all candidates are of the form $n = FR + 1$ for fixed F, one can translate the condition that none of the small primes divide n into a condition on R. This will be faster to check, since R is usually much smaller than n (and certainly less than $\sqrt{n}$). More concretely, if

α	$\rho(\alpha)$
1.5	0.59453 48919
2.0	0.30685 28194
2.5	0.13031 95618
3.0	0.04860 83883
3.5	0.01622 95932
4.0	0.00491 09256
4.5	0.00137 01177
5.0	0.00035 47247
6.0	0.00001 96497
7.0	0.00000 08746
8.0	0.00000 00323
9.0	0.00000 00010

Table 3. Distribution of the largest prime factor.

$n = FR + 1 \equiv 0 \bmod p$, then $R \equiv -F^{-1} \bmod p$. So we can precompute $-F^{-1}$ modulo each small prime used for test division, and for every candidate check for each p if R has residue $-F^{-1} \bmod p$.

Furthermore, even if a candidate passes the test division, there is no need to try immediately proving that it is prime. A better approach is to do a Rabin test with base 2 (see Section 4.1.1). Base 2 gives the most efficient Rabin test possible. Like any other base, it will exclude no prime, and from practical experience, it will exclude virtually all composites (this is also supported by theoretical results [Pom81]). If n passes this test, we have implicitly checked that $2^{n-1} \equiv 1 \bmod n$. It is therefore advantageous to use Pocklington's result with $a = 2$, since we have then already checked the first condition.

A final optimization concerns Pocklington's result, which has been improved by Brillhart, Lehmer and Selfridge [BLS75]:

> Given $n = FR + 1$, suppose we have an a that satisfies the conditions of Pocklington. Let R' be the odd part in the factorization of R, and $F' = (n-1)/R'$. Let r, s be defined by $R' = 2F's + r$, where $1 \leq r < 2F'$. Suppose $F' > \sqrt[3]{n}$. Then n is prime if and only if $s = 0$ or $r^2 - 8s$ is not a square.

This refined condition is slightly more computationally costly to verify. However, this makes little difference in practice, at least if we look at the variation using the Rabin test. For this variation, experience shows that the above result will only be used on the final candidate, and the extra computation required is only some trivial manipulations to find F', R', s, r, and perhaps a square root computation, which takes time negligible compared to the exponentiations.

Furthermore, the distribution of the largest prime factor shows that only 5% of the numbers x are expected to have all prime factors less than $x^{1/3}$. We suggest that we can easily live without these 5%, in which case we never have to generate more than one prime factor of $n - 1$. This will simplify the code and save time compared to Maurer's original version for the approximately 30% of the numbers that have their largest prime factor less than $x^{1/2}$. It will, however, bias the distribution of the primes generated slightly, compared to the uniform distribution over the primes. This is not a problem for application to RSA, though, since the modification will tend to generate primes p with larger prime factors of $p - 1$.

4.2.3   Satisfying Security Constraints

Of the conditions in Section 3.3, the ones on $p - 1$ and $r_p - 1$ are very easy to ensure with Maurer's algorithm: one simply sets up a lower limit for the size of q_1, the largest prime factor of the candidate prime minus 1. This limit may be set to, e.g., 75 and 40 bits on the first, respectively second level of recursion. In addition, one should use $a = e$ when proving primality of r_p, since this will automatically mean that demand 3 is satisfied.

The condition on $p + 1$, can be solved similarly as for probable primes (once again, our target is a prime in the interval $[low \dots high]$):

1. Using Maurer's algorithm, generate primes r, s of at least 75 bits, such that $r > \sqrt[3]{high}$.
2. Using the same method as in the *strongprime* procedure, find an odd p_0, such that $p_0 \equiv 1 \mod r$ and $p_0 \equiv -1 \mod s$.
3. Choose random values of L in some appropriate interval, until a number of the form $p = 2Lrs + p_0$ can be proved prime by Maurer's method (or based on the improvement by Brillhart, Lehmer and Selfridge).

p_0 is likely to have about the same bit length as rs, so since s must be of length at least 75 bits, this means that r can be of length at most $length(p_0) - 75$. This introduces a slight deviation from the uniformity of primes otherwise produced by Maurer's method. Table 3 indicates that for 256 bit primes and a 75 bit s, we loose at most 20% of the primes this way.

4.3   A Hybrid Method

It is possible to combine the provable and the probable method. Using the notation from the *strongprime* procedure, this works roughly as follows:

PROCEDURE HYBRIDPRIME(seed se, interval I, exponent e)

Output: a prime p chosen at random from interval I based on seed s, such that it can be used in RSA with public exponent e. Security conditions from Section 3.3 are satisfied.

1. *initrand(se)*
2. $t := probprime(c_1(I)\sqrt{I}, 1, 1)$
3. $s := probprime(c_2(I)\sqrt{I}, 1, 1)$

4. Search through numbers of the form $r = 2kt+1$, k chosen such that r is in $c_2(I)\sqrt{I}$, until r can be proved prime using Pocklington's result, with $F = t$ and $a = e$.

5. $p_0 := 2s \cdot inverse(s, r) - 1$

6. Search through numbers of the form $p = 2krs + p_0$, k chosen such that p is in I and $gcd(p-1, e) = 1$, until p can be proved prime using (the improvement of) Pocklington's result, with $F = r$.

7. return(p).

This procedure is constructed such that IF t is prime then r and p MUST be primes. Thus, we only have to worry about the error probability when generating t and s. Since these primes are generated "from scratch", the estimates for the error probability given earlier will apply directly. Moreover, this method will be faster than Maurer's method, since we can get rid of all of the recursion below the level of t. It is also faster than *strongprime* because we do not have to do many Rabin tests on r and p, in particular all the tricks for speedup of Maurer's algorithm apply here.

Finally, note that by using $a = e$ when proving primality of r, we have implicitly checked that the condition on iterated encryption is satisfied: the multiplicative order of e, i.e., the number of encryptions needed to reconstruct the plaintext, is at least divisible by t.

5   Generation of Pseudorandom Bits

If a hardware source of randomness is not available (which will be the case in many environments), it is likely that only a very limited number of random bits will be at our disposal: for example, there is a limit to how many random characters we can ask a user to type.

What is needed in this situation is a method that will take a short random bit string and stretch it to a much longer string that is SEEMINGLY random, e.g., for any practical purpose, it is as good as a really random string.

An example: suppose we have a strong encryption algorithm E, where $E_K(M)$ denotes encryption of M under key K. Then the procedure *initrand* would interpret its input as a pair of plaintext, key M, K and store this in a fixed memory location. Later, the procedure *randomchoice* could obtain a seemingly random bit string of any length by computing $E_K(M), E_K(E_K(M)), \ldots$.

Many variations on this theme are possible. Also, good methods exist that use modular arithmetic [MiSc91].

6   Conclusion, Choice of Algorithm

From a cryptographic point of view, there is not much practical reason for using provable primes rather than probable ones. Any application will rely on secrecy of a number of keys. There is always a non-zero probability that these keys are guessed by an enemy, so removing error-probability from the prime generation will never remove all error probabilities from the system.

Hence the question rather is whether one can efficiently bring down the error probability to an acceptable level. We have seen that for the Rabin test, only a small number (less than 5) tests are enough to get a probability that is comparable to the probability of guessing e.g., a random DES key.

Taking this to be an acceptable error probability, probable primes tend to be a bit faster than provable ones. Moreover, in applications where only a small amount of storage for program and data is available, probable primes have a distinct advantage: the Rabin test is simple enough to make a very compact implementation possible.

However, as we have seen in Section 4.3, the methods that provable primes are based on can still be very useful.

Finally, we discuss the security constraints: the (rather complicated) methods described by *strongprime* and *hybridprime* are necessary if we want to check with certainty that the constraints are satisfied. This is motivated by the fact that for primes of less than 300-400 bits, there is some nonnegligible (but small) probability that a random prime will not satisfy the constraints (see Table 3). With increasing size of primes, this probability rapidly becomes completely negligible, however. Therefore, a much simpler solution than *strongprime*, for example a single call to *probprime*, can safely be used for primes above 300-400 bits. For smaller primes, the simple solution may still be used, if one is prepared to take a small risk that one of the primes does not quite satisfy the demands. Depending on the application, this may be acceptable. However, it should be noted that, independently of the security considerations, there is an efficiency benefit in building a large prime p from factor(s) of $p-1$, similarly to what is done in *hybridprime*.

References

[BaSh89] E. Bach and J. Shallit, "Factoring with cyclotomic polynomials," *Mathematics of Computation*, Vol. 52, 1989, pp. 201–219.

[BDL91] J. Brandt, I.B. Damgård and P. Landrock, "Speeding up prime number generation," *Advances in Cryptology, Proc. Asiacrypt'91, LNCS 739*, H. Imai, R. Rivest, and T. Matsumoto, Eds., Springer-Verlag, 1993, pp. 440–449.

[BrDa92] J. Brandt and I.B. Damgård, "On generation of probable primes by incremental search," *Advances in Cryptology, Proc. Crypto'92, LNCS 740*, E.F. Brickell, Ed., Springer-Verlag, 1993, pp. 358–369.

[BLS75] J. Brillhart, D.H. Lehmer and J.L. Selfridge, "New primality criteria and factorizations of $2^m \pm 1$," *Mathematics of Computation*, Vol. 29, 1975, pp. 620–647.

[DLP93] I.B. Damgård, P. Landrock and C. Pomerance, "Average case error estimates for the strong probable prime test," *Mathematics of Computation*, Vol. 61, 1993, pp. 177–194.

[Gan90] M.J. Ganley, "Note on the generation of p_0 for RSA keysets," *Electronic Letters*, Vol. 26, No. 6, 1990, p. 369.

[Gor84] J. Gordon, "Strong primes are easy to find," *Advances in Cryptology, Proc. Eurocrypt'84, LNCS 209*, N. Cot, T. Beth, and I. Ingemarsson, Eds., Springer-Verlag, 1985, pp. 216–223.

[Knu81] D.E. Knuth, *The Art of Computer Programming, Vol. 2: Seminumerical Algorithms, 2nd Edition*, Addison-Wesley, Reading Mass., 1981.

[LeMa90] A.K. Lenstra and M.S. Manasse, "Factoring with two large primes," *Advances in Cryptology, Proc. Eurocrypt'90, LNCS 473*, I.B. Damgård, Ed., Springer-Verlag, 1991, pp. 72–82.

[LLMP90] A.K. Lenstra, H.W. Lenstra, Jr., M.S. Manasse and J.M. Pollard, "The number field sieve," *Proc. 22nd ACM Symp. Theory of Computing*, 1990, pp. 464–572.

[Mau89] U.M. Maurer, "Fast generation of secure RSA-products with almost maximal diversity," *Advances in Cryptology, Proc. Eurocrypt'89, LNCS 434*, J.-J. Quisquater and J. Vandewalle, Eds., Springer-Verlag, 1990, pp. 636–647.

[MiSc91] S. Micali and C.P. Schnorr, "Efficient perfect polynomial random number generators," *Journal of Cryptology*, Vol. 3, No. 3, 1991, pp. 157–172.

[Pom81] C. Pomerance, "On the distribution of pseudoprimes," *Mathematics of Computation*, Vol. 37, 1981, pp. 587–593.

[Wil80] H.C. Williams, "A Modification of the RSA Public-Key Encryption Procedure," *IEEE Trans. on Information Theory*, Vol. IT–26, No. 6, 1980, pp. 726–729.

Chapter 10

Implementation Guidelines for Arithmetic Computation

Table of Contents

1 Introduction

The integrity primitives IBC-hash (Chapter 5), RSA (Chapter 7), and COMSET (Chapter 8) are based on calculations with large integers. The implementation of such calculations is non-trivial, as the size of the numbers used is significantly larger than the word-size of computers. Therefore, this chapter gives some introductory guidelines for software implementation of large integer arithmetic. For more detailed information the interested reader is referred to [Knu81].

2 Elementary Operations

For operations on large unsigned integers a representation in radix b notation is used, where b can be in principle any integer ≥ 2. That is, an arbitrary nonnegative integer x is represented as a sequence of radix b digits $\langle x_0, x_1, \ldots, x_{k-1} \rangle$, where

$$x = \sum_{i=0}^{k-1} x_i b^i, \quad 0 \leq x_i < b \quad \text{for } i = 0, 1, \ldots, k-1.$$

The best choice for b will be determined by the computer, the programming language, and the compiler that is used. Normally b will be one of the available integer types. Since most computers nowadays are binary computers, the radix will be a power of 2 rather than of 10.

The addition, subtraction, multiplication, and division of large integers can be implemented according to the classical algorithms familiar from pencil-and-paper calculations [Knu81, Algorithms 4.3.1A, 4.3.1S, 4.3.1M, and 4.3.1D, respectively]. Whereas the performance of the classical algorithms is good in the case of addition and subtraction, one can do much better for multiplication and division. Fast algorithms are e.g., described in [Knu81, Section 4.3.3].

As an example the classical algorithm for the division of an l-digit dividend $x = \sum_{i=0}^{l-1} x_i b^i$ by the k-digit divisor $m = \sum_{i=0}^{k-1} m_i b^i$ is given. The quotient $\lfloor x/m \rfloor$ is returned in $q = \sum_{i=0}^{l-k} q_i b^i$, and the dividend x is replaced by the remainder $x \bmod m$. This algorithm is a formalization of the ordinary $l - k$ step pencil-and-paper method, each step of which is the division of a $(k+1)$-digit integer z by the k-digit divisor m, yielding the one-digit quotient q_i and the k-digit remainder r_i. Each remainder r_i is less than m, so that it can be combined with the next digit of the dividend into the $(k+1)$-digit number $r_i b + $ (next digit of dividend) to be used as the new z in the next step.

The formalization by D. Knuth [Knu81, Algorithm 4.3.1D] consists in estimating the quotient digits q_i as accurately as possible. Dividing the two most significant digits of z by m_{k-1} will result in an estimate that is never too small and, if $m_{k-1} \geq \lfloor \frac{b}{2} \rfloor$, at most two in error. Using an additional digit of both z and m (i.e., using the three most significant digits of z and the two most significant digits of m) this estimate can be made almost always correct, and at most one in error (an event occurring with probability $\approx 2/b$). The pseudocode of this algorithm is given in Algorithm 1.

```
if (x > mb^{l-k}) then {
    x := x - mb^{l-k};
    q_{l-k} := 1;
}
else
    q_{l-k} := 0;
for i := l - 1 downto k - 1 do {
    if (x_i = m_{k-1}) then
        q̂ := b - 1;
    else
        q̂ := (x_i b + x_{i-1}) div m_{k-1};
    while (q̂(m_{k-1} b + m_{k-2}) > x_i b^2 + x_{i-1} b + x_{i-2}) do
        q̂ := q̂ - 1;
    x := x - q̂ m b^{i-k};
    if (x < 0) then {
        x := x + mb^{i-k};
        q̂ := q̂ - 1;
    }
    q_{i-k} := q̂;
}
```

Algorithm 1. Classical division algorithm ($m_{k-1} \geq \lfloor \frac{b}{2} \rfloor$)

3   Modular Computations

Modular addition, subtraction, and multiplication can be implemented using the non-modular operations described above, followed by a modular reduction. For modular addition and subtraction this modular reduction consists of adding or subtracting the modulus. The result of a modular multiplication can be determined as the remainder when dividing the non-modular product of the multiplicands by the modulus.

Modular reduction for general arguments is most efficiently implemented as a division by the modulus, where only the remainder is returned. In [Bar86, Mon85] faster modular reduction algorithms using precomputations are given, where the arguments are limited in length to twice the modulus' length. The latter algorithm has the advantage that it can be combined with multiplication: the modulo reduction is started on intermediate results of the multiplication. A software library for digital signal processors incorporating these techniques is described in [DuKa90]. A comparison of the three modular reduction algorithms mentioned and their application in modular exponentiations is given in [BGV93].

An efficient implementation of modular exponentiation $a^e \bmod n$ will take the following two observations into account:

- To keep intermediate results small they are reduced modulo n whenever possible. That is, $a^e \bmod n$ is not computed by first calculating a^e and subsequently reducing the result modulo n. Instead, intermediate results (mostly of multiplications) are immediately reduced modulo n, so that they never exceed n^2.
- At most $2s$ (modular) multiplications are needed for the computation of $a^e \bmod n$, where s is the bit length of the exponent $e = \sum_{i=0}^{s-1} e_i 2^i$.

The most elementary but quite efficient way to do modular exponentiation is the binary *square and multiply algorithm* (see [Knu81, Section 4.6.3], where also an m-ary generalization of this algorithm is given). The pseudocode of the binary version is given in Algorithm 2. On return Y is equal to $a^e \bmod n$. Improvements using addition chain and vector addition chain techniques are e.g., described in [BoCo89, BGMW92, YL92].

```
Y := 1;
Z := a;
for i := (s - 1) downto 0 do {
    if (e_i = 1) then
        Y := Z * Y mod n;
    Z := Z^2 mod n;
}
```

Algorithm 2. Binary square and multiply algorithm

4   Greatest Common Divisor and Modular Inverses

The extended Euclidean algorithm ([Knu81, Algorithm 4.5.2X]) can be used for calculating the greatest common divisor of two nonnegative integers as well as modular inverses. Given two nonnegative integers u and v this algorithm determines values u_1, u_2, and u_3 such that u_3 is the greatest common divisor of u and v and such that $u_3 = uu_1 + vu_2$. The pseudocode of this algorithm is given in Algorithm 3. u is invertible modulo v if and only if $u_3 = 1$. In this case $1 \equiv uu_1 \pmod{v}$, and hence u_1 is the inverse of u modulo v.

5   Jacobi Symbol

Algorithm 4 calculates the value of the Jacobi symbol $\left(\frac{a}{b}\right)$ of two integers a and b. This is needed for the Rabin variant of RSA described in Chapter 7.

```
(u₁, u₂, u₃) := (1, 0, u);
(v₁, v₂, v₃) := (0, 1, v);
while (v₃ > 0) do {
    q := u₃ div v₃;
    (t₁, t₂, t₃) := (u₁, u₂, u₃) − q(v₁, v₂, v₃);
    (u₁, u₂, u₃) := (v₁, v₂, v₃);
    (v₁, v₂, v₃) := (t₁, t₂, t₃);
}
```

Algorithm 3. Extended Euclidean algorithm

The mathematical background may e.g., be found in [Kob87] for the Jacobi symbol and in [Sim92, Appendix J of Chapter 4] for the algorithm. On return of Algorithm 4 J is equal to $\left(\frac{a}{b}\right)$. s represents an auxiliary storage variable.

```
J := 1;
while (a > 1) do {
    if (a mod 2 = 0) then {
        if ((b² − 1)/8 mod 2 = 1) then
            J := −J;
        a := a/2;
    }
    else {
        if ((a − 1) · (b − 1)/4 mod 2 = 1) then
            J := −J;
        s := b mod a;
        b := a;
        a := s;
    }
}
if (a = 0) then
    J := 0;
```

Algorithm 4. Jacobi symbol

References

[Bar86]   P. Barrett, "Implementing the Rivest Shamir Adleman public key encryption algorithm on a standard digital signal processor," *Advances in Cryptology, Proc. Crypto'86, LNCS 263*, A.M. Odlyzko, Ed., Springer-Verlag, 1987, pp. 311–323.

[BoCo89]   J. Bos and M. Coster, "Addition chain heuristics," *Advances in Cryptology, Proc. Crypto'89, LNCS 435*, G. Brassard, Ed., Springer-Verlag, 1990, pp. 400–407.

[BGV93]   A. Bosselaers, R. Govaerts, and J. Vandewalle, "Comparison of three modular reduction functions," *Advances in Cryptology, Proc. Crypto'93, LNCS 773*, D.R. Stinson, Ed., Springer-Verlag, 1994, pp. 175–186.

[BGMW92]   E.F. Brickell, D.M. Gordon, K.S. McCurley, and D.B. Wilson, "Fast exponentiation with precomputations (extended abstract)," *Advances in Cryptology, Proc. Eurocrypt'92, LNCS 658*, R.A. Rueppel, Ed., Springer-Verlag, 1993, pp. 200–207.

[DuKa90]   S.R. Dussé and B.R. Kaliski Jr., "A cryptographic library for the Motorola DSP 56000," *Advances in Cryptology, Proc. Eurocrypt'90, LNCS 473*, I.B. Damgård, Ed., Springer-Verlag, 1991, pp. 230–244.

[Knu81]   D.E. Knuth, *The Art of Computer Programming, Vol. 2: Seminumerical Algorithms, 2nd Edition*, Addison-Wesley, Reading Mass., 1981.

[Kob87]   N. Koblitz, *A Course in Number Theory and Cryptography*, Springer-Verlag, Berlin-Heidelberg-New York, 1987.

[Mon85]   P.L. Montgomery, "Modular multiplication without trial division," *Mathematics of Computation*, Vol. 44, 1985, pp. 519–521.

[Sim92]   G.J. Simmons, Ed., *Contemporary Cryptology: The Science of Information Integrity*, IEEE Press, Piscataway, N.J., 1992.

[YL92]   S.-M. Yen and C.-S. Laih, "The fast cascade exponentiation algorithm and its applications on cryptography," *Advances in Cryptology, Proc. Auscrypt'92, LNCS 718*, J. Seberry and Y. Zheng, Eds., Springer-Verlag, 1993, pp. 447–458.

Springer-Verlag
and the Environment

We at Springer-Verlag firmly believe that an international science publisher has a special obligation to the environment, and our corporate policies consistently reflect this conviction.

We also expect our business partners – paper mills, printers, packaging manufacturers, etc. – to commit themselves to using environmentally friendly materials and production processes.

The paper in this book is made from low- or no-chlorine pulp and is acid free, in conformance with international standards for paper permanency.

Lecture Notes in Computer Science

For information about Vols. 1–945

please contact your bookseller or Springer-Verlag

Vol. 981: I. Wachsmuth, C.-R. Rollinger, W. Brauer (Eds.), KI-95: Advances in Artificial Intelligence. Proceedings, 1995. XII, 269 pages. (Subseries LNAI).

Vol. 982: S. Doaitse Swierstra, M. Hermenegildo (Eds.), Programming Languages: Implementations, Logics and Programs. Proceedings, 1995. XI, 467 pages. 1995.

Vol. 983: A. Mycroft (Ed.), Static Analysis. Proceedings, 1995. VIII, 423 pages. 1995.

Vol. 984: J.-M. Haton, M. Keane, M. Manago (Eds.), Advances in Case-Based Reasoning. Proceedings, 1994. VIII, 307 pages. 1995.

Vol. 985: T. Sellis (Ed.), Rules in Database Systems. Proceedings, 1995. VIII, 373 pages. 1995.

Vol. 986: Henry G. Baker (Ed.), Memory Management. Proceedings, 1995. XII, 417 pages. 1995.

Vol. 987: P.E. Camurati, H. Eveking (Eds.), Correct Hardware Design and Verification Methods. Proceedings, 1995. VIII, 342 pages. 1995.

Vol. 988: A.U. Frank, W. Kuhn (Eds.), Spatial Information Theory. Proceedings, 1995. XIII, 571 pages. 1995.

Vol. 989: W. Schäfer, P. Botella (Eds.), Software Engineering — ESEC '95. Proceedings, 1995. XII, 519 pages. 1995.

Vol. 990: C. Pinto-Ferreira, N.J. Mamede (Eds.), Progress in Artificial Intelligence. Proceedings, 1995. XIV, 487 pages. 1995. (Subseries LNAI).

Vol. 991: J. Wainer, A. Carvalho (Eds.), Advances in Artificial Intelligence. Proceedings, 1995. XII, 342 pages. 1995. (Subseries LNAI).

Vol. 992: M. Gori, G. Soda (Eds.), Topics in Artificial Intelligence. Proceedings, 1995. XII, 451 pages. 1995. (Subseries LNAI).

Vol. 993: T.C. Fogarty (Ed.), Evolutionary Computing. Proceedings, 1995. VIII, 264 pages. 1995.

Vol. 994: M. Hebert, J. Ponce, T. Boult, A. Gross (Eds.), Object Representation in Computer Vision. Proceedings, 1994. VIII, 359 pages. 1995.

Vol. 995: S.M. Müller, W.J. Paul, The Complexity of Simple Computer Architectures. XII, 270 pages. 1995.

Vol. 996: P. Dybjer, B. Nordström, J. Smith (Eds.), Types for Proofs and Programs. Proceedings, 1994. X, 202 pages. 1995.

Vol. 997: K.P. Jantke, T. Shinohara, T. Zeugmann (Eds.), Algorithmic Learning Theory. Proceedings, 1995. XV, 319 pages. 1995.

Vol. 998: A. Clarke, M. Campolargo, N. Karatzas (Eds.), Bringing Telecommunication Services to the People – IS&N '95. Proceedings, 1995. XII, 510 pages. 1995.

Vol. 999: P. Antsaklis, W. Kohn, A. Nerode, S. Sastry (Eds.), Hybrid Systems II. VIII, 569 pages. 1995.

Vol. 1000: J. van Leeuwen (Ed.), Computer Science Today. XIV, 643 pages. 1995.

Vol. 1002: J.J. Kistler, Disconnected Operation in a Distributed File System. XIX, 249 pages. 1995.

Vol. 1004: J. Staples, P. Eades, N. Katoh, A. Moffat (Eds.), Algorithms and Computation. Proceedings, 1995. XV, 440 pages. 1995.

Vol. 1005: J. Estublier (Ed.), Software Configuration Management. Proceedings, 1995. IX, 311 pages. 1995.

Vol. 1006: S. Bhalla (Ed.), Information Systems and Data Management. Proceedings, 1995. IX, 321 pages. 1995.

Vol. 1007: A. Bosselaers, B. Preneel (Eds.), Integrity Primitives for Secure Information Systems. VII, 239 pages. 1995.

Vol. 1008: B. Preneel (Ed.), Fast Software Encryption. Proceedings, 1994. VIII, 367 pages. 1995.

Vol. 1009: M. Broy, S. Jähnichen (Eds.), KORSO: Methods, Languages, and Tools for the Construction of Correct Software. X, 449 pages. 1995. Vol.

Vol. 1010: M. Veloso, A. Aamodt (Eds.), Case-Based Reasoning Research and Development. Proceedings, 1995. X, 576 pages. 1995. (Subseries LNAI).

Vol. 1011: T. Furuhashi (Ed.), Advances in Fuzzy Logic, Neural Networks and Genetic Algorithms. Proceedings, 1994. (Subseries LNAI).

Vol. 1012: M. Bartošek, J. Staudek, J. Wiedermann (Eds.), SOFSEM '95: Theory and Practice of Informatics. Proceedings, 1995. XI, 499 pages. 1995.

Vol. 1013: T.W. Ling, A.O. Mendelzon, L. Vieille (Eds.), Deductive and Object-Oriented Databases. Proceedings, 1995. XIV, 557 pages. 1995.

Vol. 1014: A.P. del Pobil, M.A. Serna, Spatial Representation and Motion Planning. XII, 242 pages. 1995.

Vol. 1015: B. Blumenthal, J. Gornostaev, C. Unger (Eds.), Human-Computer Interaction. Proceedings, 1995. VIII, 203 pages. 1995.

Vol. 1017: M. Nagl (Ed.), Graph-Theoretic Concepts in Computer Science. Proceedings, 1995. XI, 406 pages. 1995.

Vol. 1018: T. Little, R. Gusella (Eds.), Network and Operating Systems Support for Digital Audio and Video. Proceedings, 1995. XI, 357 pages. 1995.

Vol. 1019: E. Brinksma, W.R. Cleaveland, K.G. Larsen, T. Margaria, B. Steffen (Eds.), Tools and Algorithms for the Construction and Analysis of Systems. Selected Papers, 1995. VII, 291 pages. 1995.

Vol. 1020: I.D. Watson (Ed.), Progress in Case-Based Reasoning. Proceedings, 1995. VIII, 209 pages. 1995. (Subseries LNAI).

Vol. 1021: M.P. Papazoglou (Ed.), OOER '95: Object-Oriented and Entity-Relationship Modeling. Proceedings, 1995. XVII, 451 pages. 1995.

Vol. 1022: P.H. Hartel, R. Plasmeijer (Eds.), Functional Programming Languages in Education. Proceedings, 1995. X, 309 pages. 1995.

Vol. 1023: K. Kanchanasut, J.-J. Lévy (Eds.), Algorithms, Concurrency and Knowlwdge. Proceedings, 1995. X, 410 pages. 1995.

Vol. 1024: R.T. Chin, H.H.S. Ip, A.C. Naiman, T.-C. Pong (Eds.), Image Analysis Applications and Computer Graphics. Proceedings, 1995. XVI, 533 pages. 1995.

Vol. 1025: C. Boyd (Ed.), Cryptography and Coding. Proceedings, 1995. IX, 291 pages. 1995.